BRITAIN, ISRAEL AND THE UNITED STATES 1955–1958

CASS SERIES: BRITISH FOREIGN AND COLONIAL POLICY
SERIES EDITOR: PETER CATTERALL
ISSN: 1467-5013

This series provides insights into both the background influences on and the course of policy-making towards Britain's extensive overseas interests during the past 200 years.

Whitehall and the Suez Crisis, Saul Kelly and Anthony Gorst (eds)

Liberals, International Relations and Appeasement: The Liberal Party, 1919–1939, Richard S. Grayson

British Government Policy and Decolonisation, 1945–1963: Scrutinising the Official Mind, Frank Heinlein

Harold Wilson and European Integration: Britain's Second Application to Join the EEC, edited by Oliver Daddow

Britain, Israel and the United States, 1955–1958: Beyond Suez, Orna Almog

Britain, Israel and the United States, 1955–1958

Beyond Suez

Orna Almog

Foreword by
Donald Cameron Watt

Routledge
Taylor & Francis Group
LONDON AND NEW YORK

First published in 2003 by
FRANK CASS PUBLISHERS

This edition published 2013 by Routledge
2 Park Square, Milton Park, Abingdon, Oxon OX14 4RN
711 Third Avenue, New York, NY 10017

Routledge is an imprint of the Taylor & Francis Group, an informa business

First issued in paperback 2016

British Library Cataloguing in Publication Data
Almog, Orna
Britain, Israel and the United States, 1955–1958: beyond Suez. – (Cass series. British foreign and colonial policy) 1. Great Britain – Foreign relations – Israel 2. Israel – Foreign relations – Great Britain 3. Great Britain – Foreign relations – 1945–1964
I. Title
327.4'105694'09045

Library of Congress Cataloging-in-Publication Data
Almog, Orna, 1958–
Britain, Israel, and the United States, 1955–1958: beyond Suez/Orna Almog.
p. cm. – (Cass series–British foreign and colonial policy, ISSN 1467-5013)
Includes bibliographical references (p.) and index.
ISBN 0-7146-5246-6
1. Israel–Foreign relations–Great Britain. 2. Great Britain–Foreign relations–Israel. 3. Israel–Foreign relations–United States. 4. United States–Foreign relations–Israel. 5. Israel–History–1948–1967. 6. Middle East–Foreign relations. I. Title. II. Series.

DS126.93.G7 A55 2002
327.4105694'09'045–dc21 2002026781

Typeset in 10.5/12.5 Palatino by Frank Cass Publishers Ltd.

ISBN13: 978-0-7146-5246-7 (hbk)
ISBN13: 978-1-138-98792-0 (pbk)

Contents

Series Editor's Preface

On 15 September 1955, the British Foreign Secretary, Harold Macmillan, met with the Israeli Ambassador to London. Afterwards Macmillan recorded in his diary:

> Mr Elath painted a very realistic and impressive picture of the situation in Israel today. The population is a strange mixture, ranging from sophisticated and highly educated Jews from Hamburg and Vienna, to the latest arrivals from the miserable life of Rabat or Algiers. The party system is hopelessly confused; the electoral system (PR) makes it almost impossible to get a Govt of any authority; the extremist views have undue weight. Meanwhile, the determination, or apparent determination, of the Arabs to keep the nominal state of war and the economic boycott permanently going, makes many Israelis despair and therefore lean to violent measures.

The siege mentality of a young and vulnerable state, Macmillan recognised, was reinforced by purchases of arms by Israel's hostile neighbours, including British tank sales to Egypt. There, however, Macmillan's sympathetic appraisal of Israeli anxieties ended. For the British, Israel was only part of the Middle East, and a very problematic part at that. The prism through which they primarily viewed Israel is clear from Macmillan's comment the following month to Mr Sharett, then the Israeli Prime Minister, 'that he ought to accept our idea for a final Arab/Israel settlement. Till that was made, we shd all be easy prey to Russian intrigue.'

This Anglo-American scheme, Project Alpha, involved an adjustment of territories between Israel and the Arab states in favour of the latter. That its prospects for success were limited had already been made clear by the talks Macmillan had held with Fawzi, the Egyptian Foreign Minister. But if Fawzi's demands suggest that Alpha offered the Arabs too little, from the Israeli point of view offering anything was too much. The British willingness to do so only added to the intense Israeli suspicion of their motives that had festered from the end of the Mandate.

In such circumstances, as Orna Almog shows, the coincidence of collusion between the British and Israelis over Suez in 1956 did not fundamentally alter the parameters of their relationship. Suez was an alliance of convenience, pursued for very different reasons by the two governments. While it may have cemented British enmity towards Nasser, it did not produce a reciprocal amity towards Israel.

Anglo-American historiographies of the Middle East have tended to focus upon 1956 as a key date. Almog challenges this orthodoxy. Without downplaying the importance of the Suez Crisis of 1956, she persuasively makes the case for regarding the crises of 1958 as more of a turning point. The US deployment in Lebanon then made explicit their new position as prime Western power in the region. The Iraqi coup deprived the British of their main Middle Eastern ally. The fact that Israel was this time incidental to the political upheavals in Iraq, Jordan and Lebanon facilitated a rapprochement between it and Britain. The events of 1958 thus brought about a more fundamental realignment than 1956. The fact that on this occasion Britain and Israel were bystanders sharing similar anxieties rather than allies with different agendas was not the least of the shifts from the situation of 1956. This, and the dropping of any remaining pretensions to support Project Alpha, Almog effectively demonstrates, clears the way for a marked improvement in Anglo-Israeli relations.

This book not only challenges the chronological orthodoxy, but it is also one of those rare works that draws upon a multiplicity of archival sources. Too often – if sometimes unavoidably – international history accounts reflect the cultural and geopolitical preoccupations contained in the archives consulted. As Almog points out, the difficulties in accessing sources in most Middle Eastern countries mean that, for histories of that region, this problem is likely to persist. However, the extensive use she has made of Israeli archives ensures that this is nevertheless a genuine study of bilateral diplomacy. It casts light on the very different mindsets of the British, Americans and Israelis during these difficult years. It illustrates how limited was US support for Israel at this time, which is not only surprising in hindsight but could also catch the British out at the time, with serious consequences during Suez. And it shows how the Palestinian issue was, at best, very much secondary to the question of the existence or otherwise of Israel. Instead, Israeli policy-makers had first to secure their state, seeking, in the face of hostile neighbours, supportive Western allies. These, however, were by no means natural allies. As Orna Almog shows in her book, the British and Americans, at least until 1958, were at best reluctant in giving the support sought by the Israelis.

Peter Catterall
Queen Mary, University of London

Foreword

One of the most happy rewards of an academic career, especially if one is fortunate enough, as I was, to spend a substantial part of one's time in the care and supervision of graduate students, is to observe at close quarters the development of a new and original mind engaged in the investigation of historical phenomena with which one has a limited and imperfect acquaintance, and to learn from the student how the seemingly chaotic entanglement of events, personalities, perceptions and interactions can be metamorphosed into a plausible and satisfying narrative and analysis. This is the greater when the student is covering, as Dr Almog does in this monograph, events that one has observed and commented on at first hand when they occurred. One can at all stages compare one's memories and contemporary observations with the detailed wealth of evidence from all sides that the student of international history using the archives of the governments that were involved in the events, in so far as they are available, can produce from their research.

This is of particular value when one is dealing with the history of events in the Middle East. Unfortunately the history of international events in the Middle East is largely the preserve of those who share a common attitude to the area, one which incorporates a state of mind which regards some phenomena as 'natural' and acceptable because they conform to some sense of Natural Right inherent in the past history of the area, while other phenomena, especially the appearance in the last century of the state of Israel, are regarded as alien, intrusive and in a sense illegitimate and contrary to Natural Law. Cultural differences are taken as indicating that some states 'belong' in the area and others do not. The working out of a sense of nationalism in areas where the 'nation-state', as conceived by nineteenth century Europeans, is both an alien concept in thought and language and exists only in relation to special areas, such as Egypt, where the historical continuity provided by the ecology of the Nile valley is buttressed by historical monuments on a monumental scale, has been supported by schools of writers and cultural historians for whom the sense of identity provided to Israelis by the creation and survival of their own state is a matter of contention and regret. Israel is seen as an alien and inimical intrusion. This view is understandable is so far as it is held and advocated by opinion and propaganda in those states that claim to be part of the tradition of Arab civilisation. But for the true historian it is itself part of the problem and should not be part of the historian's mindset. But studies of the history of the Middle East since the beginning of the twentieth century have been coloured to the point of warping by partisanship more to be expected in Athenian histories of the Persian wars or Roman histories of Carthage, than in the 'scientific' historiography of today.

Dr Almog's monograph is to be read in this sense, as a contribution to the understanding of a crucial period in the history of international relations involving not only the states of the Middle East but those of the major powers of the mid-twentieth century active in the area. It is to be hoped that its readership will approach it with minds open to questioning the hitherto set values which have governed the historiography of the area; and that her work will be incorporated into a historical view which is not irretrievably locked into mindsets that are more reminiscent of the racial philosophy of the 1850s than the realities of the twenty-first century.

Donald Cameron Watt
Professor Emeritus of International History

Acknowledgements

I would like to thank everyone that helped me to write this book. In Britain I have benefited from the libraries of London University, the Lord Avon Archive in Birmingham and the Public Record Office; in Israel from the Israeli State Archive and the Ben-Gurion Centre in the Negev. I must offer special thanks to the Jewish Memorial of Jewish Culture for their financial contribution. I am grateful for the support of my friends and colleagues throughout the years; to Professor D. Cameron Watt for his initial guidance, and Professor John Young, Mrs Mary McCormick, Larry Butler, Gill Sterck and Simon Beer. To those who were willing to assist me in Israel, Michael Bar-Zohar, Ambassador Eliahu Elath, Professor Harkabi and Gershon Avner. A special thanks to Dr Kate Morris, who encouraged, assisted and supported me in very difficult moments; to my supervisor, Dr Antony Best, for leading me along the way and to Dr Peter Catterrall for his useful assistance and comments.

I would like to thank my family in Britain and give my special thanks to my family in Israel; my sisters Ilana and Rebecca. This book is dedicated to my parents: to my father Ben-Zion, who did not survive to witness the completion of this study, and to my dear mother, Hana, who has always been a source of inspiration and support throughout the years.

Abbreviations

AIOC	Anglo-Iranian Oil Company
ARAMCO	Arabian–American Oil Company
BGA	Ben-Gurion Archive
BP	British Petroleum
CENTO	Central Treaty Organization
EEC	European Economic Community
EFTA	European Free Trade Association
FLN	National Liberation Front
FRUS	Foreign Relations of the United States
GAA	General Armistice Agreements
IDF	Israel Defense Forces
ISA	Israeli State Archive
MABAR	British and Commonwealth Department, Israeli Foreign Ministry
MAHAV	United States Department, Israeli Foreign Ministry
MEAF	Middle East Air Force
NATO	North Atlantic Treaty Organization
PLO	Palestine Liberation Organization
PRO	Public Record Office
RAF	Royal Air Force
SCUA	Suez Canal Users Association
UAR	United Arab Republic
UNEF	United Nations Emergency Force
UNRWA	United Nations Relief and Works Agency
UNTSO	United Nations Truce Supervision Organization

Introduction

> Middle Eastern politics were like a game of tennis in which the only way of scoring was by waiting for the opponent to serve double faults.[1]

This book aims to examine the Anglo-Israeli relationship from 1955 to summer 1958 in the context of the Cold War, superpower rivalry and political upheaval in the Middle East. Ever since the establishment of the State of Israel in 1948, the Anglo-Israeli relationship has faced adversity and setbacks and had been overshadowed by the bitter historical experience of the British Mandate. Israel's attitude towards Britain has been characterised by two ambivalent dimensions: first, great admiration towards Britain as the democracy that gave the Jews the Balfour declaration; and second, suspicion and apprehension of British policy and motives in the region. This dualism also characterised the British attitudes towards Israel. British public opinion largely ignored Israel from 1950 to 1955 and British officials focused on relations with Arab states. Within the Foreign Office there was a general appreciation of Israel's achievements and pioneering spirit, but its presence in the region was always considered to be contrary to British strategic and economic interests. Close relations with Israel were therefore viewed as conflicting with Britain's general position in the Middle East.

A major undercurrent in the relationship and a bone of contention between the two states was the question of Israel's borders and the 1949 armistice lines. The British felt, and this was outlined publicly in Anthony Eden's Guildhall speech of November 1955, that in order to promote regional peace and stability, which would serve British interests, Israel would have to make territorial concessions.

In the period under study, Anglo-Israeli relations went through two major stages. The first, from early 1956 to early 1957, was marked by growing tension in the Middle East and cool relations between Israel and Britain, which at times became almost openly hostile. The second period, from early 1957 to summer 1958, was characterised by the growing instability of the pro-Western states in the region and by an eventual breakthrough in Anglo-Israeli relations.

The British Ambassadors to Israel recognised Israel's suspicion of Her Majesty's Government, but sometimes reported this in a negative way, with little real understanding of the Israeli mood. For example, a most significant remark can be found in a letter of 8 March 1955 from Sir John Nicholls, British Ambassador in Tel-Aviv, to Sir Evelyn Shuckburgh, the Assistant Under-Secretary at the Foreign Office: 'The centre of infection in the region is Israel and we have to treat the Israelis as sick people, their illness is psychological ... therefore it is not reasonable to expect that a nation made up of individuals so psychologically unstable, should be capable of mature foreign policy.'[2]

The period following the Suez war was marked by an improved and calmer relationship, although the real shift only came in summer 1958. It is therefore of immense importance to establish to what degree the co-operation between Israel and Britain during the Suez war paved the way for the breakthrough, or whether Suez was just an interlude followed by a retreat into old patterns of political behaviour. This book argues that it was the upheavals after Suez, and primarily the crisis during summer 1958, that finally led to a better understanding as well as a transformation of the traditional power relationship between the two states. It can thus be argued that the Suez war did not bring an end to the traditional British interests and view of the region, but rather that the fundamental change came in 1958.

In order to appreciate the nature of Anglo-Israeli relations at this time it is necessary to understand the various factors that influenced Britain and Israel, such as Israel's political and security vulnerability in a hostile environment, the internal rivalries among the Arabs, British strategic and economic interests in the region, and the ever greater role and influence of the USSR and the United States in Middle Eastern affairs. The intensification of the Cold War in the region had a major impact on Middle Eastern states and on Israel's actions. This led to great upheavals in some regional states, and encouraged the growth of Arab radicalism and nationalism. The period under study was also marked by the rise of the Arab nationalist movement and by the predominance of Nasser's influence and prestige, which had a significant impact on Middle Eastern internal affairs and on the region's position *vis-à-vis* the Western powers. Arab nationalism associated imperialism with Western domination, and consequently perceived the West as obstructing its aspirations. Therefore its resentment towards the West grew at this time. Furthermore, because of the Arab belief that Zionism and the state of Israel were the creation and spearhead of Western imperialism, the dispute between the Arabs and Israel was seen by the former not merely as a regional conflict but as an international one. The Arab–Israeli dispute was also fed by the pan-Arab movement and Nasser's pan-Arab propaganda, and by Israel's militant response. It is therefore vital for any historian examining the Middle East to acknowledge the importance of the regional forces operating in the Middle East, rather than to assume that history can be explained by studying Western actions and motivations alone. Any attempt to marginalise regional factors, and to relegate the area itself only to secondary importance compared to emphasis on the Western policy-making process, risks a narrow interpretation of the subject and would encourage false assumptions and historical misunderstanding.

There are also similar dangers when historians examine Israel's policies. In the introduction to his book *Between East and West: Israel's Foreign Policy Orientation 1948–1956*, Uri Bialer wrote: 'The entire body of research on Israel's external policy has not been systematically and thoroughly based on the political documentation of that country.'[3] Indeed, Western historians, because of their lack of knowledge of the Hebrew language, have of necessity relied solely on the use of American and British documents to analyse Israeli foreign policy. Moreover, the historian examining Israel's foreign policy must take into consideration not only Israel's defence position, but also the various components that influenced its decision-makers such as the domestic political coalition considerations, public opinion, morale and support, as well as the economic and financial limitations on its foreign policy choices.

The origins of the Suez crisis have been studied extensively. Benny Morris's book *Israel's Border Wars 1949–1956*[4] provides a very penetrating study of Israel's retaliation policy and contributes to a greater understanding of the Arab–Israeli dispute and of the policy behind Israel's decision-making. Another study that gives a broad account of the affair and its background is *Suez 1956: The Crisis and its Consequences*, edited by Wm Roger Louis and Roger Owen.[5] Keith Kyle's book, *Suez*,[6] and *The Suez–Sinai Crisis 1956*, edited by Selwyn Troen and Moshe Shemesh,[7] also provide additional information and context. Mordechai Bar-On's book, *The Gates of Gaza*,[8] provides interesting insights into the policy adopted by Israel at the time. Yet Bar-On's book is based in the main on secret unpublished material, both official and private papers, to which most researchers have no access, and this therefore makes an evaluation of his conclusions difficult.

Research has already been conducted on the issue of British attitudes towards the Arab-Israeli dispute and towards Israel in general. Ilan Pappé's book, *Britain and the Arab–Israeli Conflict 1948–1951*,[9] has examined the earlier period from the establishment of Israel in 1948 to 1951.[10] Yoav Tenembaum's thesis provides an interesting account of British attitudes towards the Arab–Israeli dispute and Israel between 1951 and 1954. However, these studies have focused on examining the British attitude towards Israel and the Arab–Israeli dispute alone, and do not provide a comparative study or a deep analysis of Israeli attitudes towards Britain.

This book, based predominantly on Israeli and British documents, seeks to provide a broader study, and to highlight issues as they were seen from both London *and* Jerusalem, and to deliver a comparative study which hitherto has been absent. Furthermore, most of the books written about Suez and Israeli foreign policy do not go beyond early 1957, and no serious study of the Anglo-Israeli relationship in the period following Suez has yet been published. This book intends to highlight not just the Suez war period, but to go beyond this. It argues that the co-operation between Britain and Israel during Suez was the result of necessity and did not represent a significant turnabout in the relations between the two countries. Rather, it was the July 1958 crisis that had a more important and defining impact on Britain's general position in the Middle East and upon Anglo-Israeli relations. In particular, as a study primarily of Anglo-Israeli political relations, this book only considers British defence policy for the Middle East when and if it had a direct bearing on the diplomatic relations between Israel and Britain.

The researcher of Middle Eastern studies faces numerous problems, above all the fact that archives in Arab states are not accessible to researchers. As for the Israeli Archives, although in principle Israel applies a 'thirty years rule', there are some archives and materials that have not been declassified. The main problem relates to the Israel Defense Forces' archive, which allows only restricted access to documents on defence and security issues. Attempts made by this writer, and by other researchers, have largely been in vain. The Ben-Gurion Archive and Ben-Gurion's diary give very interesting and useful insights into Israeli foreign policy formulation, but here again most researchers find that many documents are still classified and only accessible to certain select historians. Historians are also denied access to the records of the Israeli Cabinet and the Foreign Affairs Parliamentary Committee. However, a good source is the Israeli State Archive, which contains quite a wide range of information, including some intelligence reports.

The structure adopted in this book is a chronological one. As a comparative study it is important to examine first of all the interests of the two states in the Middle East and their general outlook on international affairs. Therefore the first chapter gives an account of British interests, with a special emphasis on the importance of oil, and its attempts to solve the Arab–Israeli dispute. The second chapter examines Israel's interests, political discourse and aims as a young pioneering Jewish state, and focuses on its attitude to the Arab-Israeli dispute in particular. The third chapter examines the Anglo-Israeli relationship since Israel's establishment, stating the main principle of contentions, mostly from Israel's point of view.

The fourth chapter deals with events during 1956, the growing radicalism in the Arab world, the development of a closer Franco-Israeli relationship and the countdown to Suez, including an examination of the so-called 'collusion' between Israel and Britain. The fifth chapter deals with the events during the Suez war itself, such as the Israeli attack on Egypt, the British–French collaboration and the limited co-operation between Israel and Britain. The chapter also examines the British and Israeli positions in that crucial period and focuses on Israel's attempt to secure its interests prior to its withdrawal, and on the political storm in Britain. The sixth chapter deals with the consequences of Suez and questions whether the war brought about any substantive change in Anglo-Israeli relations. It addresses the Israeli struggle to secure free passage through the Suez Canal and its effort to strengthen itself internally and to search for a new status quo in the region. The seventh chapter focuses on the upheavals in Jordan in April 1957 and the events leading to the crisis in the Lebanon, and the greater dependency of Britain and Israel on American decision-making and foreign policy. All of this is analysed in the context of the greater involvement of the superpowers in the region.

The eighth chapter deals with the dramatic upheavals of July 1958, their consequences for Britain's position in the region, the intervention in the Lebanon by the United States and by the British in Jordan, and focuses on the changing mood in the region and, in particular, on Anglo-Israeli relations.

NOTES

1. P[ublic] R[ecord] O[ffice], hereafter PRO, FO371/137267/VR1051/6, Lloyd(British Foreign Secretary) to Chauvel (French Ambassador to London), 3 February 1958.
2. PRO, FO371/115825/VR1051/8, Nicholls (Tel-Aviv) to Shuckburgh (Foreign Office), 8 March 1955.
3. Uri Bialer, *Between East and West: Israel's Foreign Policy Orientation 1948–1956* (Cambridge: Cambridge University Press, 1990).
4. Benny Morris, *Israel's Border Wars, Arab Infiltration, Israel's Retaliation and the Countdown to the Suez War 1949–1956* (Oxford: Clarendon Press, 1993).
5. Wm Roger Louis and Roger Owen (eds), *Suez 1956: The Crisis and its Consequences* (Oxford: Clarendon Press, 1989).
6. Keith Kyle, *Suez* (London: Weidenfeld & Nicolson, 1992).
7. Selwyn Ilan Troen and Moshe Shemesh (eds), *The Suez–Sinai Crisis 1956, Retrospective and Reappraisal* (London: Frank Cass, 1989).
8. Mordechai Bar-On, *The Gates of Gaza: Israel's Defence and Foreign Policy 1955–1957* (Tel-Aviv: Am-Oved, 1992).
9. Ilan Pappé, *Britain and the Arab–Israeli Conflict, 1948–1951* (Basingstoke: Macmillan, 1988).
10. Yoav J. Tenembaum, 'British Policy Towards Israel and the Arab–Israeli Dispute 1951–1954' (unpublished PhD thesis, St Antony's College, Oxford, 1991).

—1—
British Interests in the Middle East in the 1950s

IMPERIAL AND OIL INTERESTS

THE BRITISH PERSPECTIVE on the Middle East in the 1950s combined traditional interests and attitudes with contemporary strategic requirements. These interests can be divided into two main categories: first, economic interests and, second, political–strategic.

Britain had traditionally been one of the most interested of the great powers in the region, and had come to a position of dominance after the collapse of the Ottoman Empire. Originally, in the first half of the nineteenth century, Great Britain's diplomatic objectives in the Middle East related to the defence and preservation of its Indian Empire. However, with the completion of the Suez Canal in 1869, British interests in the region increased. The Canal drastically shortened the time it took to get to India and the other British possessions east of Suez, and thus it became of immense importance to British trade. It also helped to encourage British trade with the Middle East, and from the late nineteenth century 10 per cent of Britain's exports went to countries in this area. This meant that any interruption of free passage through the Canal would be a grave threat to Britain's financial and trading interests.[1]

British interests in the Middle East and in the Suez Canal grew even further as a result of the discovery of oil in Iran and other Middle Eastern countries in the early years of the twentieth century. (In 1939, the Anglo-Iranian Oil Company (AIOC) was Britain's largest overseas economic asset.) Thus, by the time of the Second World War, the Middle East was considered to be a region of vital strategic importance to the security of the British Empire.

Following the Second World War, British interests within the region came to be of even greater significance. One might have expected, in the light of the granting of independence to India, Pakistan, Burma and Ceylon during 1947–48, that the emphasis on the Middle East would have declined. However, the Suez Canal still remained a vital route of communication to Britain's interests in the Far East, e.g. Malaya and the empire in East Africa and Australia. Moreover, the

Middle East was becoming more important to Britain on its own account.

There were a number of reasons for the greater British emphasis on its role in the Middle East. One of the key factors was that with the withdrawal from India there was a need for Britain to forestall the impression that the empire was in retreat and that it was relinquishing its status as a world power. This meant that it was vital for reasons of prestige to preserve Britain's presence in the Middle East. By being responsible for the security of the Suez Canal and the defence of the region from the Soviet Union, Britain could emphasise that it was still a major player in world affairs and that its opinion could not be ignored.

After the Second World War, control of the Middle East assumed a greater significance for Britain as the region's main strategic raw material, oil, had become a decisive factor in the recovery of the British and western European economies. The war against Germany had clearly demonstrated the growing importance of oil as it became obvious that the traditional sources of energy – coal and hydroelectric power – were incapable of sufficient expansion to meet the needs of modern industry.[2] Much of the new industrial plant constructed to replace the facilities that had been destroyed during the war was powered by oil, and it was widely assumed that oil was the energy source for the future. If this was true it was clear that the major source of this oil would be the Middle East where there were great oil reserves and production costs were relatively cheap.

The growing importance of Middle Eastern oil can be seen in the fact that by 1955 the region produced 160 million tons, which was equal to nearly two-thirds of all the oil used by the free world outside the United States.[3] In order to reach the markets in western Europe, about 67 million tons of this oil was moved northward by tanker from the oil-producing regions through the Suez Canal and the Mediterranean,[4] which was the quickest and cheapest route for oil traffic. An alternative but more expensive route was around the Cape of Good Hope, which added 5,000 miles to the voyage from the Persian Gulf to London. A third means of conveying the oil to western Europe was by pipeline from the oil fields to the Mediterranean coast and then by tanker. This route applied to the oil from two vital sources. The first was that from the Kirkuk region of Iraq, which was taken by the Iraqi Petroleum pipeline across Syria to the Lebanese coast at Tripoli. The second was the oil from Saudi Arabia which was transported by the Trans-Arabian pipeline (Tapline) across Jordan and Syria to the port of Sidon in the Lebanon.

Britain did not depend entirely on Middle Eastern oil to power its industry, but it was one of the main sources of its energy supply. This became increasingly significant after the United States stopped Lend-Lease abruptly in 1945 and Britain could no longer afford the dollars to pay for American or Caribbean oil. In addition, the oil fields in Iraq, Iran, Kuwait and the Gulf states, which were controlled by British companies such as British Petroleum and Royal Dutch Shell,[5] contributed to British economic stability. The revenue that Britain obtained from the sale of Middle Eastern oil was crucial to its balance of payments figure and to the gold and dollar earnings of the Sterling Area. The financial benefits from oil revenue were reinforced by a further relevant point which was that the former British-occupied territories in the Middle East were members of the Sterling Area and kept their sterling reserves in London. This arrangement was extremely useful for Britain, because it made trade with the Middle Eastern countries difficult for other European states and, in particular, it meant that the American oil companies in the Middle East had to carry out much of their activities in sterling.[6] The irony of the situation for Britain, however, was that while the revenue generated by oil sales improved its financial position, at the same time it heightened the need to divert resources to defend the Middle East and, in particular, the Suez Canal and the Persian Gulf, and necessitated strenuous political efforts to maintain Arab goodwill. The importance of Middle Eastern oil, in terms of both its use by British industry and its value to the Treasury, obviously meant that it was essential for Britain to secure the passage of oil. Any interruption in the flow of oil would gravely damage the British economy and affect its balance of payments, because it would have to buy oil in dollars from the western hemisphere. In order to maintain the flow of oil, it was necessary to keep these communication lines free and this naturally meant that the security of the Suez Canal and the political allegiance of the oil-producing states and the countries traversed by the pipelines became of immense importance to Britain.

MIDDLE EAST DEFENCE: THREAT AND TREATIES

The defence of Middle Eastern oil and the perpetuation of British prestige should have been a relatively easy task considering that Britain was already the linchpin of regional security. After the end of the Second World War, Britain still had a sizeable military establishment in the Middle East based on its defence treaties with a number of the local states. These included the defence treaty with Egypt which was signed in 1936. Under this agreement, Britain had a naval base in Alexandria and was permitted to keep the Suez base including land troops and air force, with the necessary ancillary personnel for administration and technical duties.[7]

Britain also had a treaty with Iraq dating from 1930, under which it had control over two air bases at Habbaniya and Shaiba. Iraq also promised to furnish Britain with 'all facilities and assistance', including the use of railways, rivers, ports and means of communication in times of war.[8] In addition, Britain had a defence treaty with Jordan, which allowed the RAF to station units in Amman and Mafraq. The Jordanian airfields also afforded a convenient staging post in peacetime for short-range fighters en route to the Far East.[9] Britain was also allowed to move troops through Jordan's territory whenever it was deemed necessary. In return Britain provided financial aid to Jordan, and helped to organise and train its army, the Arab Legion, which was commanded by British officers employed by the Jordanian government. As well as these three main pacts, Britain also had defence treaties with other states in the region, such as that with Libya, which provided air bases for British forces and overflying rights, and the agreements to protect the sheikhs of the Aden protectorate and those of Kuwait, Bahrain, Qatar and the Trucial Coast. Britain also maintained a special treaty with the Sultan of Muscat and Oman.

On the surface this appeared to be a solid basis for the defence of the region. However, Britain's ability to maintain its interests in the post-war era was not as great as it had been prior to 1939 and it could not operate from the position of overwhelming strength – in military, political and economic terms – it had enjoyed in the heyday of its imperial power. A combination of internal weakness and external challenges made it vulnerable.

One of the most fundamental problems facing Britain was that after the sacrifices of the Second World War, it no longer had the financial resources to maintain a world-power role. With defence commitments in Europe and South East Asia, as well as those in the Middle East, and the need to meet a perceived Soviet threat, Britain was clearly overstretched.

After the return of the Conservative government in October 1951, it became clear that defence expenditure would have to be reduced considerably; it still took a major part of the budget and was a heavy burden, as defence purchases had more than tripled since 1950. In particular, calls from the Treasury for retrenchment began to mount in 1952 when Britain was faced with a balance of payments crisis and a widening dollar gap. This led to the Chiefs of Staff producing a new Global Strategy Paper of 1952, which envisaged a shift in emphasis to nuclear weapons which they believed would allow a lowering of defence expenditure by facilitating a reduction in the armed forces.[10]

This also appealed to the British government because of the belief that Britain needed its own nuclear strike forces in order to be sure of knocking out Russian bases, which would be a threat to Britain but to which the Americans might assign lower priority. The Global Strategy Paper also emphasised that nuclear weapons would enable Britain to be an independent power, free from domination by the United States, and would maintain British prestige within Europe and the world.[11]

The greater importance attached to the nuclear deterrent satisfied the government and the strategists who saw nuclear weapons as an answer to remaining a world power on the one hand, and the need to reduce defence expenditure on the other. The concept of nuclear power should have replaced the concept of an overseas base chain and reliance upon air mobilisation. Nevertheless, the strategists had no evidence for believing, at that stage, that the new scheme would permit a gradual running down of overseas bases. The belief was that the chain of bases linked by sea and air remained as necessary and as extensive as ever. This was particularly true for the Middle East as British interests there, such as maintaining its prestige and defending oil supplies, demanded a permanent, conventional military presence. This was especially important as there was an unwritten understanding with the regimes tied to Britain that the latter would help to maintain internal security if called upon. A complete retreat from the region and reliance on nuclear weapons was thus impossible. At the same time, however, the financial constraints meant that defence cuts had to be made.

The problem of where and how to make cuts was particularly acute as one of the key claims of the British was that their presence in the Middle East helped to defend the region against any possible Soviet offensive. In order to cope with light Russian attacks during the initial phase of a future war with the USSR, the British had argued that local forces in the Middle East should be built up and that a British garrison within the region should be maintained in peacetime in order to support them. However, it was soon realised that Britain alone could not provide a sufficient covering force, and that it would have to be combined with extra contributions from the friendly Middle Eastern states and the United States. The problem was, however, whether the Arab states and the United States were willing to prop up a permanent British presence.

Britain's difficulties were compounded by political changes taking place within the region, which began to erode the basis of its economic and military power. At the beginning of 1955, the Middle East was entering 'a revolutionary era'[12] and the rise of the Arab national movement endangered British interests. The nationalist trend within the Arab world had increased after the Second World War and reached a climax after Gamal Abdul Nasser and the 'Free Young Officers' came to power in 1952. The unity of the movement was based on their hatred of the West and, in particular, Britain and the oil companies, which represented Western colonialism and imperialism. According to Nasser, the difference between the Arab states and the Western world was an essential and fundamental one, and could only lead to one of two conclusions: the defeat of the Arab world or that of the West.[13] In his book *The Philosophy of the Revolution*, Nasser affirmed that he aspired to guide all Arab countries, to establish Egyptian hegemony in North Africa, and to exert influence over Central and West Africa, and throughout the Moslem world.[14] Nasser believed that the Western powers were imperialistic, that their rule had left the Arabs bitter and divided, and asserted that his aim was to oust the Western powers (especially Britain) from their positions in the Middle East.[15] The main threat from this movement was the possibility that Nasser might be tempted to interrupt the flow of oil by closing the Canal and influencing other Arab states to follow his example. Such action would have forced the British government to use the route around the Cape of Good Hope, and would have compelled them to use American tankers, which would add to the cost of oil.

A crucial problem raised by Egyptian nationalism was that it led to a challenge to the British desire to maintain its hold over the Suez Canal base. The facilities for the defence of the Canal were considered by the British to be central to the defence of the region. However, from as early as 1945 it was clear that Egypt wished to see the withdrawal of British forces and thus began a longer and bitter dispute between the two countries that would last for the next nine years. By 1951 tensions were so great that Egypt abrogated its 1936 treaty with Britain and began a large-scale campaign of harassment. All British attempts to continue to use the base, even as part of a multilateral defence agreement for the region, met with solid opposition. Finally, a combination of Egyptian intransigence and domestic financial weakness forced Britain to retreat. In 1954, an agreement was signed which passed the base to Egypt on the condition that Britain could return if the security of the Canal was endangered or the Straits of Bosphorus came under threat.[16]

The confrontation with Egypt was not the only challenge to British interests in the region. Relations with Iran deteriorated markedly in the early 1950s. The problems with Iran centred around the position of the Anglo-Iranian Oil Company (AIOC), which was a great source of revenue for the British Treasury. For the Iranians, on the other hand, the company represented a British tool of economic and political hegemony over Iran. A dispute erupted in 1951 due to the decision by Premier Mossadeq to nationalise the AIOC. The AIOC, however, refused to accept the validity of nationalisation, and the company's stand was supported by the Labour government and the Conservative government after 1951.[17] For the next two years there was a bitter stand-off between the two countries, with Britain being restrained from using force only due to pressure from the United States. Finally, the crisis ended in August 1953 when a CIA–MI6 coup in Teheran led to the fall of Mossadeq and the return of the Shah from exile. In contrast to the case of Egypt, this might appear to have ended in triumph, but it came with a high price. The main concession was that Britain was forced to allow American oil companies to operate in Iran, thus removing the AIOC's monopoly. Furthermore, the crisis placed Britain once again in opposition to the nationalist forces in the region, thus portraying it as an imperialist–colonialist power rather than as the benevolent protector of the Middle East.

Although the breakdowns in relations with Egypt and Iran were the most significant examples of the problems in Britain's relations with the region, they were not isolated cases. There was also hostility towards Britain within other states. In 1948, there was an attempt by Britain to renegotiate the defence treaty with Iraq, but when the new pact was placed before the Iraqi assembly it met with great opposition and had to be abandoned.[18] Perhaps of even greater significance was the decision of the oil-rich state of Saudi Arabia to remove itself from the British orbit completely by aligning with the United States. This raised the frightening possibility for Britain that there might be a shift in power in the region from London to Washington.

In order to safeguard its interests, in the light of its economic weakness and the increasing challenges to its position, Britain had to co-operate with the United States and, to a great extent, rely on the Americans to execute a policy that would take these interests into account. Unfortunately for Britain, its imperial interests did not always coincide with those of the United States, which had in any case a tradition of opposing empire. British interests combined strategic and economic needs, as well as obligations to countries with whom it had defence treaties, and were based on upholding British prestige. American interests, on the other hand, were initially economic but increasingly became centred around the need to prevent Soviet penetration into the region. In addition, although American oil companies were heavily involved in Iran, Kuwait and Saudi Arabia, the United States itself was not dependent on Middle Eastern oil for domestic consumption.[19]

These contrasting attitudes manifested themselves in the economic as well as the political sphere and came into play, in particular, in regard to oil. Although the United States had sufficient oil reserves from domestic sources, from the 1930s there were growing concerns about the need to explore other sources in case of a crisis. This led to a search for overseas supplies and especially an interest in the Middle East. The large oil reserves in the Middle East and the relatively cheap price of the region's oil attracted the American oil companies. The belief that it was essential to get hold of oil resources encouraged the US government to support the American oil production companies to exploit Middle Eastern resources further. American oil companies succeeded in obtaining concessions in the Middle East, a move which Britain did not favour. The British view was that the American companies were intruding in their sphere of influence.

The American international oil companies operating in the Middle East argued that for political, economic and security reasons, the future of the United States would be dependent on oil supplied from sources outside the United States. (Domestically provided oil was much more expensive than imports from the Middle East.) For a while, the British aim was to maintain Anglo-American oil co-operation, in order to avoid giving concessions to Middle Eastern countries. The American oil companies, however, believed that they could safeguard the flow of oil by concessions to the Arabs, and by avoiding any measures that would arouse their suspicion and antagonism.

The clearest example of this trend was the American oil consortium involved in Saudi Arabia, the Arabian–American Oil Company (ARAMCO). Oil in Saudi Arabia in commercial quantities was only discovered in 1939 and by 1941 it was becoming apparent that the Saudi oilfields were of immense importance. The main companies involved in ARAMCO were Socal and Texaco, but they lacked sufficient market outlets to cope with the production, and in the late 1940s Socony Vacuum and New Jersey Standard entered the consortium. ARAMCO was the first company to introduce into the Middle East the idea of an equal division of profits between the oil company and the concession government, which accrued up to the stage when the oil left the latter's territory. For this purpose the profits were calculated on the basis of the posted prices.[20] This move created unrest in other Arab states, which wanted to reach the same agreement. Saudi Arabia had agreed on a 50 per cent profit-sharing plan and the agreement eventually replaced the former system of fixed royalty payments.[21]

The British argument against ARAMCO was that while the latter declared they were only 'oil men', they were, in fact, supported by the American government and deliberately increased Saudi Arabian suspicion of Britain. The British government claimed that ARAMCO appeared to be consistently favourable to those forces working for the elimination of British influence in the Middle East, and made it more difficult for Arab demands to be resisted elsewhere.[22] The British suspicion was fuelled by the fact that the crisis in Iran in 1951 was in part precipitated by the ARAMCO royalty-sharing deal with the Saudis. To add insult to injury, after the crisis the AIOC was forced to allow American oil companies to operate in Iran. By 1956, the American companies controlled 57 per cent of the Saudi Arabian oil and had a share in the rest.

The growing significance of the American oil companies had the effect of increasing US concerns about the security of the region. However, perhaps an even more important factor in the development of US interests in the Middle East was the need to contain the Soviet Union in the wider context of the Cold War.

The Soviet Union had already begun to develop its role in the region in 1947, when it voted in favour of the United Nations partition plan for Palestine. Nevertheless, between 1947 and 1955 it was not involved directly in the Arab–Israeli dispute, and perceived the issue as part of global policy, rather than a local one.[23] However, a change in Soviet policy emerged after Stalin's death in 1953. Moscow tried to change its foreign and internal policies, and to conduct them with new flexibility. It discovered that it could exploit the Arab national movement to increase its influence and field of manoeuvre.[24]

Consequently, the Soviet Union's efforts to gain a greater foothold in the Middle East intensified during 1954–55. This reached a peak in the autumn of 1955 with the signing of an arms deal with Egypt (although officially it was between Egypt and Czechoslovakia). The anti-Western ethos within the Arab national movement made it easy for the Soviets to gain access in the region, particularly among Arab states which, unlike Turkey and Iran, had no common border with the Soviet Union and were not directly exposed to Soviet pressure. The Soviets were perceived by the Arabs as a powerful but distant country, whose support against the encroachment of the West should be enlisted. Although the Soviet Union supported the UN 1947 partition plan for Palestine, and in fact supported the establishment of Israel, the Arabs did not hold this against them. Among the Arab young generation, the Soviet Union represented the progress, social change and revolution that they desired and it was therefore welcomed. France and Britain, on the other hand, had dominated the area previously and co-operated with rulers who were not always popular among the people. They represented reaction instead of progress. All these factors facilitated the Soviet expansion in the Middle East.

Both Britain and the United States were worried that Soviet access to the Middle East posed a real threat as it could potentially cut the supply of oil to the West and control the communications lines through the Suez Canal. The consequences of such a step would damage British shipping and financial interests. It was assumed that the Soviets aimed to deny oil to the West, both in peace and in war. The Soviet task was seen as being to explore new areas of energy supply they could not produce within their own boundaries. From this assumption it was predicted that the USSR would seek access to Middle Eastern oil, not on a commercial basis but through purchases from the producing companies, within the framework of a political attempt to support the growing nationalist movement in the Middle Eastern countries.[25]

Northern Tier and the Baghdad Pact

The potential Soviet threat lead to a new direction in US policy. In May 1953, John Foster Dulles, the US Secretary of State, visited the Middle East. This visit brought Dulles to the conclusion that Egypt was the main factor in building foundations for a military defence in the region and the need for the United States to conduct a policy independent of Britain. He realised that the British were not popular in the region and wanted to avoid the United States being associated with an 'old imperialist power'. Furthermore, Dulles also decided that the United States would end its unlimited support of Britain in the Anglo-Egyptian talks and asked the British to compromise over the status of the Suez Canal base.[26] Dulles began to put forward a new concept for the defence of the Middle East based on co-operation with the Northern Tier states of Turkey, Iraq and Iran. This idea was encouraged by recent developments in the eastern Mediterranean.

In February 1952, Greece and Turkey had joined NATO, which enabled the organisation for the first time to extend its influence into the Balkans and defend the Straits of the Bosphorus. Turkey's accession to NATO was particularly important as it controlled the exits from the Black Sea on which Russia's only warm water port lay, and provided bases from which air attacks on the oilfields of the Caucasus and the industrial area of the Ukraine could be launched.[27] Turkey was also important because it raised the possibility that a forward defence strategy could be developed for the Middle East.

To facilitate this concept the United States began by encouraging a friendship pact between Turkey and Pakistan which was signed in April 1954. This was then followed by a Turco-Iraqi pact, signed in February 1955. In support of these initiatives Washington announced its willingness to provide military aid to these states and signed agreements with Iraq on 21 April and with Pakistan on 19 May 1954.[28] This American interest in Middle East defence was welcomed by the British and there was hope that the United States would commit itself directly to the defence of the region. However, despite its initial enthusiasm, the United States subsequently grew cautious about making any firm commitment. The major reason for American apprehension was the fear that the Northern Tier might alienate Nasser, whom they saw as a major partner for any future Arab–Israeli settlement. The US administration was also worried that if they committed themselves to the Baghdad Pact then Israel might require similar security guarantees, which the US government was not willing to grant prior to an Arab–Israeli agreement.

The lack of a direct American commitment left it to Britain to take the lead in the establishment of a Northern Tier and to tailor it to its own needs. Britain was initially unenthusiastic about the Northern Tier due to its own concerns about the Egyptian response, but after a while came round to seeing the potential advantages. It is important to stress here that although both the United States and Britain supported the Northern Tier they were motivated by different reasons. The Americans saw it first and foremost as a defence against Soviet expansion into the region, while the British viewed it as an 'umbrella' for its Middle Eastern treaty commitments.[29] To Britain, the Northern Tier concept had the advantage of providing a framework within which it could redefine its presence in the region. By 1954 this was urgent, due to the forthcoming Suez Canal Base Agreement and the need to renegotiate the 1930 defence treaty with Iraq.

The difficulties caused by the withdrawal from the Suez Canal base could, in part, be met by the redeployment of forces to the remaining British colonies and bases in the region, such as Libya, Aden and Cyprus. In December 1954, the joint headquarters of the army and the RAF was transferred to Nicosia. The Ministry of Defence and the Secretary of State for War argued that Cyprus should be developed as an airbase, because it provided a stepping stone to the Middle East and was useful in the context of encircling the Middle East beyond the reach of Arab nationalism and the Arab–Israeli dispute. In addition, it had a military importance to NATO strategy and the Western position in the region. Although Cyprus had its limitations as a major base – its harbour was inadequate for large ships and its facilities could not support large land, sea and air operations – it seemed to be the best replacement. It fitted well into the idea of a regional strategic reserve which could be located in Cyprus, Benghazi and Tripoli.[30]

The bases in the eastern Mediterranean were, however, not sufficient to meet British requirements for the security of the region, let alone the maintenance of British prestige. For these purposes it was essential for Britain to maintain close ties with and to retain its influence in Iraq. Britain looked upon its position in Iraq as a means of protecting its strategic needs, and as a useful staging post in the air route to the Far East and Australia. The defence of Iraq had become more important than ever because it had oilfields and refineries, and was also adjacent to the oil regions of the Persian Gulf. The strategists believed that Iraq was more suited to the defence of the Persian Gulf than Suez because reinforcements could arrive from there faster than from the Suez base. The Iraqi airbases could also serve the RAF on flights from Cyprus, and were regarded as sufficient to enable Britain to strike at any Soviet force that might attempt to penetrate Iran and other areas in the Middle East. It would also guarantee Britain's ability to use the air corridor in the area, and thus would eliminate the need to maintain bases in Egypt.

The defence links with Iraq could, however, be continued only if the nature of the British military presence could be renegotiated to meet Iraqi sensibilities. In September 1954, after a failed attempt at rapprochement with Egypt, Nuri el-Said, the Iraqi Prime Minister, suggested the replacement of the Anglo-Iraqi treaty, due to expire in 1957, with a multilateral system and continued British use of its bases in Iraq.[31] Nuri's policy was characterised by a strong, almost fanatical concern with the threat to Iraq from the Soviet Union. He also favoured an alliance with Britain because he realised that Britain was the only great power that was prepared to provide Iraq with support.[32]

The British agreed to Nuri's terms, especially in view of the fact that the Northern Tier concept proved to be a useful umbrella for such diplomacy. It allowed Britain to tie a new defence arrangement with Iraq to a regional collective security organisation, and thus, under the cover of Britain joining the Turco-Iraqi treaty, to form the Baghdad Pact. It was able to hand over sovereignty of the two airbases to the Iraqis without losing prestige, and establish a more equal relationship with the Iraqi government without the previous imperialistic overtones. Although the airbases now came under Iraqi command, the RAF was still allowed to use them and maintain their rights of overflight and landing. In addition, British personnel were allowed to remain in Iraq to help to train its forces and to install and maintain equipment and aircraft.[33]

As well as helping to perpetuate its military presence, Britain saw the Baghdad Pact as a useful tool for bolstering the Anglophile regimes in the Middle East. In particular, the British government was keen to support Iraq's claim to Arab leadership as an alternative to Nasser. In order to strengthen the Baghdad Pact and Nuri's position, the British government hoped that Jordan would join the Pact as well. They were aware of the danger of the pro-Nasserist elements' desire to gain greater power in Jordan and therefore wanted to avoid a situation in which the country would become a satellite of Egypt. They thought that Iraq's influence on Jordan might be useful in this context.[34]

However, King Hussein did not desire accession to the Pact, in spite of British pressure. He preferred not to damage his relationship with Nasser and antagonise the radical elements within his kingdom.

The Iraqi government's decision to renew the alliance with Britain was of the greatest significance for regional politics because of Iraq's relations with the rest of the Arab world and, in particular, Egypt. Nuri's great ambition to link his country to a defence system outside the Arab League alienated Nasser, who believed that the Arab League could give sufficient safeguard to every Arab country and that there was no need to seek an outside alliance, especially one based on a pact with a Western state. Egyptian–Iraqi relations had begun to deteriorate soon after Nasser came to power. The major conflict between the two was over predominance in the Arab world. Iraq objected to Nasser's aspirations of control. Nasser's philosophy and claims seemed from Iraq's point of view to be too controversial and lacking in legitimacy and historical justification.

Another state that Britain wanted to include within the Baghdad Pact was Iran, as its membership would work to the advantage of the Middle East defence system. If Iran, adjacent to Soviet territory, was to fall into Soviet hands then greater communist pressure would be placed on Afghanistan and Pakistan. In addition, it would enable the Soviets to threaten the oil of Northern Iraq, Kuwait, Saudi Arabia, Oman and Bahrain. From Iran, Soviet communications by land with the Arab states of the Middle East would be direct and would supplement or replace communications through the Bosphorus.[35] Following a visit to Teheran by a Turkish delegation in October 1955, the Shah decided to join the Pact.

By mid-1955, US policy was still hesitant, which disappointed the British government who desired a stronger commitment from the United States in the area, especially towards the Baghdad Pact. The British government believed that support for the Pact was the most effective way of making the Soviet government aware that the United States was interested in the Middle East. Macmillan noted in his memoirs that 'if only they [the Americans] had taken the plunge themselves a great sense of confidence would have been created'.[36] The initial British lack of enthusiasm for the Pact, on the grounds that it would invoke the hostility of Egypt and destablise the region, was soon forgotten once it became clear that it could be an instrument for the renewal of its treaty right with Iraq and, more importantly, a potential vehicle for the maintenance of its influence throughout the area.[37]

The US administration, however, did not make any direct move towards the Middle East, and, in a way, preferred Britain to play a major role, especially in areas that were traditionally under British influence. Although supporting the idea of the Northern Tier, they were not prepared to join such a defence arrangement until a settlement of the Arab–Israeli dispute was reached. The United States continued to avoid commitments outside NATO, though limited support for Britain, in both Egypt and Iran, was given in 1954, and the existence of American airbases in North Africa and Saudi Arabia under bilateral agreements provided some reassurance. However, it was not prepared to join the Northern Tier for a mixture of reasons.

One of the most important was that the State Department wished to preserve relations with Saudi Arabia and Egypt. In addition, it had no wish to antagonise Israel and did not want to antagonise the Soviet Union any more than necessary. The American administration believed that the major defence burden for the Middle East should be left to the United Kingdom. In a State Department report to Eisenhower on 11 July 1955, it was recommended that Washington should not be formally associated with the Baghdad Pact because it might affect its influence and ability to reduce Arab–Israeli tension.[38] This stand aggravated the British government, especially in view of its desire to reduce defence expenditure and also because it believed it was pushed into acceding to the Northern Tier by the Americans and then left to carry the burden virtually on its own.[39]

Dulles believed that the Pact was not of primary importance because he perceived that it was not 'an instrument for collective defence against the Soviet Union, but has become an instrument of Arab intrigue.'[40] Dulles' unwillingness to sanction US accession to the Pact represented not just a minor tactical disagreement with Britain, but a major disagreement with British strategy in the region.[41]

The US government was fully aware of Nasser's strong rejection of the Pact. In a conversation with Robert Anderson, Eisenhower's special envoy to the Middle East, on 19 January 1956, Nasser stated that the Baghdad Pact was viewed by him and his government as a conspiracy designed to isolate Egypt. In his view the Pact was not just a regional defence agreement, but had a political philosophy. He thought that a pact between outside powers and the Arab world was not desirable. Furthermore, besides the ideological factors, Nasser objected to the Pact because it aimed to strengthen Iraq as the major force in the region.[42]

Nasser's apprehension about the formation of the Baghdad Pact was not something that could be ignored, as the likelihood of divisions within the Arab world would weaken rather than strengthen the security of the region and perhaps open up a path for the Soviets to exploit. It was therefore essential to minimise any rift between the West and Nasser, and to initiate policies that were designed to placate him. In order to achieve this it was necessary to go beyond simply making offers of aid or acknowledging his influence in the Arab world, for there would also have to be an effort to solve one of the major problems in Middle East politics, the continuing Ara–Israeli dispute. Without a settlement of this conflict it would be impossible to achieve complete regional alignment with the West, and the Soviet Union would still have an issue to exploit to its own advantage. However, it was clear that a solution to this dilemma would not be easy to achieve. It would require the negotiation of a wide-ranging agreement to address the many issues arising out of Arab–Israeli antagonism. In addition, it relied on the US and British powers being able to ensure that Israel was willing to make concessions to Egypt. There was, however, no guarantee that it would be possible to achieve the latter. British and US relations with Israel were strained and they lacked the necessary leverage to force concessions outside of direct coercion. In particular, there were grave tensions in Anglo-Israeli relations, which arose out of a fundamental clash of national interests. To understand the nature of this relationship it is essential to look at the foundations of Israeli foreign policy and the history of its relations with Britain since 1948.

NOTES

1. Royal Institute of International Affairs (RIIA), *British Interests in the Mediterranean and the Middle East: A Report by Chatham House Study Group* (Oxford: Oxford University Press, 1958), p. 25.
2. General Staff of the Israel Defense Forces, 'The World Oil Market', *Skeira Hodshit* (Israeli military monthly review), (November 1957), p. 25.
3. RIIA, *British Interests*, p. 27.
4. General Staff of the Israel Defense Force, *The World*, p. 25.
5. Daniel Yergin, *The Prize, the Epic Quest for Oil, Money and Power* (London: Simon & Schuster, 1991), p. 45.
6. RIIA, *British Interests*, p. 27.
7. J.C. Hurewitz, 'The Historical Context', in Wm Louis Roger and Roger Owen (eds) *Suez 1956: The Crisis and its Consequences* (Oxford: Clarendon Press, 1989), pp. 19–20.
8. Richard Jasse, 'The Baghdad Pact: Cold War or Colonialism?', *Middle Eastern Studies*, Vol. 27, No. 1, January 1992, p. 140.
9. Jacob Abadi, *British Withdrawal from the Middle East: The Economic and Strategic*

Imperatives (Princeton, NJ: Kingston Press, 1982), p. 88. See also: PRO, DEFE6/37/JP(56)61, October 1956.

10. John Kent, 'The Egyptian Base and the Defence of the Middle East, 1945–1954', in Robert Holland (ed.) *Emergencies and Disorder in the European Empires* (London: Frank Cass, 1994), p. 52.
11. Abadi, *British Withdrawal*, pp. 156–7.
12. Nigel Ashton, *Eisenhower, Macmillan and the Problem of Nasser: Anglo-American Relations and the Problem of Nationalism 1955–1959* (Basingstoke: Macmillan, 1996), p. 26.
13. Gamal Abdul Nasser, *Egypt's liberation: The Philosophy of the Revolution* (Washington, DC: Public Affairs Press, 1955). In his book Nasser broadly addresses British imperialism and its role in creating the Zionist state. On imperialism in general, see pp. 98–102, and *passim*.
14. Ibid.
15. Ibid.
16. Kent, *The Egyptian Base, passim.*
17. For a wide account of the Anglo-Iranian dispute see Benjamin Shwadran, *The Middle East, Oil and the Great Powers* (Jerusalem: Israel Universities Press, 1973), Ch. 5, pp. 89–112.
18. Jasse, 'The Baghdad Pact', p. 144.
19. For further details on the operation and politics of the American oil companies see Daniel Yergin, *The Prize, passim.*
20. PRO, FO371/133257/UES 1179, Petroleum attaché (Washington) to Foreign Office, 3 July 1959.
21. Fiona Venn, *Oil Diplomacy in the Twentieth Century* (London: Macmillan, 1986), p. 113.
22. PRO, FO371/120782/ES1531/22, Riches (Foreign Office) to Nutting (Foreign Office), 2 July 1956.
23. *Skeira Hodshit*, p. 23.
24. Uri Bialer, *Between East and West: Israel's Foreign Policy Orientation 1948–1956* (Cambridge: Cambridge University Press, 1990), pp. 133–4.
25. Ya'acov Roi, *Soviet Decision Making in Practice: The USSR and Israel 1947—1954* (Somerset, NJ: Transactions Book, 1980), p. 483.
26. W. Scott Lucas, *Divided We Stand, Britain, the US and the Suez Crisis* (London: Hodder& Stoughton, 1991), pp. 25–6.
27. PRO, DEFE4/66/COS(53)118, 29 October 1953. .
28. Lucas, *Divided We Stand*, pp. 32, 42, 67.
29. Ibid., p. 38.
30. PRO, CAB134/2340/GEN 622/1/3, brief prepared by the Foreign 0ffice on United Kingdom interests in the Middle East, 12 December 1957.
31. Lucas, *Divided We Stand*, p. 38.
32. Ashton, *Eisenhower, Macmillan*, p. 120.
33. Jasse, 'The Baghdad Pact', p. 141.
34. Jules Menken, 'Problems of Middle Eastern Strategy', *Brassey's Annual* 1956, p. 136.
35. PRO, AIR20/9896 JP(56)57, 13 March 1956.
36. Harold Macmillan, *Riding the Storm, 1956–1959* (London: Macmillan, 1971), p. 91.
37. Ashton, *Eisenhower, Macmillan*, p. 59.
38. *FRUS*, 1955–57, Vol. 12, State Department position paper, 11 July 1955, pp. 129–32; Hoover To Dulles, pp. 132–3, 11 July 1955, cited in Ritchie Ovendale, *Britain, the United States and the Transfer of Power in the Middle East* (London: Leicester University Press, 1996), p. 122.

39. Ibid., pp. 122–3.
40. PRO, CAB134/2340/GEN622/113, brief by the Foreign Office, 12 December 1957.
41. Ashton, *Eisenhower, Macmillan*, p. 78.
42. *FRUS*, Vol. 15, 1955–57, message from Robert Anderson to the State Department, 19 January 1956, pp. 31–3.

— 2 —
Israeli Interests in the Middle East

SECURITY-DOMINATED FOREIGN POLICY

ON 15 MAY 1948, the last British soldier left Palestine, marking the end of 30 years of British rule and the birth of the new Jewish state, Israel, which aimed to be the homeland of every Jew who wanted to participate in building the new country.

Since its foundation, Israel's interests in the Middle East have been conditioned by one dominant factor – its security position as a result of the Arab–Israeli dispute. This basic factor underlined Israel's foreign policy. It led to a drive for military superiority over its Arab neighbours; to a consistent search for arms supply as well as security guarantees by other major powers. It also meant that Israel's main diplomatic efforts were made towards countries that could potentially help it militarily and economically.

At the time, the main figure was David Ben-Gurion, the Prime Minister and Defence Minister between 1948 and 1953, who took the leading role in the conduct of Israel's defence and foreign policy. Ben-Gurion and the elite of the Israeli government took a broad view of security, which included military strength, settlements, advanced technology and science. This view arose for two main reasons: first, the feelings of isolation, and, second, the constant feeling of threat caused by the Arabs' non-acceptance of Israel's right to exist. The centrality of defence and the need to rely on Jewish self-defence were also influenced by past experience. The 1880s pogroms in Russia and the defenceless position of the Jews had a strong impact on Ben-Gurion's generation, who experienced some of the horrors themselves. It contributed to the feeling that the young Jewish state must have a strong Jewish defence force, and led to the conclusion that Israel could not rely on any other force but its own. This attitude also explains the central position of the Israel Defense Forces (IDF) within Israeli political life. The IDF was seen as a model for the fulfilment of the Zionist dream, a new creation where the *Sabras* (the Israeli native-born) were the dominant element; it represented the rebirth of the Jewish nation. The great emphasis on security caused Israel's foreign policy to become more or less an instrument of its defence needs, and therefore not independent of the military. There was, in effect, hardly any distinction between foreign and defence policy. Furthermore, Ben-Gurion did not take many people into his confidence; only a very small group was consulted on military issues. The security decisions were therefore a result of a small circle of advisers (in Israel it was common to call this group *Anshie Shlomenu*, or in a free translation, 'one of us, one of the net') and this phenomenon continued during many successive Mapai governments though not to the same extent. In Golda Meir's premiership it was known as 'Golda's kitchen'. It meant that those who were close to Ben-Gurion enjoyed great influence on him. The Israeli Foreign Ministry was largely excluded from this intimate group, and its failure to obtain arms agreements with the West, despite all its efforts, decreased its influence even further.

Throughout the first years of independence, Israel's foreign policy was formulated against a backdrop of economic stress. The absorption of large numbers of immigrants in a very short time entailed enormous expense. The situation became more acute due to the fact that Israel was deprived of the possibility of trading with its neighbours (as the Arab countries imposed economic blockade on Israel), which had been such an important economic benefit in the Mandate period. This meant that Israel's goods were prevented from reaching the Arab countries and Arab goods from reaching Israel. From 1951, the Arab boycott effort greatly intensified. Arab League was active against Israeli commercial firms as well as third parties doing business with Israel. The Arab League members set up an elaborate network of boycott offices in all their capitals and commercial centres, and attempted to prevent foreign companies from doing business with Israel. At the same time, there was an air blockade and flights to and from Israeli airfields were forbidden to fly over Arab territory.[1]

In such an atmosphere it was not surprising that an Arab–Israeli peace settlement was regarded as unrealistic for the time being. Ben-Gurion stated in one of his political essays that although peace was desirable, there was no prospect for it in the near future. 'We do not think', he said, 'that today or tomorrow we will achieve a peace settlement between Israel and the Arabs, but we should not be restricted to the present.'[2] In his view peace could be achieved under two conditions: first, the Arab states should become democratic, and, second, Israel's political, military and economic position should be strengthened, because that would diminish the Arab hopes that Israel would collapse. Consequently, the Israeli government was determined not to show any sign of weakness and to use its 'armed fist' whenever it felt it was necessary. This policy meant that Israel would not take the risk of being militarily inferior, even if this were to reduce the tensions between Israel and its Arab neighbours.

The firm line adopted by the Israelis from 1954 onwards was based upon the idea that Israel had 'to teach the Arabs a lesson', the reasons for this policy being the Fedayeen activities and their effect on the Israeli population. Until 1953 the Fedayeen operated mainly from Jordan, although the first attack took place in 1951 from Syrian territory. From 1954, however, most of the Fedayeen activities came from Egypt. These were large-scale operations in contrast to the earlier incursions, which had been on a limited scale. The close proximity of the Gaza Strip to Israel could only worsen the situation, as many Palestinian refugees who fled Israel in the 1948 war had settled in refugees camps in Gaza. The Palestinians who had lost their homes and villages, and who faced great hardship, were bitter and hostile towards Israel and were therefore an easy target for those governments that wanted to exploit their hatred. By violating the 1948 armistice agreement and supporting the Fedayeen, the Arab countries had demonstrated their unwillingness to compromise with Israel and reminded it constantly of its vulnerability and of their animosity towards its existence. Moreover, the fact that many Palestinian refugee camps were located near the Israeli border, either in Gaza or the West Bank, added more fuel to the fire, as these Palestinians could see across the border and watch their former villages and fields being occupied by Israel. The fact that they were the forgotten victims of the Arab–Israeli dispute and were hardly assisted by their new host governments added more fuel to this inflammable situation. Yehoshafat Harkabi, former head of Israeli military intelligence, pointed out in an interview with the author that the Israeli government and IDF were aware that quite often, and especially in the early period of the Fedayeen raids, these infiltrations were mainly motivated by economic reasons, e.g. by Palestinians who crossed the border in order to harvest their crops in their former villages.[3] They led to a firm response from Israel across the borders of both Jordan and Egypt, in order to 'teach' the Arab leaders that the Israeli government saw them as responsible for these activities, even if they had not directly conducted them. By adopting this policy the Israeli government expressed a basic belief, which can be described as the 'deterrent concept'. It meant that Israel could not take any risks regarding the balance of power in the region. Retaliation was carried out because of the predictable effect it might have, rather than due to the actual severity of the Fedayeen actions. It was presented by the

Israeli government as an instrument which made it clear to the Arabs how far they could go. According to Horowitz, this policy in regard to the rules of the Arab–Israeli dispute contained an element of bargaining founded on violence.[4] It represented a recognition of an unsolved situation.

Ben-Gurion expressed this view in his memoirs by saying that 'We could not sit with our hands folded in the face of attempts on the life of our citizens by murderers sent into our sovereign territory ... if the Armistice lines were to be open to saboteurs and murderers, they could not be closed to the defenders'.[5] 'Our borders,' he said, 'are no less important to us than they would be to a Soviet, American or British leader, and I am sure' he added, 'that they would not agree that their people would be subject to constant terrorist activities'.[6] He also believed that the Jews, who had finally achieved their right to return, should be welcomed by the Arabs (because of the economic prosperity they brought to the country), but that instead they were treated in a hostile way, a view which was common among most Mapai members from the 1930s onwards. Moshe Dayan, the Chief of Staff, shared Ben-Gurion's view and said that the retaliatory policy was not an act of revenge, but a punishment and a warning to the governments concerned of the potential danger to their inhabitants if they did not control the infiltrations along Israel's border. He also believed it forced the Arab governments to consider whether their aim of destroying Israel was realistic.[7] Dayan felt that retaliatory action was the only way to convince the Arab countries that, for the safety of their own people, they should stop infiltration by the Fedayeen. 'We are not able', he said, 'to protect every man, but we can prove that the price for Jewish blood is high.'[8]

The Dayan–Ben-Gurion relationship was very special and very close. Ben-Gurion saw Dayan as more than just a military adviser and consequently Dayan enjoyed great freedom in his actions. This relationship also reflected the importance of the defence circles in Israeli foreign policy. Dayan, with the support of some commanders in the field, portrayed himself as spokesman of the armed forces in order to strengthen his position. Ben-Gurion's and Dayan's approach to the question of the Arab–Israeli dispute can be described generally as militaristic and uncompromising. However, there was a difference between the two. As the Prime Minister, Ben-Gurion was more aware of the implications that retaliatory actions had upon Israel's relations with the West and was willing, up to a point, to take note of Western sensitivities, although he was convinced that Israel should have military superiority, and that if found in danger of losing, Israel would have to react before it was too late. Moshe Dayan, who masterminded the reprisals, generally shared Ben-Gurion's views but took them in a more radical direction. To him, retaliation on a small scale did not serve the purpose. There was a need for operations on a large scale.[9] He favoured mass retaliation on the grounds that he knew it might escalate the whole situation and bring about a war. Dayan believed war was the only real long-term solution to the Fedayeen activities. He was a *Sabra*, a native-born Israeli, and had been a military man from an early age. He had been a commander in the Hagana (the Jewish underground movement during the Mandate period), lost an eye in an operation in Syria during the Second World War, and later, after the foundation of Israel, became a symbol of heroism, youth and courage. To Ben-Gurion and his generation, Dayan represented the new-born Jew, an image that was highly admired and promoted at the time. The 'Diaspora' Jew represented the past, helplessness and misery, the *Sabras*, on the other hand, symbolised the future, rebirth, courage and hope.

When analysing Israeli retaliatory policy one should also take into consideration Israeli public opinion. Although very occasionally some newspapers criticised government policy, usually the public was fully behind it. In general there was little criticism of the retaliation policy. The new immigrants who had recently arrived in Israel were largely placed in the new settlements along the borders, and suffered constantly from the Fedayeen attacks. For them the retaliatory policy was evidence that the government would protect them. Furthermore, the majority of the public believed that it was within Israel's rights to adopt this policy because the 'Arabs' provoked it by their actions. One could conclude, therefore, that the one main advantage of the reprisal policy was that it boosted public morale. However, the reprisals had a devastating impact on Israel's external relations, and did not provide a decisive military answer to the problem.

The question is, therefore, why did Israel continue to pursue this policy despite its obvious disadvantages and the worldwide criticism it provoked? The answer can be found if we examine Israeli policy from a wider viewpoint. The Zionist movement and the founders of the Jewish state had a very strong belief that their cause was just. In their view, criticism and hesitation over fundamental Zionist issues could weaken the Zionist effort to create a new, fresh and courageous society. One of these fundamental beliefs was that Israel had the right to exist despite its neighbours' rejection, or injustice to them. If its Arab neighbours would not accept Israel's existence and tried to destroy it, Israel was justified in employing any means necessary to eliminate the threat. There was also a growing belief during the 1950s that the only 'language' the Arabs understood was force. There was also a conviction that if Israel did not respond, its neighbours might see it as a sign of weakness and would be encouraged to try to destroy it.

The firm line adopted by Ben-Gurion, Dayan, the military circles, as well as by the majority of Mapai, did, however, meet with some opposition. Moshe Sharett, Israel's Foreign Minister from 1948 to 1956 and Prime Minister from 1953 to 1955, represented a different outlook. He believed that adopting a firm line, and especially the tactic of retaliatory action, was fruitless, and could damage Israel's interests rather than benefit them. The only advantage of such a policy, he thought, was the effect on public morale. Although Sharett recognised that this was an important factor, he believed that there should nonetheless be a limit on how far it should affect Israeli policy. He admitted that sometimes security considerations might force Israel to take actions that might damage world sympathy and its foreign relations, and increase the tension between itself and its Arab neighbours, but that such action should be kept to the minimum.[10] Sharett's different outlook resulted from the way he perceived the Arab-Israeli dispute. He saw it from a broader perspective, which meant that he recognised the Arab–Israeli dispute to be only one of many regional and international disputes in the world. He was aware that one single, dramatic military action could not solve this dispute, but that it would be a long and slow process before any fundamental change in Israel's relations with its neighbours would occur. Therefore, in Sharett's view, Israel had to adopt a cautious and moderate policy, which might eventually lead to a peace settlement.

In retrospect, Ben-Gurion's and Dayan's belief in retaliation proved to be misplaced. Captured documents found after the Six Day War showed that up until the Gaza raid in February 1955, the Egyptian government did not conduct the Fedayeen activities directly; on the contrary, it sometimes tried to limit them. It was only after the Gaza raid that Nasser gave his support to these actions and started to organise them.[11] However, the Israeli government was not aware of this at the time. Instead, it was sure that if only the Egyptians wanted, they could stop the Fedayeen raids. This belief, combined with the anger and frustration the Israelis felt, meant the Israeli government was determined that the retaliation raids were the only effective way to deal with the problem. Taking into account the important role of the IDF circles upon Ben-Gurion and foreign policy in general – especially the unique influence Dayan had on Ben-Gurion – it is little wonder that there was no place for any other attitude.

THE INFLUENCE OF THE JEWISH DIASPORA

Another key and unique aspect of Israeli foreign policy was its relationship with the Diaspora Jewry. As a Jewish state Israel aimed to be a base for millions of Jews from the Diaspora who would come and create an 'ingathering of the exiles'. Jewish immigration to Israel was seen as essential to Israel's strength, and was visualised as an act of redemption. Consequently, Israel placed a very important emphasis on its relations with Jewish communities outside Israel, and this, in turn, had a unique influence on Israel's foreign policy. The significance of the relationship arose from the fact that Israel and the Diaspora Jewry felt a deep concern and obligation towards each other. The question is whether and how far this factor influenced Israeli foreign policy and whether we can see the Diaspora Jewry as a significant interest group.

Ben-Gurion certainly viewed them as a group with a legitimate function and an obligation to assist Israel to achieve its foreign policy goals. This can be understood on the grounds that the Israelis had a constant feeling of isolation and therefore viewed the Jewish communities abroad as their only loyal allies. He thought that an attachment between Israel and the Jewish Diaspora was important, because it prevented the Jews of the Diaspora from total assimilation.[12] Apart from these religious–national reasons, the Jewish communities, especially in the United States, played a significant role on Israel's behalf. The Israeli government did not hesitate to demand actual political and economic aid from them. This should be understood in terms of the complicated relationship between the two. For most of the Israelis, Zionism meant to live in Israel and therefore they felt that the Diaspora Jews, who were not sharing the daily burden, could at the very least help Israel politically and economically.

As a pragmatic politician, Ben-Gurion did not challenge their self-identification as Zionists. On the contrary, he let them believe that they had an important role to play. He praised American Jewry's contribution to Israel, and described the mutual relations between the state of Israel and the American Jewry in the following way. While Israel was a 'pillar of strength and enhancement of dignity and stature, in turn it [the American Jewish community] makes to us [Israel] a contribution with which no other Jewry can vie'.[13] Indeed, American Jewry operated as a useful lobby for Israel, both before and after the Sinai war.

However, the limitation of these activities should be recognised. The US Secretary of State, John Foster Dulles, sharply criticised the activities of the American Jews, holding mass meetings and creating a situation where the Arabs felt it was not safe for them to rely on the United States. He made it clear to Ambassador Eban on 2 March 1956 that the President and he had made a decision to: 'formulate our foreign policies without reference to the effect upon domestic politics'.[14] This continued to be the case after the Suez war, when the American government threatened the Israelis by making it clear that if Israel would not withdraw from Sinai, it might affect the economic contribution of American Jewry to Israel. In spite of the huge demonstration held by the American Jews in Madison Square Gardens, it did not cause the American administration to change its policy. It must be noted that, although the Jewish vote played an important role in the United States, Eisenhower carried the 1956 elections in New York and California against the Jewish vote. The Jewish communities at the time largely voted for the Democrats and therefore, unlike Truman, Eisenhower was freer to carry out his policies without taking the Jewish lobby into consideration. Anthony Eden, the British Prime Minister, did not understand this and relied upon the American Jews to restrain Eisenhower.

However, despite American Jewry's assistance to Israel and his belief that there should be a strong bond between the Diaspora Jewry and the state of Israel, Ben-Gurion, along with most Israeli decision-makers and most of the Israeli people, strongly believed that if a Jew wanted to influence Israeli policy, the only way to do it was to come and settle in Israel. This explains the fact that, despite their financial aid to Israel, the Diaspora Jews did not win any political power over Israeli policy. Furthermore, the Diaspora Jewry had no decision-making mechanism or central control body. It can be therefore be described as an interest group which had an important role in Israel, but it cannot be seen as a vital factor in the Israeli decision-making process.

THE SEARCH FOR ARMS SUPPLY: ISRAEL'S EXTERNAL RELATIONS WITH THE GREAT POWERS

As a country that felt constantly under threat and isolation, Israel aimed to acquire an arms supply of high quality and gain security guarantees. By the early 1950s, it was clear to the Israeli leaders that it was only from the West that Israel could obtain the facilities necessary to train the officers for its young army, and consequently, from 1950 onwards, Israel's foreign policy orientation shifted towards the Western powers. This was a shift away from the policy in the early days after its foundation when Israel had tried to maintain neutrality towards the West and the East. However, if closely analysed, Israeli interests show that a shift towards the West was inevitable.

The first clear shift in Israeli policy *vis-à-vis* the West was marked by its attitude towards the Korean War, when it declared its support for the West. One of the central aims of Israeli policy from that stage was therefore to obtain arms and security guarantees from the United States. Israel viewed the United States with great sympathy and admiration. Ben-Gurion thought that the United States of America represented a magnificent phenomenon in history and that there was a similarity between Israel and America, since they both pursued a pioneering goal. Apart from that, he was aware that a great number of Jewish people lived in America who could serve as 'a bond and bridge between Israel and the country in question'.[15]

Early in 1951, Israeli leaders had already decided to aim to ally themselves with the United States. During the first half of 1951, Israel sent the American government a secret memorandum on its economic and industrial capacity to co-operate with the American military.[16] The American government, on the other hand, had quite a hesitant policy towards the Middle East, and they had no interest in creating a special relationship with Israel. This, however, did not reduce Israel's determination to persuade the Americans that it was in their best interests to support the State of Israel. In 1955, the Israeli government tried to obtain a specific security guarantee and arms supply from the United States. The discussions were secret and conducted mainly by the Israeli Ambassador in Washington. Israel offered the Americans bases and, in exchange, asked for security guarantees, in particular a defence treaty, which would include the supply of arms. Moshe Sharett, who was Foreign Minister at the time, appealed to Secretary Dulles to consider: 'Further urgent thought to the crucial question of whether the conclusion of a defence treaty should be deferred till after tangible progress towards a settlement has been achieved, or whether it should not rather be proceeded with alone and itself pave the way for such a progress.'[17] He tried to convince Dulles that a security treaty with Israel would give Israel a sense of stability. Sharett said that it would promote a more realistic spirit within the Arab states, encourage them to make peace, and make the Arabs eager to secure for themselves the advantages accruing from association with the United States.[18] This was a line the Israeli diplomats tried constantly to put forward. Ben-Gurion himself tried to convince the American government that if Israel was given arms, it would not be driven to launch a preventive war.[19] However, the Americans at that stage were determined not to supply Israel with any substantial arms. This could be explained by the feelings that existed at the time in Washington, that arms supply to Israel would identify the Americans as supporters of Israel while the Soviets would appear to be the Arabs' allies. The United States was keen at that stage to be seen as maintaining all Western interests in the Middle East rather than being just an ally of Israel. This was seen as the main task of US policy, especially in view of the growing Soviet intervention in the region. According to Bar-On, as long as the US administration believed that there was a chance for ALPHA (see Chapter 3), they did not want to supply arms as a means of keeping Israel under constant pressure to agree to some territorial concessions. Dulles was sure that arms supply to Israel would cause anger in the Arab world against the United States and it would limit its influence in the Middle East and upon oil supply.[20] It was not surprising, therefore, that in those circumstances Israel had no chance of getting the arms it desired. This is not to say that the United States was not aware of Israel's desperation and was ready to supply a few items such as helicopters, but they preferred that Israel look to other sources such as Canada and France for arms.

As already emphasised, Israel tried in its early days to adopt a more neutral position in the unfolding Cold War and established good relations with the Soviet Union. However, from the beginning, Israeli leaders were suspicious and apprehensive of the Soviets. Although the Soviet Union had supported the 1947 UN partition resolution, this was seen by the Israeli leaders as a temporary aberration in the long history of Soviet hostility towards Zionism. There were two basic factors in Soviet policy which were bound to clash with Israeli aims. The first was the position of Soviet Jewry within the USSR. The second was Israel's basic identification with Western democratic ideology, rather than with communism, despite the Zionist parties on the left who were, however, in favour of close relations with the Soviet Union. Most of the Israeli leaders were antagonistic towards communism, an attitude which had developed due to the Russian, and after 1917 Soviet, hostility towards the Jews and Zionism.[21]

This view was expressed by Moshe Sharett, the Israeli Foreign Minister, who believed that Israel should oppose communism, be its mortal enemy, and that the unity of the Jewish people necessitated 'abolishing the Communist regime in the world'.[22] The attitude towards the Soviet Union was debated in the inner circle of the Mapai party, which was the dominant party throughout the 1930s and after Israel's establishment. It was a Zionist–Socialist party and included members such as Ben-Gurion, Golda Meir and Abba Eban. It was a relatively moderate party in its foreign policy, but did not hesitate to demonstrate its 'armed fist' if it felt necessary. Ben-Gurion thought that it was important that Israel should not appear as an open enemy of the Soviet Union, but he also believed that the Soviet regime represented a contrasting ideology to the State of Israel and to the close relations between Jewish communities worldwide. In his view, every totalitarian regime would strangle the State of Israel and stop its growth, nourished from the Diaspora. Furthermore, he believed that, even if the Soviet bloc did not espouse the destruction of Zionism and deny the unity of the Jewish people, it would be dangerous for Israel to be associated with it, because, as a totalitarian regime, it would try to dominate Israel, showing her in a negative light *vis-à-vis* the Western world.[23]

The relationship worsened in 1952 as a result of the Prague trial where the Jewish secretary of the Czech Communist Party was accused of conspiracy against Soviet Jewry. This was accompanied by a wave of anti-Semitism throughout the Eastern bloc, which confirmed the Israeli government's deep suspicion towards the Soviets. This also caused Israeli leaders to turn completely to the West, which looked more promising as a source of arms.

Another bone of contention between the two countries was the position of Soviet Jewry and their very limited religious freedom or right of contact with Israel or even Israeli representatives. As a Jewish country, Israel felt that it had a responsibility for Jews that were discriminated against because of their beliefs. This was the case in the Soviet–Israeli relationship where Israel could not establish good relations with a regime that did not allow freedom for the Jews, which tried to assimilate them by force and did not allow them to emigrate to Israel. In a meeting between Golda Meir and Israeli diplomats in Paris in 1958, there was a consensus among the Israeli diplomats and Meir about the grave situation of the Soviet Jewry in the USSR and its implications for the Israeli attitude towards the Soviet Union. This factor thus led the Israeli government to follow a very cautious policy towards the Soviets, while avoiding attacking them openly.[24]

Following its failure to form a close alliance with the United States or to come to some accommodation with the Soviet Union, Israel had to keep searching for other potential sources from which it could obtain modern weapons. Israel's new hope was France. A major decision was taken in 1954 to try to make France a primary source of arms supply. This marked a turning point in Israel's foreign policy and should be viewed from the background of the Israeli failure to obtain arms from the United States. This determination was especially dominant among the military and defence circles, who thought that Israel should try elsewhere. Ben-Gurion was sceptical at first, but he was convinced by Moshe Dayan and by the General Director of the Defence Ministry, Shimon Peres, who argued that the possibility of gaining arms from the United States was small because it was not in the latter's interests to supply arms to Israel.

Shimon Peres and Moshe Dayan built their relationship with the French through French defence circles. Both defence ministries enjoyed great importance and prestige in their respective countries, and the French military were receptive to Israeli overtures because of the Algerian conflict and their fear of Nasser as a radical element who inspired the National Liberation Front (FLN). The French government thought that the Israelis could help them to eliminate the power of the rebels in Algeria.

However, the French did not want to be seen as the sole supplier of arms to Israel, as this might harm their remaining interests in the Middle East. The problem was that because of the northern Africa issue the French position had become very delicate, with Egypt, Saudi Arabia and, to some extent, Syria all having the potential to damage French interests in the region. The French Foreign Minister therefore believed that it would be better if Britain, France and the United States could reach an agreement on arms shipment to the Middle East, and that to create a rough equilibrium in the arms capabilities of Israel and its Arab neighbours would require delivery of arms from the West to Israel. In the French view there were only two possibilities: either the Western powers would allow Israel to defend itself or they would sacrifice it to the Arab states.[25]

Although the relationship between the two countries was close, the French were constantly suspicious of Israel's motives. They believed that Israel would prefer to ally itself with the Americans and the British, and that the Israelis chose to ally with France only because they had no alternative. Being aware of this sensitivity, Moshe Sharett told the Cabinet that real friendship with France could not rely only on a cultural exchange, but there should be a wider framework. He did not specify particular fields, but from 1955 onwards there were intensive negotiations between Israel and France at a military level. Israel could offer the French intelligence assistance and the French could supply Israel with arms, technical and scientific aid, and assist with its plan to build an oil pipeline.

However, on two points there were conflicting opinions between the two countries. First, the Baghdad Pact, and, second, the approach towards Soviet penetration in the Middle East. Regarding the first issue the Israelis were not in favour of the Pact, but did not object to it entirely, while the French opposed it totally. The French government opposed the Pact because they were against Arab unity and anxious about the possibility that Arab nationalism might become an influential factor in the international arena. On the second issue, the

French government's view of Soviet intervention in the region was very different to that of Israel and the other Western countries. The French government believed that more consideration should be given to the Soviet Union, while the Israelis thought that any kind of Soviet arbitration in the region was very dangerous to Israel and to future stability. The French believed that it was important to come to some agreement with the USSR, thereby neutralising its ability to stir up the nationalists in northern Africa against France. In addition, France had a strong Communist Party which it depended upon to some degree. If one combines all these factors together one can understand the French anxiety to keep amicable relations with the Soviet Union.[26] The French government was also very sensitive about any Israeli retaliation against Syria, because they retained some influence in that country and were afraid that reprisals might endanger this position.

Despite these difficulties there were, however, many common interests between the two countries, such as their attitude towards Nasser and the Arab National Movement. The similarity in perspective and needs enabled the two countries to reach a close relationship, based on military and economic interests, and for Israel, France was the only ally it had at the time.

In its constant search for an arms supply, Israel also appealed to the Canadian government. Canada was perceived by the Israelis as a friendly country which understood Israel's needs. Canada did not have an elaborate Middle East policy and its main concern was over refugee relief and keeping stability in the region. However, its Foreign Minister, Lester Pearson, who was a pragmatist on Middle Eastern affairs, had a marked preference for Israel.[27] Furthermore, as a country with few interests in the region, Canada originally had little to do with arms sales to the region. Israel first raised the possibility of purchasing Canadian Sabre fighter aircraft in April 1953, but an official request for 24 planes was not submitted until a year later. The Israeli Ambassador to Canada emphasised that the aircraft were absolutely essential as a deterrent to aggression and to give Israel and its people some confidence in their ability to defend themselves.[28] But Dulles' opposition to the request caused the Canadians to cancel the proposed sale. However, the changing circumstances in the Middle East gave Canada more freedom. That summer the American government supplied arms to Iraq, and in October 1954, with the signing of a new Anglo-Egyptian agreement, Great Britain lifted its arms embargo on Egypt. At the same time, Canada opened embassies in Tel-Aviv, Cairo and Beirut. With Western arms flowing to the Arabs and with Canada trying to demonstrate its political independence in the region, Lester Pearson was willing to supply a range of equipment, including anti-tank and anti-aircraft guns, although Washington remained a major obstacle. However, under great pressure from Israel, and in the light of the Egyptian–Czech arms deal, the United States agreed that other Western states could sell arms to Israel as long as the latter lifted the pressure on Washington. It seems that at that stage the United States realised the necessity of selling arms to Israel. Dulles said to the French Foreign Minister, Christian Pineau, that if Israel were to be attacked the United States would take action, but that he was well aware that American aid might come too late to be of immediate assistance. 'There was, of course,' he said, 'no assurance that it would be possible to give Israel adequate means of defending itself alone after an attack should occur.'[29] Dulles resented the constant pressure from the Zionist lobby in the United States and emphasised that supplying Israel with arms at that particular moment would make it appear as if they were giving in to that pressure and turning away from a position of neutrality.[30] It is important to emphasise this point that the Eisenhower administration was not giving way to Zionist pressure and wanted to avoid any impression that they conducted a favourable policy towards Israel because of the Jewish lobby. It highlights again that, contrary to the common belief among American Jewry and Israeli leaders in the enormous power of American Jews, this was not the case at that time. If anything it seems that the Zionist lobby's pressure made Dulles and Eisenhower even more determined to conduct a policy they believed was solely in the best interests of the United States.

The tacit American approval of Israel obtaining arms from other states in the West can be seen at a tripartite meeting at the Quai d'Orsay on 6 May 1956, between British, French and US representatives. At the meeting, Pineau, the French Foreign Minister, raised the subject of Israel's vulnerability and the necessity to supply it with arms. Dulles emphasised that on this occasion he was very concerned about the pressure on the United States to supply Israel with arms and said that the United States preferred if Israel could obtain arms from sources other than themselves. However, he added that if Israel was in a grave danger the United States would reconsider its position, and concluded: 'We would not sit idly and watch Israel destroyed.'[31] However, when Pineau pointed out to Dulles the grave situation that Israel faced as a result of Egyptian air superiority, Dulles replied that it was nonsense to believe that this problem could be solved by supplying Israel with large quantities of bombers; the only answer to the problem was deterrence. He therefore saw the benefit of supplying Israel with some aircraft as a deterrent against the Arabs' intentions. Dulles continued by saying that he did not like Israeli pressure on his government and that the United States was not in a position to supply Israel with arms. The excuse Dulles gave at the time was that American public opinion would dramatise a situation in which the Soviet Union supplied arms to one side and the United States to the other, and that 'we will all be dragged out much further than we wished to go'.[32] Dulles therefore hoped that Israel could obtain arms from other sources such as Canada and France.[33] Finally, in September 1956, Canada announced that it would sell 24 Sabre aircraft to Israel.[34] In the end these aircraft were not delivered, due to the Suez War and the United Nations resolution of an arms embargo on Israel and Egypt.

We can conclude that in this early period Israel's efforts to gain arms were only partly successful, as were its attempts to gain security guarantees from the West. The Dayan–Ben-Gurion partnership and their determination to carry out the reprisal policy did not help Israel's stand. Israel only gained a close relationship with France, but the overall feeling among Israeli leaders and the Israeli public was that 'The people shall dwell alone' (Numbers, 23:9).

NOTES

1. ISA, HZ232/9, survey by Israeli Foreign Ministry, research department, 22 April 1956.
2. David Ben-Gurion, 'Our Foreign Policy', in *Hazon Vaderech* (Hebrew), Vol. 3 (Tel-Aviv: Am-Oved, 1957), p. 245.
3. Almog interview with Yehoshafat Harkabi, Jerusalem winter 1993.
4. Dan Horowitz, 'Doctrinat Habitchon shel Israel, Hatfisa Ha-ysraelit shel Bytachon Leumi (1948–1972)', in Benjamin Neurberger (ed.) *Diplomatia Betzel Eymut* ['Israeli Security Doctrine', in *Diplomacy and Confrontation*, Selected Issues in Israel's Foreign Relations, 1948–1978], (Tel-Aviv: Everyman's University, 1984), p. 117.
5. David Ben-Gurion, *Yehud Veichud* [Singularity and Mission], (Tel-Aviv: Ma'arachot, 1971: 1982), p. 230.
6. Ibid., p. 231.
7. Moshe Dayan, 'Military Activities in Peace Time', *Bamachane* (Israel Defense Forces' weekly magazine), Vol. 51, 26 October 1954, p. 5.
8. Ibid.
9. Moshe Dayan, *Avnei Derech* [Story of my Life] (Tel-Aviv: Edanin, Jerusalem: Dvir, 1976), p. 242; see also Moshe Sharett, *Yoman Ishi* [Personal Diary], entry for 28 March 1955 (Tel-Aviv: Ma'ariv, 1978), p. 591.
10. Ibid., p. 872.
11. Ehud Yehari, 'Egypt and the Fedayeen 1953–1956', cited in Mordechai Bar-On, 'Haiska Ha-Checit-Mizrit, Shela shel-Tiaruch' [The Czech–Egyptian Arms Deal – A Question of Date], *Ma'arachot*, Israeli Defence Ministry, December 1986–January 1987, 306–7, p. 29.
12. Ibid., p. 208. For A wider account on the relationship between the State of Israel and the Diaspora Jewry see Arthur Hertzberg, 'Israel and the Diaspora: A Relationship Re-examined', *Israel Affairs*, Vol. 2, Nos 3–4, Spring–Autumn 1996.
13. David Ben-Gurion, *Rebirth and Destiny of Israel* (London: Thomas Yosselof,

1959), p. 396.
14. *FRUS*, Vol. 15, 1955–57, memorandum of conversation, State Department, 2 March 1956, p. 281.
15. David Ben-Gurion, *Israel: A Personal History* (New York/Tel-Aviv: Funk and Wagnalls/Sabra Books, 1971), p. 501.
16. Uri Bialer, *Between East and West: Israel's Foreign Policy Orientation, 1948–1956* (Cambridge: Cambridge University Press, 1990), p. 243. See also David Tal, 'The American–Israeli Security Treaty: Sequel or Means to the Relief of Israeli–Arab Tensions, 1954–55', *Middle Eastern Studies*, Vol. 31, No. 4, October 1995.
17. *FRUS*, Vol. 14, 1955–57, telegram from Lawson (Tel-Aviv) to the State Department, 5 May 1955, p. 172.
18. Ibid., p. 171.
19. *FRUS*, Vol. 14, 1955–57, telegram from Lawson (Tel-Aviv) to the State Department, 17 February, p. 65.
20. Mordechai Bar-On, *Sharei A'za, Medinut H'chuz Vehabithon Shel Medinaht Israel 1955–1957* [The Gates of Gaza: Israel's Defence and Foreign Policy 1955–1957] (Tel-Aviv: Am-Oved, 1992), p. 172.
21. Michael Brecher, *Diplomatia be-Tzel Imut, Sugiot Bemedinut Hachz shel Israel 1948–1978* [Diplomacy and Confrontation, Selected Issues in Israel's Foreign Relations 1948–78], ed. Benjamin Neuberger (Tel-Aviv: Everyman's University, 1984), p. 61.
22. Uri Bialer, *Between East and West: Israel's Foreign Policy Orientation 1948–1956* (Cambridge: Cambridge University Press, 1990), p. 42.
23. Ben-Gurion, *Yehud Veichud*, p. 196.
24. ISA, HZ 2449/8, A meeting of Israeli diplomats in Paris, 24–25 February 1958.
25. *FRUS*, Vol. 15, 1955–57, telegram from the delegation at the North Atlantic ministerial meeting to the State Department, 3 May 1956, p. 596.
26. HZ2595/6, a report on Franco-Israeli relations, 10 April 1956.
27. Michael G. Fry, 'Canada, the North Atlantic Triangle, and the United Nations', in Wm Roger Louis and Roger Owen (eds) *Suez 1956: The Crisis and its Consequences* (Oxford: Clarendon Press, 1989), p. 286.
28. PRO, FO371/121334/V1192, Foreign Office memorandum, March 1956.
29. *FRUS*, Vol. 15, 1955–57, telegram from the delegation at the North Atlantic ministerial meeting, 3 May 1956, p. 597.
30. Ibid.
31. PRO, DEFE7/10/V10713/14, Tripartite meeting at the Quai d'Orsay, 6 May 1956.
32. Ibid.
33. Ibid.
34. Michael Oren, 'Canada, the Great Powers, and the Middle Eastern Arms Race, 1950–1956', *International History Review*, Vol. 12, No. 2, May 1990.

—3—
The Anglo-Israeli Relationship

IN ITS CONSTANT QUEST for Western allies and an arms supply, Israel also looked towards Britain. Yet the relations between the two countries were complicated by past experience. The formal British attitude towards Israel was based on the fact that 'A Jewish state in Palestine was brought into being in accordance with the will of the United Nations General Assembly.' Britain did not vote for the 1947 resolution but promised to 'respect the wishes of the majority of member nations'.[1] Britain had given Israel *de facto* recognition only after five aircraft flying over Israeli–Egyptian territory had been shot down by the Israelis, and only extended *de jure* recognition after the armistice lines were signed and King Abdullah of Jordan had formally annexed the West Bank.[2] British policy towards Israel after this was shaped by its general attitude towards the Middle East, which was centred around the regional defence system between Britain and the Arab states. In this context, Israel had very little significance for Britain other than as a potential obstacle to British interests.[3] Israel had little strategic or economic importance for Britain. It had no oil resources and it was not close to borders with the Soviet Union, which had to be defended. Israel could not provide the British with any strategic advantage they needed and did not have already. Furthermore, the Foreign Office believed that 'Israel by the mere fact of her existence represents a constant threat to our economic and strategic interests in the Middle East.'[4] Therefore any alliance with Israel risked Britain's friendship with certain Arab countries, co-operation with whom was much more essential than any link with Israel.[5]

Her Majesty's Government strongly opposed Israeli reprisal actions, as it felt that this policy caused disturbances in the target countries, and consequently created regional problems. Britain was especially concerned by Israel's actions against Jordan, because an escalation between the two might activate the defence treaty between Jordan and Britain, bringing Britain into dispute with Israel. The British government tried to avoid a situation where they might have to make a military stand against Israel. The possibility that the British government would face a situation where it would have to stand militarily either with the Arabs or against Israel was therefore of great concern. The British realised that an Arab–Israeli war would have serious consequences for Britain as it would gravely endanger oil supply and its own influence. They also realised the military capacity of Israel, and yet they were aware of the vulnerability of Israel in a joint Arab attack and admitted that the ultimate Arab aim was to destroy Israel. Therefore Britain sought a solution to the dispute.

Early in the 1950s, despite the above concerns, there were some attempts to find a scheme that would deepen the relations between the two countries on a military basis. In January 1951, William Strang, the Permanent Under-Secretary at the Foreign Office, asked the Israeli Ambassador in London to obtain his government's authorisation for a visit to Israel by General Sir Brian Robertson, Commander-in- Chief, British Middle East Land Forces. The idea was to use this visit to explore the possibility of a pact with Israel, or some kind of alliance. One of the ideas was to establish British bases in Gaza, which might be connected by a corridor to Jordan. The other consideration was the construction of British bases in Israel itself. Discussions between the two countries on strategic co-operation were held in both 1951 and 1952. However, by 1952 these negotiations had come to an end. One of the main reasons was the very sceptical attitude of Ben-Gurion towards the British. In a discussion at the Israeli Foreign Office between Ben-Gurion; Sharett; Michael Comay, the Head of MABAR (British and Commonwealth Department at the Israeli Foreign Ministry); Walter Eytan, the Director General of the Israeli Foreign Office, and Reuven Siloah, a security and intelligence expert, the Prime Minister expressed his apprehension and total reservation about the British suggestion. Although this discussion belongs to an earlier period than this book is concerned with, it is important to take it into consideration as it explains the fundamental attitude of Ben-Gurion towards Britain. Ben-Gurion emphasised that the British government under Bevin had conducted a hostile policy towards Israel, that their proposal aimed only to get back into Israel and that it was not in Israel's interests to give the British any such opportunity. He went on to stress the differences between Britain and the United States. Ben-Gurion stated that the United States provided Israel with financial aid and demanded nothing in return and therefore the Israelis were always ready to talk with the Americans. He stressed that Israel wanted the Americans to provide some security guarantees, and concluded that the United States had never done anything to harm Israel, if anything they had only helped. This was not the case with Britain.[6]

There were other considerations in Ben-Gurion's rejection of the proposal, but what is important to this study is the deep suspicion, bitterness and dislike Ben-Gurion had towards the British government and its policy in the Middle East. This suspicion was evident during the major part of the period being studied.

On the other hand the British made no real attempt to explore the possibility of significant and active Israeli involvement in their defence plans. This is because Britain put the security of the region well above the security of Israel and also they had a very different outlook on Middle Eastern defence strategy. The British government believed that in order to secure its position in the region it was of immense importance not to appear to have very close relations with Israel, while securing its traditional area of influence in countries such as Jordan and Iraq.

The relationship from the early 1950s to October 1956 was therefore purely formal, without any co-operation between the two. Any suggestions of co-operation were rejected by the British on the grounds that it might lead to the end of British influence in the Middle East. For instance, the Israeli request to join the Commonwealth in March 1956 was ruled out by the British Foreign Office because 'It would confirm Arab arguments that Israel is a spearhead of Western Imperialism in a new guise.'[7] The Israeli request to join the Commonwealth might seem strange. According to Bialer, Ben-Gurion did not really wish to join the Commonwealth but rather to indicate that Britain's attitude towards Israel should be the same as if she was in the Commonwealth. For Ben-Gurion, this was the type of relationship between the two countries that should form a basis for any future military or political commitment.[8]

It seems that the overall perception of Israel by the Foreign Office was one of suspicion and apprehension, combined with some appreciation and admiration of Zionism's pioneering work and Israel's determination. The British view was also that the Israelis were stubborn, self-righteous, and lacking an understanding of the overall Middle Eastern situation, in addition to the problems that the foundation of Israel had created. Furthermore, the British argued that Israel's statements about its desire for peace and harmony with its neighbours were not compatible with its actions, which were often violent and demonstrated Israel's unwillingness to make concessions.

The British Ambassador in Tel-Aviv believed that this behaviour was caused by the Israeli belief that there could be only two views: 'The Israeli view and the wrong one.'[9] Israel was seen as a very interesting experiment which was largely admired by the Foreign Office, although one often gets the impression that it was with some scepticism about whether a 'Jew' could be transformed into a new Israeli. They were also aware of Israel's great sensitivity to the possibility of foreign powers forcing a settlement on it; as Sir Roger Makins, the British Ambassador to Washington admitted: 'It must be recognised that the Israelis dislike the idea of the US and UK agreeing between themselves on suitable terms for a settlement and there are signs of this apprehension.'[10]

However, it was also recognised that 'Fear and suspicion are the driving forces behind the policies of both sides ... The Israelis after centuries of persecution see danger lurking behind every boundary stone and pride themselves on the success of their policy of retaliation.'[11] The British government was aware of the limited influence they had on Israel's policy and that they were viewed as the 'bad guys' while the Americans were seen as the 'good guys'. Therefore the best way of encouraging Israel to adopt a more moderate policy depended on American policy.

Sir John Nicholls, the British Ambassador to Tel-Aviv from 1954 to 1957, had a very critical view of Israel and the Israeli people in general. His overall outlook combined a deep understanding of Israeli society and politics with sharp criticism, which at times betrayed a general and cynical dislike of Israel. He had a very interesting perception of Israel, and his views appear to have been widely shared by the Foreign Office. He thought that the Israelis were 'queer customers individually and collectively'.[12] He believed that Israelis were sentimental, grasping and generous, brash and different, realistic and visionary, but they were not yet equipped with steady nerves or an understanding of other people, were sure of their own superiority and rightness, and were convinced that they represented progress in the Middle East. Nicholls also felt that the Israelis had a special talent for 'saying and doing the wrong thing at the wrong time in the wrong way'.[13] He repeated what his predecessor had said that 'No other people has ever shown such an aptitude for jerking the rug of sympathy away from under one's feet.'[14] He compared the Israelis' personal and political behaviour as follows.

> At the very moment when one has weighed the good qualities of an Israeli against the bad and decided that the former predominate, he will do or say something so gratuitously foolish or offensive that the impulse to like and even admire is immediately stifled ... There is no measure in Israeli behaviour; it is normal only momentarily as it oscillated between too much and too little.[15]

The Ambassador realised that it was hard to generalise about the Israeli character because, in a country which had imported more than half its population in the last ten years and which had drawn Jews from every continent, there was little homogeneity. Nevertheless, Nicholls thought that it could be said that most Israelis were intelligent, cultivated, conscientious and honest, but none of them thought that it was important to heal the wound that Arab pride had suffered as a result of the 1948 war, and naively expected that finally the Arabs, with the help of outside power, would come to them. Consequently, they accepted their isolation in the region as a price they had to pay. The Ambassador believed that the 'ghetto syndrome' that the Jews suffered before had not disappeared and that Zionism therefore succeeded 'in exchanging a thousand ghettos for a single comprehensive one'.[16]

Nicholls realised that Israel's geographical and territorial difficulties resulted from its 'absurd shape' and its subsequent lack of resources. He felt that the land itself 'produced the same effect of uneasiness as its inhabitants'.[17] Against this background, the Ambassador concluded that one may say of Israel's moral and material development the same as of a dancing dog, 'that one does not ask whether it is well done, the wonder is that it should be done at all'.[18] In spite of his criticism and cynicism, the Ambassador saw Israel as an example of 'a unique, admirable achievement, the product of ruthless determination, hard work, enterprise and devotion to an ideal on the part of the ruling few'.[19] Nevertheless, he also commented that 'The question still remains as to the validity of the Zionist experiment because it still is to be shown that the Jew who has maintained his separate way of life in an alien environment for two thousand years is capable of learning how not to be an alien in the Middle East.'[20] He thought that Israel's aspiration to build a technological civilisation on the Western model set them even further apart from their neighbours, and that Israel only paid lip service to the slogan of integration in the region. In his view Israel's leaders feared the possibility that, under the influence of the climate and immigration from Asia and Africa, Israel would become Levantine, thus losing its European and Western character which for the Israeli leaders meant modernity and progress, and be brought down to the Arab level with everything that would denote in Western eyes.

Nicholls's understanding of Israel's difficulties did not produce sympathy towards Israel. His overall perception as stated in one of his dispatches was that:

> The centre of infection in the region is Israel. I believe we must treat the Israelis as sick people, their illness is psychological … Therefore, it is not reasonable to expect that a nation made up of

> individuals so psychologically unstable, should be capable of a mature foreign policy.[21]

In the same telegram, the Ambassador outlined what can be seen as a summary of British expectations and hopes for the future of Israel's policy:

> We wish them to calculate exactly the weakness of their position, to discount the violently expressed hostility of their Arab enemies, to rely on the assurance of ultimate support from the Western powers while accepting that for various reasons these powers are unable to offer them any support but on the contrary are obliged to provide military assistance to the Arabs.

Realising the difficulties and contradiction in the demands this posed on Israel, Nicholls continued to say that in spite of this situation, Britain still would like Israel to realise that this was the only realistic analysis and they should consequently adopt a policy of accommodating themselves 'to their Arab enemies and accept the irritations, dangers and crippling economic burdens in their present situation in the hope that one day things may get better'.[22] Taking into account this complicated situation and the knowledge that British expectations of Israel were therefore not going to be fulfilled in the short term, the realistic way to deal with the problem was as follows:

> To devise some way of getting the Israelis into a psychological condition which would enable them to adopt a more modest and conciliatory attitude which ... can only lead to the Arab acceptance of Israel which is essential to her continued existence ... the best hope lies in steadily feeding the Israeli passion for being appreciated and understood by going as far as we possibly can to satisfy the growing sense of insecurity which however imaginary – and it is of course by no means entirely so – unfortunately poisons all Israel's policies.[23]

It is difficult to ascertain the major reasons for Nicholls' jaundiced view, as there is nothing in the Ambassador's background to indicate any motive. Sir John Nicholls served as an Assistant Under-Secretary of State in 1951 and prior to his arrival in Israel had acted as an adviser at the British embassy in Lisbon. We can only assume that the fact that Nicholls served in Israel during a very stormy period contributed to his outlook. His time in Israel was characterised by a very militant, aggressive Israeli policy which was mainly demonstrated by retaliation actions against its Arab neighbours. This policy did not win Israel many supporters, but drew worldwide condemnation instead. The pre-Suez era was also a time when Britain still believed that it could maintain its status and economic–political interests in the Arab world, and Sir John Nicholls was aware of this.

The Israeli attitude towards Britain in this period was marked by two ambivalent lines: first, admiration for Britain as a democratic country that gave the Jews the Balfour Declaration, and, second, a deep suspicion towards British motives and interests in the Middle East. From the Israeli point of view the British had done everything in their power to prevent the establishment of Israel. The bitterness towards Britain was further enhanced by Britain's active participation in the Baghdad Pact. It increased Israel's feelings of isolation and projected Britain as an ally of the Arab world and especially Iraq.

Israeli leaders were worried about the tendency towards Arab unity, assuming that Arab unity might be a danger to its security, and saw the Pact as a possible step in this direction in the long term. On the other hand, the Pact was viewed positively in that it divided the Arab world. It was assumed that the best situation for Israel would be if Jordan joined the Pact, because this would provide clear proof of the obvious divisions in the Arab world. They also favoured the Pact because they assumed that the non-Arab countries would have a moderating influence.[24] However, Israel in the end did not support the Pact for two main reasons: first, the French objected to the Pact and Israel did not want to appear to be in opposition to the one ally it had. Second, the potential to weaken Israel's position *vis-à-vis* the United States. Israel's main argument was that it was the only country in the region that was not a member of any Pact. If Israel supported the Baghdad Pact, it might lose its main argument for close alignment with the United States and ease the way for American entry into the Pact. In a conversation between the American Ambassador to Israel, Edward Lawson, and Moshe Sharett, the latter admitted that with the Pact's existence, 'Israel's isolation and exclusion from the Middle East defence system became more highly emphasised in the mind of people and government.'[25]

However, the main bones of contention between the two countries were the questions of arms supply and frontiers. Regarding the first issue Israel felt that Britain's attitude towards it was discriminatory, that it adopted a policy of 'trickle' on arms supply to Israel, while at the same time supplying Jordan and Iraq with modern weapons under its treaties with these countries.

In 1955, Nasser claimed that he had to get arms from the Russians because the West refused to sell him arms while they poured arms into

Israel, but the fact was that Britain supplied Nasser in 1954 with 32 Centurion tanks and 45 aircraft. In addition, they agreed to release considerable quantities of tracked vehicles, 25-pounders, 17-pounders and other guns. Although Israel's efforts to gain arms from Britain were not very successful, there were some deliveries and the Israelis never gave up hope. After the Czech arms deal, Moshe Sharett tried to impress upon Selwyn Lloyd in October 1955 that Israel's position had become critical.[26] However, despite the hostility in Anglo-Egyptian relations, the British government did not change its attitude towards arms supply to Israel and, as the Israeli Ambassador in London, Eliahu Elath, noted, the animosity between Britain and Egypt did not bring Israel and Britain any closer.[27] This feeling also continued after the Suez War and Ben-Gurion told Sir Francis Rundall, Nicholls' successor, that the attitude of the British Foreign Office had not changed since 1945. He accepted that the latter was neither pro-Arab nor pro-Israel, but it did not change the fact that their policy towards Israel had remained unfriendly.[28] The British government was well aware that as a result of the Arab–Israeli dispute the issue of arms supply to the region had further political importance, far exceeding the actual extent of supplies.[29] Officially, the British policy on arms supply was based on the Tripartite Declaration of May 1950. This declaration between the United States, Britain and France registered their joint desire to prevent an Arab–Israeli arms race by monitoring the flow of weapons into the zone and restricting their own sales; the three states enjoyed a monopoly of the modern arms market. The Declaration announced the right of the Arab states and Israel to maintain a certain level of armed forces, to acquire arms for security and legitimate self-defence, and to play their part in the defence of the area as a whole. The British government claimed in early 1956 that Her Majesty's Government 'have supplied and continue to supply strictly limited quantities of arms in accordance with this declaration.'[30]

Yet, a deeper analysis of this statement might give a different answer. It is interesting to note that later, in 1958, the Foreign Office had to admit that in the years since Israel's establishment there was no balance in Britain's arms supply to the Middle East and that Israel was discriminated against.[31] First of all, arms supply to Israel was often used as a bargaining chip for Israel's 'good behaviour'. It was always suspended in a case of reprisals. For example, in 1956, as a result of an Israeli attack on Syria in the Sea of Galilee, the British Cabinet decided on 3 January to suspend delivery of certain arms to Israel.[32] In addition, Britain had treaty obligations with Middle Eastern countries. Under these treaties, Britain supplied countries such as Jordan and Iraq with arms. Britain also supplied large quantities of arms to countries with which it had no treaty, such as Syria and Egypt. From 1948 to 1956, the value of the United Kingdom's exports of aircraft, tanks and military equipment to Egypt, Iraq, Jordan, Syria and Lebanon, totalled just under £31 million. In 1955 Egypt received from Britain alone more than the total amount sold to Israel in the previous seven years (1948–55). From 1956 to 1958 there was almost an embargo on arms export to Israel. The British government at no time made any gift of arms to Israel or sold any items which were not surplus to British requirements. They never sold Israel any of the latest types of arms.[33]

The British arms supply to Israel up to 1955 amounted to 9 jet aircraft and 20 Sherman tanks, which was hardly sufficient to meet Israel's needs. Moreover, Britain reneged upon a promise to provide Centurion tanks, which would have significantly increased Israel's military capacity. Therefore, as the Foreign Office stated at the time, 'There has never been any question of our policy under the Tripartite Declaration being designed to establish parity as between Israel and the Arabs.'[34] In spite of this, the Foreign Office still believed that 'Israel was in a position to defend itself against any Arab combination.'[35]

The British government argued that the result of supplying Israel with large quantities of arms equal to those supplied by the Soviets to the Arab states would be that the Israelis would be surrounded by Arabs armed to the teeth.[36] Yet Israel was the only country that was not a member of any regional defence system. It was the only country in the region to which Britain adopted a 'trickle' policy regarding arms supply. One of the arguments for adopting such a policy was the hope that it would enable the West to persuade Nasser to co-operate with them and to achieve a permanent settlement. The failure of these efforts convinced the British Foreign Office that limited quantities of arms, necessary for Israel's defence, should be released. The British believed that any direct supply of weapons to Israel would symbolise to the Arabs the identification of the West with Israel, but they thought that in order to reduce Israel's anxiety and sense of isolation it would be a good idea if Israel could obtain arms from other countries that previously had provided it with arms, like Canada.[37] The British government was strongly opposed to the French supply of arms to Israel. Shuckburgh explained to Sir Gladwyn Jebb, the British Ambassador in Paris, that 'The existence of Israel cannot be guaranteed by the number of weapons which she possesses.'[38]

It would be wrong to assume that Israel was not aware of British interests in the region. Elath, the Israeli Ambassador to London, warned the Israeli Foreign Office that the question of British relations *vis-à-vis* Israel should not be viewed in a vacuum, but that other relevant factors should be taken into consideration, such as the United States and the Soviet Union. In a lengthy account to the Israeli Foreign Office in April 1955, the Ambassador stated that Britain was not the only and decisive international factor in the region, and while the Foreign Office policy towards Israel was cautious, Israel enjoyed great support among public opinion and the Labour Party, and that these two factors were of immense importance.[39] However, the Ambassador and the Israeli Foreign Office were aware that 'The Arab countries and not Israel have oil, and while control of these routes are so vital to Britain they will always see Israel against the background of the general Middle Eastern picture.'[40] Ben-Gurion told Sir Francis Rundall, British Ambassador to Israel, 1957–59, that he was well aware that British policy in the region accorded with British interests such as the oil supply.[41] Yet he argued against the view that British interests, namely maintaining good relations with the Arabs, necessarily clashed with warmer relations with Israel. It was wrong to assume, he advocated, that Arab hatred towards the West could be reduced by a hostile attitude towards Israel, and argued against the British belief that any alliance with Israel would damage their relationship with the Arab world.[42] The Israeli government tried to emphasise this line constantly, both to the United States and Britain, though without much success. Despite Israeli complaints of British discrimination in their arms supplies to the region, they had to admit that most of their arms since 1948 had originally come from Britain. (This was true up to the point when the French started to supply Israel with arms.) Ben-Gurion, summarising the subject, reflected the very ambivalent attitude of Israel towards Britain: 'The White Paper [of 1939] causes us to forget that Britain gave us the Balfour Declaration. The same applies to the United Kingdom's latest attitude towards Israel, which leads us to forget the arms it sold us.'[43]

Another basic disagreement between Israel and Britain was over the question of Israel's frontiers. When Britain gave Israel *de jure* recognition in April 1950, they added that the boundaries of Israel should be arranged in a final agreement, and that until such an agreement was reached, Her Majesty's Government would not consider the present borders as final.[44] Israel was very sensitive towards any suggestion that it should revise its borders. The determination to keep Israel's borders in their present shape was one of the most important pillars of its foreign policy. The Israeli decisions-makers suspected that Britain might try to push towards a settlement that would reduce Israel's territory. The Israeli Ambassador to London warned that the real danger, should there be any negotiations between Israel and its neighbours, would come from the

United Kingdom.[45] Ben-Gurion was very suspicious of the British. He believed that if Israel started a war, Britain would be the country that would militarily support the Arabs. 'Why do I say England?', he asked, 'I am not an English "anti-Semitic", on the contrary, I appreciate the British people. When I was in Britain during the Second World War, I saw their moral strength. I have no anti-English complex, but, I know the British Foreign Office'.[46] Although Ben-Gurion was aware that British policy was not conducted out of love for the Arabs, he said that the situation in 1956 was like that of 1939 when British policy was aimed at not losing a foothold in the Middle East, and he was afraid that Britain might find an event such as a preventive war a suitable opportunity to gain Arab sympathy, in addition to a military base in the Negev, which, he believed, was desired by Britain.[47]

Unfortunately this awareness and understanding of each other's motives did not lead to a closer relationship. It is quite obvious that Ben-Gurion's attitude to Britain was heavily influenced by memories of the Mandate period. Hence his admiration on the one hand, and his deep resentment and suspicion on the other.

It is clear, therefore, that in the period from the start of 1955 to early 1956, the Anglo-Israeli relationship was characterised by suspicion and resentment. The Israeli distrust towards Britain was further enhanced in the spring of 1955 due to the British participation in the ALPHA plan, which would have required Israel to make territorial concessions, especially on its southern frontiers, as part of an Arab–Israeli peace settlement.

BRITAIN , ISRAEL AND THE ALPHA PLAN

Evelyn Shuckburgh, the Under-Secretary of State for Middle Eastern affairs at the British Foreign Office, led the initiative behind the plan in league with officials from the US State Department. In May 1955, an agreement was reached between the United States and Britain. The plan attempted to achieve a settlement between the Arabs and Israel. At the centre of the proposals was the idea that Israel should make territorial concessions in the southern Negev, which would have enabled Egypt to secure a land link with Jordan and Saudi Arabia.[48]

Both the United States and Britain believed that the key to any Arab–Israeli settlement was Egypt. The plan therefore focused on Egypt and Israel, with the possibility that it would involve other Arab states later on. The plan also considered the Palestinian refugees, and it was suggested that Israel, with Western aid, would help to resettle some of the refugees or give them compensation. The agreement also called for an undertaking by the Arab states to repeal legislation based on the existence of a state of war and to raise the economic blockade. In addition, the proposal considered the question of Jerusalem and the *de jure* division of the city, with supervision of and access to the holy places in a way that would be satisfactory to Jordan and Israel, and would also include an agreement on the distribution of the water of the Jordan river. The proposal also included some special inducements to Egypt as a key factor in the settlement. Provided the settlement was acceptable to the parties concerned, the United States and Britain would give specific security guarantees of the new frontiers to both sides.[49] In making these proposals, the British government was influenced by its concern not to do anything that would risk losing Arab friendship, which it needed more than ever. The Foreign Office admitted that 'If we are ever to bring about a Palestine settlement, we shall have to be nasty to Israel at some stage.'[50] It was also emphasised that Britain should maintain itself in a position in which the blame for the failure of the plan could be laid wholly or at least partly on Israel.[51]

Evelyn Shuckburgh, the key figure behind ALPHA, wanted to make it clear to the Israeli government that the plan was its great chance; if Israel rejected the proposal it would be responsible for the failure of the peace effort within the region, and consequently it might face economic and military sanctions from the United States.[52] He believed that the main point of the plan was the question of the Negev. Shuckburgh pointed out to State Department officials that if they failed on this point, the other proposals would collapse as well. In his view Israel was the party that had to make the concessions because, for the Egyptians, any step towards a settlement with Israel already represented a major concession on their part, and that a settlement provided more for Israel than for the Arabs.[53]

Evelyn Shuckburgh had a deep resentment towards Israel, which was clearly evident in his role in the ALPHA project. His comments, statements and ideas were based not just on narrow political calculations; one gets the impression that he had personal animosity towards the Israelis and the State of Israel in general. He believed that British interests in the Middle East could be best served by maintaining friendly relations with the Arab world, even if this upset the Israelis. On several occasions, he expressed his deep resentment towards Israel's policy and leaders. For example, in response to one of Sharett's memorandums which raised the issue of Israel's exclusion from the Baghdad Pact, he commented:

> It is impossible to read Sharett's memorandum without indignation at the arrogance and logic chopping of the Israelis.

> They seem to assume that they have the right to look after their interests quite regardless of our own interests in the Middle East. ... they seem to assume that all our actions in the area ought to be determined in relation to Israel and her problem.[54]

Furthermore, he noted in his diary that the 'State of Israel was founded, both from the Jewish and from the Western point of view, on a false premise and in unnatural, impermanent conditions.'[55] In his view Britain had to consider and realise its growing dependency on Arab goodwill for oil and also as an area defence against communism.[56]

The American administration at that time adopted a similar view to the British. Dulles had made repeated efforts to get Israeli officials to see that Israel could not rely upon arms supplied by Western powers.[57] Dulles did not accept the Israeli thesis that the surest way of protecting Israel was a United States arms supply on a substantial scale. The US government also agreed with the British view that territorial adjustment by Israel was essential, but had some reservation about the approach suggested by Shuckburgh. Francis Russell, in the State Department's Office of Near Eastern Affairs, believed that if the first issue was to be the Negev, they would find it very difficult to make any progress.[58]

The American attempt to initiate a settlement was not new. The Johnston plan was one of the United States' efforts to find a solution to the dispute over the Jordan river water sources. Between 1953 and October 1955, Erik Johnston, the President of the Movie Picture Association of America, made five visits to the region. The idea behind the Johnston plan was to get some compromise on the distribution of the River Jordan's water for the benefit of all the inhabitants in the region. Dulles hoped that such a solution might also alleviate the refugee problem and lead to negotiations on an Arab–Israeli settlement. However, his plan was accepted only reluctantly by Israel, and rejected by the Arab League.[59]

The first step in initiating the ALPHA plan came in early April 1955, when prior to the formalising of the plan, Nasser was approached by the United States Ambassador in Cairo, Henry Byroade.[60] Nasser did not object to the plan in principle, but at the same time was not very optimistic about its chances of success. In addition, he pointed out that the Anglo-American intention to establish a corridor in the Negev linking Egypt and Jordan was not adequate and that Israel should be forced to give up the whole Negev region.[61]

Discussions between the Israeli and the Egyptian governments had already taken place in the first half of 1953 but had achieved little progress. In 1954, an exchange of formulated messages took place between President Nasser and the Israeli Prime Minister, Moshe

Sharett, in which they expressed their desire to reach a peaceful solution.[62] However, the talks stopped after two young Egyptian Jews were sentenced to death in Cairo. They were members of an underground movement, led by Israeli intelligence, which aimed to sabotage British targets in order to prevent the latter from evacuating the Suez base.[63]

Both Egypt and Israel were unenthusiastic about the plan, but they did not reject it entirely because they hoped to get some favours from the United States. Israel hoped to get arms and security guarantees, while Egypt hoped to get economic aid, especially for the Aswan Dam project.

Although ALPHA was a secret plan between Britain and the United States, Dulles revealed some of its contents in a speech on 26 August 1955, during which he announced that it was necessary to find a peace settlement in the Middle East, and that some minor territorial adjustment should be accepted.[64] Dulles' decision to make this speech was mainly for domestic purposes. The speech was in a sense an indication of the US government's policy towards the question of the Middle East. Britain's Foreign Secretary, Harold Macmillan, was not in favour of any public statement that referred to ALPHA, because of the fear that it might cause chaos in the Arab states and the suspicion that the Palestinian refugees in the camps of Gaza might cause trouble. In addition, there was the danger that the Arab states might reject the plan as a whole, because they would see it as a further attempt to pressure them towards a peace settlement with Israel against their will, and this might even lead to a rejection of the Northern Tier and present a threat to their treaty with Iraq. Also there was the problem that it might put Nuri in an unfavourable position, because of his alignment with the West.[65] In a letter to Dulles of 20 August, Macmillan stated that it would be better if the latter did not specify that only minor territorial adjustments were required, as it might endanger any scheme to bring Egypt to negotiation because they would conclude that their demand for a land link through the Negev had been ignored.[66]

Dulles's speech did not arouse any special reactions, but did lead to some confusion. Although it was understood that Dulles had to make a speech for internal purposes, and the speech gave some assurances in regard to Israel's security, the Israeli Foreign Ministry suspected that Dulles's speech revealed little and concealed twice as much, and that his speech was just a small part of a more far-reaching plan.[67] Abba Eban, the Israeli Ambassador to the UN, tried to find out if the United States had any specific thoughts about possible frontier adjustments. He expressed the view that Dulles's statement did not endorse the permanency of Israel's present frontiers. These frontiers, he said, although based on military victory, had endured for seven years; they were real and the Arabs had come to accept them. Israel, he said, would not give up the Negev in whole or part.[68] However, by early September 1955, it was concluded that the two most important parties were ready to talk.[69]

The real blow to the Western attempt to get some agreement with Nasser came in September when the arms deal between Egypt and Czechoslovakia was announced. On 21 September 1955, Egypt signed an 'open agreement' with the USSR for five years, under which the Soviets agreed to furnish a supply of arms at bargain rates in exchange for Egyptian cotton, and to provide Warsaw Pact advisers to instruct the Egyptians in maintenance and operation; a package which gave Egypt qualitative and quantitative superiority in combat aircraft over Israel.

The US government felt that the arms deal with Egypt represented the most dramatic move yet in the Soviet campaign to increase its influence in the Middle East. They believed that a major objective of this campaign was to stiffen Arab resistance to Western policies in the area.[70] The Americans also feared that the Soviet arms supply would increase the chances of Arab–Israeli hostilities and raise the risk that, in the short term, Israel would launch a preventive war. Over the longer term, it was thought that increased Egyptian military strength might stimulate it to embark upon a 'second round' against Israel.[71] As a result, Dulles believed that it was essential for Israel to make a settlement, while the military balance was still weighted in its favour, a position which it might lose eventually.[72] The problem for the ALPHA plan, however, was that the Soviet arms deal did not lead to any sudden Israeli desire to negotiate. In the months preceding the arms deal, Israel's sense of isolation had grown even further in the face of the rise of the Arab National Movement, led by Egypt's Gamal Abdul Nasser, who was seen increasingly as the greatest single danger to Israel's very existence. Ben-Gurion argued that the Egyptian–Czech arms deal had caused a sudden shift in the balance of power and worsened Israel's security. He believed that the balance had changed, not just in terms of quantity but in quality as well.[73] Nasser's close links with the Soviet Union and the Soviet–Egyptian arms deal in 1955 increased the domination of the 'activists' over the Israeli government. Ben-Gurion emphasised the weapons Nasser had received from the Eastern bloc were accepted with only one aim in mind, which was to destroy Israel.[74] The threat from the Soviet Union was common to all Western countries, but the Israelis saw it differently to the European powers or the United States. While Europe and the United States viewed the danger on a global scale, the Israelis perceived it in local terms and felt the threat to them was more real, because in effect the Soviets had now become their neighbour. The Israeli government assumed that the Soviets would not like to see a war between Israel and the Arabs, but that they were in favour of instability because it could benefit their interests.[75]

Israel had never enjoyed superiority as far as quantity of arms was concerned. However, prior to the Czech arms deal the IDF assumed that it had the military capacity to defeat the Arab countries in the case of war, and this knowledge served as a deterrent against an Arab attack. Until that point, none of the regional states had ever got the quality or quantity of arms on that scale, and Israel always did its best to be on an equal level with its neighbours. As emphasised earlier, it was always an important aim of its leaders to gain arms; with the Czech arms deal this became a matter of urgency.[76]

It therefore gave the green light to Israeli officials to increase their efforts to obtain weapons from the United States. Yet, in spite of all these fears, Ben-Gurion and the Israeli Cabinet were not in favour of a preventive war. Ben-Gurion clearly recognised the ill effect it might have on the economy and upon Israeli defence; he also considered the impact of a preventive war by Israel on its external relations, and was especially worried about the possibility that it would give Britain a chance to fight on Egypt's side and thus re-establish good relations with the Arab world and possibly annexation of the Negev.[77] However, it is important to note the dilemma Ben-Gurion felt in regard to the issue of preventive war. He perceived that Israel might shortly face a situation in which it would have to launch a preventive war against Egypt in order to prevent Nasser from attacking Israel with his new Soviet arms. But he was also aware that Israel might face grave international condemnation and isolation if it attacked Egypt without a justifiable *raison d'être*. Therefore he thought that at least for a while it was better to try the diplomatic channel and to concentrate Israel's efforts on obtaining arms from the United States.[78] Hence the Israeli government was on the alert and intensified its efforts to gain security guarantees from the West and from the United States in particular.

Israeli diplomats tried to convince the American government that Nasser was not only a danger to Israel, but to the West as a whole, because he had allowed the Soviets to step into the Middle East and therefore in order to ensure that the USSR would not further expand its influence in the region, the United States should strengthen Israel because it was the only insurance for the West. In a discussion on 11 October between Eban, George Allen (Assistant Secretary of State for Near Eastern Affairs), and Donald Bergus (Near Eastern Affairs in the

State Department), Eban told his American colleagues that the regime in Egypt was willing to superimpose an international conflict onto a local one and to bring the horrors of an arms race to the area.[79] Any illusions Israel had, he said, had been shattered by this deal. 'If Nasser were going to bring the Communist to Israel's doorstep, if behind him there should arise a hinterland of Soviet support, this was a menace to Israel's survival ... Israel could not bear such a development.'[80] Eban added that Israel hoped that the West would assure it that it would not be overtaken in the quest of arms. It hoped that the United States would sympathetically consider its request.[81] Ben-Gurion took a tough line and told Robert Anderson, a personal friend of Eisenhower and a former Deputy Secretary of Defence, that he could not believe that the Americans could now decline Israel's arms request on moral grounds.[82] The American government, however, perceived the situation from a different angle. The United States government aimed to keep Nasser on the side of the West in order to reduce Soviet influence and to bring Nasser to a peace settlement with Israel. Since the US government believed they were the only Western power that still had some influence in the region, they considered any arms shipment to Israel would 'entail adverse effect on the United States position in the Arab States'.[83]

The United States wanted to convince Israel that their security could not depend upon receiving large quantities of arms. The Americans advocated that Israel should be included in the Tripartite Declaration from 1950, and that it should rely on international law and international institutions. This indicated the United States' desire at that time to strengthen the United Nations as an instrument of peace-keeping. In a conversation between Abba Eban and Dulles on 2 March 1956, the latter said that the American–Israeli relationship was not the working relationship that ought to exist between the two countries. He accused the Israelis of being selfish, and not perceiving US global interests such as the vital interests of NATO and the need for accessibility to oil and the other resources in the Middle East. Furthermore, he added, it seemed that the Israelis had decided on a form of political warfare against the American administration.[84] The Israeli leaders were very disappointed by this response. They had hoped that at least in view of the Soviet-Egyptian arms supply they would be able to convince the American administration to consider their arms request with sympathy. But the American government, more than ever, wanted to stress the need for a peace settlement.

In order not to lose the opportunity to reach a settlement, especially after the Czech arms deal, Dulles sent Robert Anderson to investigate the prospect for ALPHA. The code name of Anderson's mission was

GAMA. Meanwhile, in London, Evelyn Shuckburgh still believed that the ALPHA plan did not make any significant concessions to the Arabs, and he anticipated that Nasser would not react positively and that they would perceive it as just another peace proposal. In his view, the initiative would be successful only if the British came up with 'something which the Israelis will detest'.[85] Shuckburgh's suggestion to Anthony Eden was mentioned in the latter's annual foreign policy speech, which hinted, 'The 1947 resolution is a factor to be taken into account in any settlement.'[86]

In his speech at the Guildhall on 8 November 1955, Anthony Eden suggested that there should be a compromise between the Arabs' demands that Israel be reduced to its 1947 boundaries, and the Israeli desire to maintain the status quo of the armistice lines of 1949. The Arab world, especially Nuri el-Said, reacted positively. The Israeli government, on the other hand, was furious at the fact that the 1947 UN resolution had been mentioned. There had been growing suspicion in Israel for some time that a plan was being 'cooked' in the British Foreign Office. In the winter of 1955 these suspicions had been confirmed in a meeting on 13 April between Shuckburgh and the Israeli Ambassador to London, Eliahu Elath. Shuckburgh had told the Ambassador that Israel was an obstacle to peace in the region and that unless a settlement was reached between Israel and its neighbours, the situation would escalate. He warned Elath that Israel would be the cause of it. Shuckburgh added that Israel's annexation of territories (which were occupied during the 1948 war) was the main cause of the entire situation, and that therefore it should be willing to make sacrifices in order to achieve peace. He warned Israel that if it rejected the proposed basis for discussions, the responsibility for the failure of the peace initiative would lie with them.[87]

By the spring of 1956, it was obvious that there was no prospect of a positive outcome. Robert Anderson on 5 March told Dulles that Nasser had concluded that he did not believe a settlement could be made in a matter of a few months, and that he was unwilling to take the responsibility for making concessions that might compromise his popularity in Egypt and the Middle East.[88] The US government, therefore, reached the conclusion that Nasser was not going to make any effort towards a settlement with Israel. They also believed that if other Arab states absorbed large amounts of arms from the Soviets, they would become more arrogant and disregard the interests of western Europe and the United States in the Middle East region. As a result, the State Department suggested in March 1956 that, 'In view of the negative outcome to bring Colonel Nasser to adopt a policy of conciliation towards Israel, we should now adjust certain of our Near

East policies.'[89] Therefore the primary purpose would be 'to let Colonel Nasser realise he cannot co-operate as he is doing with the Soviet Union and at the same time enjoy most favoured nation [status]'.[90]

It was suggested, therefore, that while it was important to avoid any open break with Egypt, which might give Nasser Soviet satellite status, the United States and the United Kingdom should continue to delay the conclusion of negotiations on the financing of the Aswan Dam. Although the Americans wanted to avoid any direct measures against Nasser, they aimed to shield the Saudis from Egyptian influence and to isolate Nasser from other Arab countries. It was believed that by adopting such a policy Nasser would find that the only ally he had left was the USSR, a situation which would be unbearable to him, so finally he would be forced to change his policy.[91]

Britain's reaction was much more extreme. The British government argued that since Nasser's decision to obtain arms from the Soviets his attitude to the West had steadily deteriorated. They thought that he was deeply committed to the Soviets, and that he was not prepared to take a real initiative towards a settlement. The British Ambassador to Washington, Sir Roger Makins, told Dulles on 21 March 1956 that Nasser was determined to eliminate British and other Western influence in the whole area. He even compared Nasser to Mussolini, saying that both of them had become beholden to a ruthless power.[92] The British government argued therefore for a new tougher approach towards Nasser.

The question is whether there was any chance for the ALPHA plan to be accepted and whether we can assume that Nasser's attitude would have changed if the Israelis had agreed to make more territorial concessions, especially in the Negev. It is difficult to answer and one can only point to the fact that Nasser's main aims at that time were internal rather than external. He hoped to develop and strengthen the Egyptian economy. Therefore we might conclude that at that point Nasser did not desire a war with Israel, yet at the same time, he did not wish to reach any settlement. Nasser also felt more confident of his strength, due to the huge amount of weapons supplied by the Soviet Union, and admitted that he was not willing to risk his position in the Arab world for a settlement with Israel.[93] Furthermore, according to Ashton:

> The ALPHA project was never to advance to the stage of direct negotiations between Israel and Egypt. It foundered on the British side in the wake of King Hussein of Jordan's dismissal of General Glubb, and on the American side once Robert Anderson's mission to the region had made it clear to the Administration that Nasser was unwilling to cooperate.[94]

The British government felt that the collapse of ALPHA removed the hidden linchpin of their Middle East policy and they were left 'without a Middle East policy of any kind'.[95] Anthony Eden's speech at the Guildhall created a cloud over the Anglo-Israeli relationship, overshadowing relations between them in the years under study. Israeli leaders, primarily Ben-Gurion, were sure that the Foreign Office remained committed to the adoption of what they called 'The Guildhall Plan'. It was only in the late summer of 1958, when circumstances in the Middle East had changed, that Israel's leaders were finally convinced that this plan no longer existed.

In view of the collapse of ALPHA and the failure to bring Nasser to take a moderate view towards Israel and to reduce his co-operation with the Soviet Union, the Americans thought that there should be some revision in their arms policy towards Israel. Dulles told Abba Eban, the Israeli Ambassador in Washington, that the United States would not abandon Israel, and that there should be some way by which Israel could get defensive arms. He also added that the United States should consider giving some security guarantees to Israel against Egypt.[96] This attitude should be underlined because it demonstrated the basic difference between the US policy and the British attitude towards Israel. This is not to say that US policy was very different from Britain's, nevertheless it revealed the very basic attitude which the United States took into consideration in its Middle Eastern policy to safeguard the existence of Israel.

The British government's attitude towards Israel and the Arab–Israeli dispute did not change despite the collapse of the ALPHA plan, and there was no major revision in Middle Eastern policy as far as Israel was concerned. Although both Israel and Britain became obsessed with the threat from Nasser, it did not bring them any closer. The only contribution of ALPHA to the frigid relations between the two countries was that it added more suspicion and bitterness on Israel's part. Although ALPHA proved to be a total failure and was concealed in the back drawers, there was no sign of any real transformation in Anglo-Israeli relations.

In the summer and autumn of 1956 conditions in the Middle East changed rapidly. The nationalisation of the Suez Canal and Nasser's policy intimidated the British government to such a degree that Britain drifted into a scenario which, some months before, would have been a fantasy.

NOTES

1. PRO, FO371/128126/VR1081/83, Lloyd to Dixon (New York), No. 158, 10 January 1957.
2. ISA, HZ2592/23, A survey by the Israeli Foreign Office Research Department, 4 December 1955.
3. ISA, HZ4301/3, Israeli Foreign Office survey, 4 April 1955.
4. PRO, FO371/128082/VR1015/3, Nicholls to Lloyd, 11 February 1957.
5. Ibid.
6. Uri Bialer, *Between East and West: Israel's Foreign Policy Orientation, 1948–1956* (Cambridge: Cambridge University Press, 1990), p. 236.
7. PRO, FO371/121855/VR2211/2, Hadow (Foreign Office) to Morris (Washington) March 1956.
8. Bialer, *Between East and West*, pp. 239–40.
9. PRO, FO371/128087/VR1015/10, Nicholls (Tel-Aviv) to Foreign Office, 1 August 1957.
10. PRO, FO371/115869/VR1076/106, Makins to Lloyd, 1 June 1956.
11. PRO, FO371/115880/VR1076/321, Foreign Office to Tunton (MP) 29 September 1955.
12. PRO, FO371/128087/VR1015/3, Nicholls to Foreign Office, 5 February 1957.
13. PRO, FO371/128087/VR1015/3, Nicholls to Lloyd, 5 March 1957.
14. Ibid.
15. Ibid.
16. Ibid.
17. Ibid.
18. Ibid.
19. Ibid.
20. Ibid.
21. PRO, FO371/115825/VR1051/8, Nicholls to Shuckburgh (Foreign Office), 8 March 1955.
22. Ibid.
23. Ibid.
24. ISA, HZ2449/8, Israeli diplomatic conference in Paris, 24–25 February 1958.
25. *FRUS*, Vol. 14, 1955–57, State Department memorandum, 11 October 1955, p. 571.
26. Ibid., p. 572.
27. ISA, HZ/2592/29, Elath to Golda Meir and MABAR (Israeli Foreign Office British and Commonwealth Department), 21 September 1956.
28. ISA, HZ/331/8, MABAR to London, 12 June 1957.
29. PRO, FO371/1217773/V1192/16/G, draft paper for Middle East Official Committee, 18 June 1957. For detailed background on British arms policy towards Israel see Zach Levey, 'Anglo-Israeli Strategic Relations, 1952–1956', *Middle Eastern Studies*, Vol. 31, No. 4, October 1995.
30. PRO, FO371/121369/V1195/5, White Paper on supply of war materials, January 1956.
31. PRO, FO371/134295/V1076/6, Foreign Office to certain HMS representatives, 17 October 1958.
32. PRO, FO371/V1192/111, memorandum by the Ministry of Defence, 3 January 1956.
33. PRO, FO371/134295/V1076/6, Foreign Office to certain HMS representatives, 17 October 1958.
34. Ibid.
35. PRO, CAB133/1237/PM(W), 21 October 1957.
36. PRO, FO371/121755/VR1075/15, Dodds-Parker (Foreign Office) to W.J. Taylor,

16 December 1956.

37. PRO, FO371/121336/V1192/440, Makins (Washington) to Lloyd, 21 April 1956.
38. PRO, FO371/121755/17, Shuckburgh to Jebb (Foreign Office), 22 February 1956.
39. ISA, HZ2382/9, Elath to Israeli Foreign Office, 15 April 1955.
40. ISA, HZ331/8, MABAR to Israeli embassy London, 12 June 1957, and HZ331/8, Elath to MABAR, 4 January 1957.
41. Ibid., 12 June 1957.
42. ISA, HZ331/8, MABAR to London, 12 June 1956.
43. ISA, HZ4331/1, discussion between Ben-Gurion and Sharett, 10 April 1956.
44. ISA, HZ2592/23, Israeli Foreign Office, research department survey, 4 December 1955.
45. ISA, HZ2382/9, Elath to Luria, 11 February 1955.
46. David Ben-Gurion, *Yehud Veichud* [Singularity and Mission], articles on Israel's security (Tel-Aviv: Ma'arachot, 1971: 1982), p. 222.
47. Ibid., p. 223.
48. *FRUS*, Vol. 14, 1955–57, memorandum from Francis Russell to the Under-Secretary of State, 2 February 1955, p. 35.
49. Ibid., pp. 35–41.
50. PRO, FO371/115880/VR/1076/331, memo by Arthur (Foreign Office), 4 November 1955.
51. PRO, FO371/115879/VR1076/314, Arthur minute, 19 September 1955.
52. PRO, FO37/115864/VR1076/10, Shuckburgh to Kirkpatrick, No. 311, 2 February 1955.
53. *FRUS*, Vol. 14, 1955–57, minutes of meeting of UK and US representatives, 20 September 1955, pp. 486–7.
54. PRO, FO371/115868/VR10Y6/86/G, Shuckburgh, minute, 17 May 1955.
55. Evelyn Shuckburgh, *Descent to Suez, Diaries, 1951–1956* (London: Weidenfeld & Nicolson, 1986), p. 264.
56. Ibid.
57. *FRUS*, Vol. 15, 1955–57, Dulles to Eban and Shiloah, 2 March 1956, p. 278.
58. *FRUS*, Vol. 14, pp. 486–7.
59. Scott W. Lucas, *Divided We Stand: Britain, the US and the Suez Crisis* (London: Hodder & Stoughton, 1988), pp. 32–3.
60. Keith Kyle, *Suez* (London: Weidenfeld & Nicolson, 1992), pp. 70–1.
61. Ibid., p. 71.
62. Michael Bar-Zohar, *Ben-Gurion* (Tel-Aviv: Am-Oved, 1977), p. 1163.
63. Ibid., pp. 105–3. Bar-Zohar gives in both the Hebrew and the English version a full explanation on this matter which later caused a political storm in Israel.
64. Shimon Shamir, 'The Collapse of Project ALPHA', in *Suez 1956: The Crisis and its Consequences* (Oxford: Clarendon Press, 1989), p. 82, and Lucas, *Divided We Stand*, pp. 50–1.
65. PRO, PREM11/945, No. 376, Macmillan to Dulles, 20 August 1955.
66. Ibid.
67. ISA, HZ230/26, a discussion at the Israeli Foreign Office, 12 September 1955.
68. *FRUS*, Vol. 14, 1955–57, memo of conversation at the State Department, 6 September 1955, p. 452.
69. PRO, FO371/11879/VR1076/314, memo by Arthur, 19 September 1955.
70. *FRUS*, Vol. 14, 1955–57, special intelligence estimate, p. 583.
71. Ibid., p. 578.
72. US declassified documents, US88/2155, a meeting between Eisenhower and Dulles, 11 January 1956,
73. Ben-Gurion, *Kochavim Vaefer* [Like Stars Like Dust], essays from the government yearbook (Ramat-Gan: Masada, 1976), p. 219.
74. Ben-Gurion, *Yehud Veichud*, p. 233.

75. ISA, HZ545/10, Israeli Foreign Office to the Israeli Ambassador Moscow, 30 April 1957.
76. Mordechai Bar-On, *Sharei A'za Medinut H'chuz Vehabithon shel Medinaht Israel 1955–1957* [The Gates of Gaza: Israel's Defence and Foreign Policy, 1955–1957] (Tel-Aviv: Am-Oved, 1992), pp. 30–1.
77. Ben-Gurion, *Yehud Veichud*, p. 223.
78. For a wider account on Ben-Gurion and his attitude towards a preventive war see Bar-Zohar, *Ben-Gurion*, pp. 1152–8, and Bar-On, *Sharei A'za*, Ch. 4.
79. *FRUS*, Vol. 14, 1955–57, State Department meeting, 11 October 1957, p. 571.
80. Ibid.
81. Ibid., p. 572.
82. *FRUS*, Vol. 15, 1955–57, message from Robert Anderson to Dulles, 9 March 1956, p. 334.
83. *FRUS*, Vol. 15, 1955–57, special national intelligence estimate, 28 February 1956, p. 249.
84. *FRUS*, Vol. 15, 1955–57, discussion between Dulles, Eban and Shiloah, 2 March 1956, pp. 278–9.
85. Shuckburgh, *Descent to Suez*, p. 297.
86. Ibid.
87. Eliahu Elath, *Mibhad Leharafel Haymim* [Through the Mist of Time] (Jerusalem: Yad Izhak Ben-Zvi, 1989), p. 69.
88. *FRUS*, Vol. 15, 1955–57, message from Anderson to Dulles, 5 March 1956, p. 311.
89. US declassified documents, US89/1151, memo from Eisenhower, 28 March 1956.
90. Ibid.
91. Ibid.
92. *FRUS*, Vol. 15, 1955–57, Makins (Washington) to Dulles, 21 March 1956, p. 384.
93. *FRUS*, Vol. 15, 1955–57, message from Anderson to Dulles, 5 March 1956.
94. Nigel Ashton, *Eisenhower, Macmillan and the Problem of Nasser: Anglo American Relations and the Problem of Nationalism 1955–1959* (Basingstoke: Macmillan, 1996), p. 59.
95. PRO, FO371/121235/V1054/70, Shuckburgh to Kirkpatrick, 10 March 1956.
96. *FRUS*, Vol. 15, 1955–57, memo of conversation, 28 March 1956. p. 432.

— 4 —
From Apprehension to Co-operation, January–October 1956

THE YEAR 1956 WAS a dramatic and crucial one in the history of the Middle East and left vivid scars on the history of France and Britain. The storm of the Suez episode overshadowed the earlier events leading to the crisis. However, one cannot comprehend these events without understanding the entire complexity of the region's history and the part played by the superpowers in influencing affairs in the Middle East. The period prior to the Suez crisis was marked by increasing hostility between Israel and its neighbours, greater Soviet penetration and a decline in the British position in the region.

THE LAKE TIBERIAS INCIDENT

The episodes that occurred in early 1956 were a continuation of the stormy winter of 1955. On the eve of 11 December 1955, an Israeli parachute unit commanded by Ariel Sharon attacked Syrian military posts at Betenia farms and Kounsi on the north-east bank of the Sea of Galilee. Some troops crossed by boat while another small force including armoured vehicles advanced northward from Kibbutz Ein Gev located on the eastern shore of the lake. The offensive resulted in heavy casualties to the Syrians: 37 soldiers and 12 civilians were killed and 30 Syrian soldiers were taken as prisoners of war. Six Israeli soldiers were also killed.[1] This retaliatory action named Operation 'Olive Leaves' by the Israelis and more widely known as the Lake Tiberias incident, caused widespread shock not only in Israel but worldwide.

The Syrian–Israeli border was a constant bone of contention between the two countries. According to the armistice agreement, the demarcation line was situated 10 metres east of the Sea of Galilee. Nevertheless, the Syrians' positions were stationed on the seashore itself. The situation was exacerbated when the Syrians fired on Israeli fishermen as they tried to get close to the north-eastern shore. Israel, in turn, objected to the Syrian fishermen fishing in the lake unless they were granted special permission by the Israeli authorities.[2]

Prior to this operation there had been minor incidents along the Syrian–Israeli border, but nothing serious enough to justify a major operation. The scale of the incident was somewhat surprising because it was known that the Israeli government had, in late 1955, decided against the aggressive policy favoured by Ben-Gurion and Dayan. Towards the end of 1955, Ben-Gurion thought that now, in view of the Czech arms deal, it would be preferable for Israel to launch a preventive war against Egypt. However, aware of the difficulties such an action might cause, Ben-Gurion preferred to adopt a policy of escalation along Israel's border with Egypt in the hope that it would provide the excuse for a massive Israeli attack. This policy faced opposition in the Knesset, led by Sharett, who believed that a preventive war or escalation along Israel's southern border would risk Israel's position, with potentially disastrous consequences for Israel's relations with the Western powers as well as with its neighbours.[3]

At the time of the operation, Moshe Sharett, the Israeli Foreign Minister, was in the United States endeavouring to secure an arms deal with the American administration and was shocked and furious when he heard of the action. Sharett differed from Ben-Gurion and Dayan in his view on reprisal policy (see Chapter 2). He believed that in a democratic country such a decision should not be left exclusively to a few people, and resented the fact that the Foreign Ministry was excluded, especially at such a crucial time, when he was trying to secure the arms that Israel desperately needed. Thus, Sharett viewed the operation as a disaster. 'The world around me', he wrote in his diary, 'has been darkened and the prospect of an arms deal with the United States and Canada was quashed.'[4] 'Israel', he concluded, 'has again given the impression that she was seeking blood and provoking war.'[5] Although Sharett believed in using the 'iron fist' he did not consider this necessary in every instance, and in this case he told members of Mapai that the ramifications of the raid were horrendous and stressed that Israel was reliant on the United States and the support of American Jewry and that it could not afford to ignore this fact.[6] He concluded later in the year that 'The devil himself could not have thought of a better way of preventing an arms supply to Israel.'[7] Sharett acknowledged that even if the operation had not taken place, it was still not certain whether the US government would have supplied Israel with arms, but the more immediate question was whether such a policy made any sense and he argued that those who were responsible for it should be aware of the wider implications of the retaliation policy. Sharett also addressed the wider issue of Arab–Israeli relations, expressing the view that one must not forget that the Arab people were intelligent with similar feelings.

> I do not know what has happened to us; I cannot inculcate upon you to have the same experience that I had whilst living in an Arab village for two years in order for you to realise that the Arabs are also human beings. They have brains, sense, dignity and human feelings ... [8]

Ben-Gurion took the responsibility himself for the operation, justifying it on the familiar grounds of security. He criticised an Israeli newspaper that expressed objections to the raid, and argued that it was morally wrong to condemn the operation even before the matter was brought up before the Security Council. Furthermore, he argued that the newspaper would have reacted differently if their workers had been shelled instead of the fishermen of Tiberias. Ben-Gurion emphasised that the government of Israel had a duty to protect its rights and the lives of fishermen in the Sea of Galilee. He said that those who aimed to guide Israel's public opinion from their quiet and safe houses in Tel-Aviv should understand the simple and tragic truth that as long as Israel's borders were not secure there would be no security for Tel-Aviv either, and concluded that 'All Israeli citizens from Metula (in the north) to Eilath (in the south) are in the same boat.'[9]

It is possible, however, that the operation had a wider political motive. In his diary, Dayan pointed out that on 19 October 1955 a joint Egyptian–Syrian Military Command was established. Dayan was certain that this move, due to its aggressive nature, put Israel in a fragile position.[10] The possibility therefore exists that the operation was intended to test Egypt's willingness to assist Syria, and to spread suspicion between Damascus and Cairo, thus undermining any move towards Arab unity which would endanger Israel's security. The operation also demonstrated the anti-democratic inclinations of Ben-Gurion and especially of Dayan, which they justified in the name of security. Despite the Cabinet's decision to avoid an aggressive policy, they nonetheless perpetrated an act which jeopardised Israel's international position.

BRITAIN'S ARMS SUPPLY TO ISRAEL

It is difficult to ascertain whether Israel would have gained the arms it desired from the United States had the operation not been launched. It is, however, obvious that any slight chance that existed before the incident was now defunct. After the Israeli raid the United Nations Security Council met to consider what action to take.

In light of the ALPHA operation and the British effort to reach some kind of settlement between Israel and its neighbours (even if that meant that the main sacrifice was on the Israeli side), the British government was very concerned that the recent Israeli escalation of tensions could jeopardise its peace efforts and therefore was determined to 'teach Israel a lesson' and to 'hit' it at its most sensitive point, namely by suspending arms supply. Sir Pierson Dixon, the British Ambassador to the UN, conveyed his government's feelings to Abba Eban, the Israeli Ambassador to the UN and Washington, on 22 December, stating that it was his belief that there was no justification for such an operation, and that it would sabotage Britain's efforts to reach an amicable solution between Israel and its Arab neighbours.[11] Eban, in turn, said that he hoped that the UN resolution would not call upon Israel to pay compensation for the loss of civilian life, and informed Dixon that it would be wrong to make this one incident subject to compensation while so many earlier incidents carried out by Syria had resulted in the loss of Israeli lives. He said that such a suggestion could set off a chain reaction whereby both sides asked for compensation after every trivial incident, and added that public opinion in Israel would be seriously inflamed by such a decision. Eban also indicated his desire for the Security Council to address the issue of Syrian interference with Israeli rights on the lake, and expressed the hope that the incident would not be condemned as 'a threat to peace'. He pointed out that even in the case of Korea the Security Council had not gone to that extreme and that clearly the Israeli action was not in any way comparable with the aggression of North Korea. Dixon replied that they were not contemplating adopting an extreme stance which would condemn the action as an act of aggression and had no intention of imposing economic sanctions. He explained, however, that the aim of the British government was to ensure that Israel understood that this kind of operation did not pay and to make certain that it would not be repeated. 'Our general policy', the Ambassador concluded, 'was to condemn Israel and to convince her that the consequences would be extremely serious if it did the same again.'[12]

Addressing the Security Council on 12 January 1956, Dixon noted that his government was aware that on many occasions Israel had been provoked but that in this instance there was no excuse that could justify an operation on this scale. He therefore had no hesitation in asking the Security Council to condemn it as a flagrant violation of the ceasefire provision of the resolution of 15 July 1948, stating the conditions for the general armistice agreement between Israel and Syria. The Ambassador stressed that such an operation was bad in itself, but was all the more heinous since it came as the latest of a series of retaliatory operations which his government was opposed to on moral and political grounds. He concluded by stating that it was about time the Israeli government understood that such a policy was not just and would not pay in the long run.[13] Following this, on 19 January, the Security Council condemned Israel's action and arms shipment from Britain was suspended.

Subsequently, in a parliamentary debate on 24 January 1956 concerning Operation 'Olive Leaves', Selwyn Lloyd, the new Foreign Secretary, directly addressed the question of arms supply to Israel and said that one of the difficulties the British government faced in supplying Israel with arms was that the latter had clearly indicated that it had adopted a policy of retaliation. He mentioned some of the major Israeli retaliatory actions such as Qibya in October 1953, the Gaza incident in February 1955 and the Lake Tiberias incident, adding that all of these operations had been condemned by the Security Council.

> The putting of arms, particularly those suitable for that sort of reprisal, into the hands of people condemned for such behaviour, who had behaved in that way whatever the motives and pressures upon them may be, is something which requires very careful consideration. The problem is being made much more difficult by these calculated reprisals on the part of Israel.[14]

He argued that the problem of Israel's security in the face of Soviet arms supply to Egypt could not be countered by a supply of arms to Israel: this would only result in an arms race, with the Soviets supplying Egypt and other Arab countries with even more weapons. He said that Israel could find herself surrounded by Arab states armed to the teeth with Soviet arms and assistance, which would be a dangerous situation not just for Israel's security but for world peace. The best way to give Israel security, Lloyd contended, was to try to convince the Arab states of the grave danger of becoming dependent on Soviet arms. He denied that it was within the British government's power to control or to prevent the traffic of arms as other countries were eager to supply Middle Eastern states with military weapons. He believed that if the West delivered an appreciable quantity of arms to Israel, Egypt would take this very badly and be driven further into the Soviets' grasp. On the other hand, if Britain did not supply arms to either country the Soviets would be in a position gradually to acquire a monopoly over arms supply to Egypt. But, he stated, even if Britain could reduce arms to a trickle it would still result in additional problems because, as Sir Humphrey Trevelyan, the British Ambassador to Cairo, had pointed out, the supply to Israel would have to be sufficient to create a balance of arms.[15]

The result of this tough stance towards the Lake Tiberias incident was that from January 1956 Britain moved towards an even stricter arms supply policy in regard to Israel. The only notable concession made in the forthcoming months was that Israel did receive Meteor night fighters in March 1956. Their delivery was justified on the grounds that it was best not to drive the Israelis into a situation where they felt desperate.[16] These aircraft were the first jet fighters the Israeli Air Force had received and were designed as combat fighters. This proved that, to some extent, the British government clearly understood the general feeling of anxiety among Israeli leaders, although the latter still doubted whether Britain was sympathetic and, in general, it did not change the feeling the Israeli government had towards Britain. This concession, however, needs to be seen in context, for these fighters were no longer considered by Britain to be front-line aircraft. The British reaction was very different when it became clear that the French intended to deliver much more modern and efficient Mystere fighters. This caused some alarm in Whitehall. The French Ambassador to Washington told Sir Roger Makins on 6 March that France believed that the arms embargo imposed on Israel after the Lake Tiberias incident was no longer valid. He said that to continue to refuse arms to Israel would give the impression that it was being abandoned.[17] The Foreign Office, however, opposed the supply of Mysteres to Israel on the grounds that the RAF would be placed at a disadvantage against the Israeli Air Force if they had to fight Israel under the Anglo-Jordan treaty or the Tripartite Declaration.[18] The British view, although it did not prevent the French deliveries, was symptomatic of its concern.

In addition to aircraft, Britain was also to prove unco-operative in the naval sphere. For example, in May 1956 Israel requested that the destroyers it had received from Britain should undergo a working-up period with the Mediterranean Fleet. The Admiralty, however, rejected the presence of the destroyers at Malta because it might have undesirable repercussions in the Arab world (as the same class of ships had been sold to Egypt). In the Admiralty's view, refitting in Britain was less likely to lead to problems and be read as open co-operation with the Israeli navy. In addition to the political factor, the Admiralty stressed it could be even worse if there was another eruption along the Gaza Strip while the Israeli ships were based in Malta. The Foreign Office stood firmly behind the Admiralty over this issue. Lawrence wrote to W. Botton at the Admiralty on 27 September that, should Israel's request be granted, there was the danger of placing Britain's interests in jeopardy, and he added that it would supply more fuel to Arab newspapers which were already printing stories about alleged military collaboration between Israel, France and Britain.[19] An Israeli request for Centurion tanks was also rejected. In early 1955, Britain had promised to supply Israel with six Centurions but suspended this commitment after the Gaza raid in February that year. Ever since, the Foreign Office had avoided giving Israel a direct answer as to whether it planned in the future to adhere to Israel's request. In a Foreign Office memorandum in August 1956, Edward Rose of the Levant Department stressed that selling Centurions to Israel would be against Britain's arms policy of 'trickle' and might have a disastrous effect on British relations with Iraq and to some extent with Jordan, on which Britain increasingly depended during the present crisis in the region.[20] A different unconventional view was argued by Sir Ivone Kirkpatrick. In a letter to Rose in August 1956, Kirkpatrick contradicted the latter's view, stating that it would be incorrect to tell Israel they could not have the tanks. Kirkpatrick envisaged a scenario where there might be revolutions in the oil countries, 'and we might find ourselves not only without a single Arab friend but without a drop of Arab oil'.[21] Hence, Kirkpatrick argued, if one accepted this assessment, the Foreign Office should be more careful not to offend Israel and should take a more diplomatic tactical approach. He suggested that they should tell the Israeli Ambassador that for practical reasons they were unable to supply them with the tanks, but as production was accelerating they would review Israel's request in two months' time.[22] Although Kirkpatrick's approach was more forthcoming than Rose's, Israel, in fact, had to wait another two years, until the summer of 1958, when the scenario in the Middle East had drastically changed, for its request to be met.

The Israeli anxiety to obtain arms and their immense disappointment at Britain's reaction was evident in several discussions between Israeli officials and their British counterparts. In early January, Eliahu Elath, the Israeli Ambassador to London, told Sir Evelyn Shuckburgh that it was painful for him to see Britain entirely throwing away the sympathy it enjoyed in Israel (because of Eden's speech and by its refusal to supply Israel with arms). Elath added that his government understood the British concern for oil supplies and could only surmise that Britain was willing to see Israel disappear in order to protect those interests. Shuckburgh denied this accusation and stressed that British policy was primarily directed to securing an Arab–Israeli settlement. He concluded by saying that he had no doubt that one day Israel would realise that Britain was more honest and reliable than they appeared to think.[23] Later in the month, Elath met with Lloyd to discuss the same issue. Lloyd emphasised at their meeting on 21 January that Britain could not sell arms to Israel because of the incident with Syria and the subsequent Security Council condemnation, but denied the accusation that the British government had permanently decided to cease supplying arms to Israel.[24] He argued that there was no point in competing with the Soviet Union because this would only facilitate Soviet penetration of the region. He assured the Ambassador that the British government recognised Israel's right to defensive arms, but indicated that the Lake Tiberias incident had jeopardised Israel's opportunity to procure them. He acknowledged the fact that the arms balance in the region had changed, even though Britain did not consider Israel's existence to be at risk, and concluded the discussion by saying that he recognised that Israel had very little trust in Britain's willingness to assist.[25]

In the midst of this controversy, Sir John Nicholls, aware of the immense distrust by Israel towards Britain, noted on 20 February: 'Israel's growing regard and respect for the United Kingdom suffered a serious setback in 1955'. 'It would be tedious,' Nicholls wrote, 'to describe in detail the misunderstanding and unfounded suspicions which led by degree from disillusionment to something like hostility.' 'Until the Guildhall speech', the Ambassador explained, 'the dominant emotion was perhaps regret that the UK could be so blind to its own interests as to reject Israeli friendship on Israeli terms. Thereafter regret gave way to the suspicion that British interests might after all lie with the Arab states rather than Israel, and that British policy was not so much misguided as deliberately antagonistic.'[26] Still, the Ambassador tried to gain some comfort from the fact that, despite the deteriorating relationship, Israel's admiration for Britain's political wisdom and maturity remained unchanged.[27]

Israeli disappointment at the British attitude towards it, and especially towards the supply of the quantities of arms it desired, was also evident in Lloyd's discussion with Ben-Gurion in March 1956, when the Foreign Secretary visited several Middle Eastern countries, among them Israel. This tour was initiated by the Foreign Office, who believed that 'Lloyd's visit to Israel might help to lessen Israel's sense of isolation and strengthen the hand of the moderates.'[28] However, even prior to Lloyd's arrival, his visit raised tensions due to the fact that the Foreign Secretary did not wish to meet Ben-Gurion and Sharett in Jerusalem. Following Israel's war of independence in 1948, the Israeli government had moved all its government offices from Tel-Aviv to Jerusalem, as it considered the latter its capital. However, the status of Jerusalem was still disputed as, according to the UN partition of 1947, Jerusalem was an international zone and most embassies were therefore situated in Tel-Aviv.

Lloyd was determined that he should not go to Jerusalem to talk to Israeli Ministers, and Nicholls conveyed this view to Sharett, adding that he hoped that the Israeli government would understand the difficulties surrounding Lloyd's visit to Jerusalem, which could be perceived as *de facto* recognition.[29] He said that Lloyd would prefer to visit Sharett in his Tel-Aviv office, and then meet Ben-Gurion in Jerusalem. Sharett rejected this suggestion, explaining that Tel-Aviv's status was no different to that of any other city in Israel and that he could not agree to regarding Tel-Aviv as joint capital. Sharett argued that the world, including Britain, would have to accept the fact that, in Israel's view, Jerusalem was its capital. He assured Nicholls, however, that Lloyd's visit to Jerusalem would not be interpreted by Israel as *de facto* recognition. He told Nicholls that he was under the impression that Lloyd was cleaving to the 1947 UN resolution which decreed the internationalisation of Jerusalem. He concluded by assuring the Ambassador that Israel would do its utmost to prevent the press from conveying the impression that Lloyd's visit indicated a change in Britain's attitude towards Jerusalem.[30]

On 1 March Lloyd was welcomed by Ben-Gurion as the first British Secretary of State to visit Israel. In a meeting between the two men, Ben-Gurion said that for Britain it was natural to see Israel in the context of its global interests, while Israel saw itself as a 'world problem'. Ben-Gurion expressed his anxieties over the increase in military arms being supplied to Egypt, thus placing Israel in an extremely vulnerable position. He warned Lloyd that if Britain and the United States continued their present arms policy they would be responsible in the annals of history for any subsequent war.[31] Lloyd said that he understood Israel's anxiety but commented that it was in Israel's best interest to avoid anything which might consolidate Arab unity.[32]

The result of this exchange was that Lloyd's visit to Israel ended having achieved nothing substantial. It certainly did not in any way improve Anglo-Israeli relations. Lloyd had some reservations about the Israeli Prime Minister, although he noted later in his memoirs, 'One could not but be impressed by Ben-Gurion the diminutive figure, combative, provocative, distrustful of Britain, with the shock of white hair standing out in all directions.'[33] Once more, Ben-Gurion and the Israeli government felt let down and were convinced that the British government was as unsympathetic as ever towards Israel's needs. However, a closer analysis would have demonstrated that there was some understanding and awareness of Israel's anxieties. Anthony Eden, whom the Israelis considered to be their arch-enemy, was aware of the fact that Israel might get desperate if it was unable to obtain arms. He noted in his diary that Israel was bound to become increasingly uneasy as supplies of arms were delivered to Egypt, and he explained that it was the wish of his government to prevent an arms race between the Arab states and Israel, although he recognised that this would be no comfort to Israel if, as a result of the Soviet–Egyptian arms deal, it were placed at a disadvantage with Egypt.[34] Harold Macmillan noted in his memoirs that if Britain and the other Western powers armed Israel, they might lose their influence over the Arabs, but at the same time he recognised that a total refusal to supply Israel with arms might drive Israel into a preventive war.[35]

In spite of the fact that Britain did supply Israel with some of the arms it desired, the Israeli government felt that they were only a 'token' and could not be compared with the quantity of arms Britain had supplied to Jordan and Iraq, or those delivered to Egypt by Moscow. In Israel's view it seemed that the surrounding Arab states had a dependable source of arms supply while Israel was forced to grovel in order to get the arms it needed.

Israel's impression was that Britain was doing its utmost not to be associated closely with Israel. The British government tried to avoid a real break with Israel but at the same time attempted to limit relations as much as possible. Macmillan in his memoirs revealed that Randolph Churchill had suggested to him that Britain should make a definite treaty with Israel, thus guaranteeing Britain's communications with Jordan and Iraq which had been endangered by the withdrawal from the Canal Zone. However, Macmillan noted that, although this might have been accepted by Israel, there was no point in taking such action without US support, which he was doubtful of obtaining, 'and without it other larger issues would be imperilled'.[36]

The British apprehension towards Israel was also demonstrated in other ways. For example, Sir John Nicholls' idea of closer relations with Israel was totally rejected by the Foreign Office. Nicholls suggested in June 1956 that Ben-Gurion and Sharett should to some extent be taken into Britain's confidence. There were, in his view, several advantages in renewing Israel's belief in the essential realism of British policy. He believed that Ben-Gurion and Sharett, like all the Israelis, were prone to exaggerating the strength of pro-Arab feeling in Whitehall and would come to the conclusion that if there were no change the British government had to be seen 'either as simple and gullible or fundamentally anti-Israeli'.[37] He thought that these suspicions could diminish British influence, and therefore requested to be given the authority to relay information about British intentions, thus enabling Israeli leaders to see the wisdom of Foreign Office policy, and thereby be persuaded to listen to British advice.[38] Nicholls' suggestion was eventually rejected by the Foreign Office on the grounds that 'every previous experience has shown that when we open the door an inch the Israelis try and fling it wide open. Furthermore, it was assumed that within a week of initiating such a policy there would be a string of demands for fleet co-operation, joint air exercises and demands for arms supply'.[39] The belief that the Israelis if given an inch would take a mile was also expressed by the British Ambassador to the United States, Sir Roger Makins, who thought that the Israelis had 'devious ways of achieving their ends'.[40]

Michael Hadow of the Levant Department stressed that there was no advantage in taking Israel into their confidence and believed that Israel might only manipulate the situation to its own advantage. It was also his belief that previous experience had shown that when Britain had opened the door an inch, Israel had tried to open it wider.[41] Evelyn Shuckburgh, the Under-Secretary of State at the Foreign Office, rejected this idea on the grounds that any specific security guarantee to Israel should only be part of a general settlement in the region. Furthermore, Shuckburgh thought that if, in spite of all the British efforts to improve or maintain the present situation, Britain had to make a choice, it should be remembered that British interests lay with the Arabs and not with the Israelis.[42]

The above demonstrates that 1956 was initially a very bad year for Anglo-Israeli relations. The deterioration in relations, which had begun with Eden's Guildhall speech suggesting that there should be a compromise on Israel's present borders, was profound. The fact was that Israel's and Britain's interests did not coincide and, indeed, were growing apart. Israel's retaliatory strikes against the Fedayeen along its borders could not be expected to encourage a sympathetic view in Whitehall. In turn, Israel's leaders believed, as did the Israeli public, that the world was united against them (with the exception of the 'good French') and therefore envisaged that the only option open to them was to use the 'iron fist'.

JORDAN AND THE BAGHDAD PACT

While the Israeli leaders were intensifying their efforts to gain more understanding in Whitehall, the British government's main focus of concern was the instability and upheavals in Jordan, caused by Nasser's successful propaganda and by the general anti-Western feeling in the region. During the winter of 1955–56, the situation in Jordan deteriorated sharply. This was triggered in the main by the growing rumours that Jordan was to accede to the Baghdad Pact. The Turks and the Iraqis were anxious that Jordan should join the Pact. The Turkish President, who visited Amman, reached the conclusion that Hussein was on the point of joining the Pact and that all that was required was more persuasion from the British.[43] Anthony Eden therefore sent General Sir Gerald Templer, the Chief of the Imperial General Staff, to Jordan on 6 December 1955 to convince Hussein. Templer told the King that if Jordan joined the Pact, the British government would pay its subsidy to the Arab Legion directly into the Jordanian treasury, instead of paying it to the Arab Legion bank account in London, a change which the King greatly favoured. Templer also stressed that the accession of Jordan to the Pact imposed no terms on its relations with Israel.[44] The Jordanian Prime Minister, Al-Mifti, expressed his consent in principle but he was afraid of the repercussions at home and abroad, and, indeed, the growing rumours that Jordan was about to join the Pact created a wave of riots.[45] These started on 16 December and by the following day there was mayhem in the country. The riots were scattered throughout the Kingdom and the refugee camps erupted in violence. In Jerusalem, the Turkish and French counsellors were wounded in attacks and a general strike was declared in Amman. In addition, British property was slightly damaged.[46] The reason for the troubles was that public opinion in Jordan, and especially in the West Bank largely populated by Palestinians, was against the Baghdad Pact because the pro-Pact arguments were all about the Russian menace, while they were concerned about the Palestinian issue. Furthermore, Nasser, who was admired by many Palestinians, objected to the Pact and added fuel to the fire.[47]

At this juncture, Hussein was still in two minds about whether to join the Pact. Considering Jordan's delicate position within the Arab world and its great dependence on outside sources and subsidies, it was not surprising that the country was an easy target for hostile attack by Egypt and Saudi Arabia. In addition, Jordan had a large number of Palestinian refugees in the West Bank, an element which added to the destabilisation of Hussein's Kingdom and frequently resulted in dissent. The Palestinians were also heavily influenced by Nasser's slogan of pan-Arabism and were a useful tool for the King's opponents. As a result of the unrest, Hussein decided to dissolve Parliament and call for elections, in order to decide officially on the future of the Baghdad Pact.

This quick succession of events all within one week was viewed as a dramatic defeat of the regime. On 5 January 1956, the Diwan Khass, the Jordanian supreme council for the interpretation of the law, declared the dissolution of Parliament invalid on a technicality and cancelled the elections. The reversal of the decision was seen as stemming from the government's fear of elections. Once again riots erupted, but this time Hussein and the security forces were ready. Glubb Pasha, the Commander-in-Chief of the Arab Legion, brought in the army and the soldiers cleared the streets of Amman and then sealed off the refugee camps, but with considerable bloodshed on both sides. Samir Rifai became the new Prime Minister on 8 January, and immediately declared that Jordan would not join the Pact.[48] The British belief was that the Baghdad Pact was a matter with 'which the prestige of Her Majesty's Government is deeply concerned'.[49] It was feared that if Britain's effort to get Jordan into the Pact failed, British influence in the country would quickly diminish. At the same time, Britain's effort to extend the Pact risked Egypt's increased hostility towards British policy throughout the Middle East.[50] Therefore, despite the British desire to see Jordan accede to the Pact, the British government was aware of Hussein's difficulties. It realised that it would be difficult for Jordan to join the Pact because of the impact on inter-Arab relations, namely its position *vis-à-vis* Egypt and Saudi Arabia. Bearing this in mind, it was clear that the King could not ally himself with a pact that was unpopular at home and would generate strong criticism abroad.

Therefore, the British government had to admit defeat. Eden noted in his memoirs 'After what had occurred, I considered that we should not continue to press Jordan to enter the Baghdad Pact at this time, ... I felt it is important to show that, in spite of what had happened, we were still good friends to Jordan'.[51] He agreed with the view that the King had expressed at the time to the British Ambassador in Amman, Sir Charles Duke, that Jordan's accession to the Pact could be discussed again in the future, but that too much pressure in the current environment could spoil it all.[52] The British government, which was aware of the weakness of Hussein's position as well as Jordan's status in the Arab world, denied the accusation that Britain had played a major role in pressuring Hussein to join the Pact. In a parliamentary debate on 24 January, the Foreign Secretary, Selwyn Lloyd, addressed the question and emphasised that the British government had neither put pressure on Jordan to join the Pact nor that the initiative had come from the British government.[53] In view of the Templer mission, this was simply not true.

The Israeli government, meanwhile, viewed the events in Jordan with anxiety. In a special survey by the Israeli Foreign Ministry Research Department, it was assumed that the continuation of the present tension in Jordan was not in Israel's favour. The survey revealed that Israel was anxious for the status quo in Jordan to be maintained, but that was not its only fear. Israel was also greatly apprehensive about British involvement in Jordan. It was concluded that Britain did not wish to see its influence in Jordan diminished and that therefore the British government would do everything possible in order to strengthen the Legion and the pro-British elements.

Additionally, Israel's anxiety lay in the belief that Britain would side with the Arab world and improve its relations by colluding with them at Israel's expense.[54] The survey also emphasised that Israel was generally in favour of Jordan's accession to the Pact, and hoped that the Lebanon would join too, as this would mean that the non-Arab members in the Pact might possibly have a moderating influence. Moreover, it would strengthen Israel's request to the United States for security guarantees and weapons.[55]

Sir John Nicholls was aware of the great anxiety that the situation in Jordan had created in Israel. In a letter to Lloyd on 23 January, the Ambassador emphasised that Israeli officials and public opinion were inclined towards the belief that any change in Israel's position *vis-à-vis* her neighbours would be for the worse. The Ambassador also believed that Israel was in two minds regarding Jordan's accession to the Baghdad Pact, but that the Israelis feared that such a step would increase Western arms supplies to the Arab world.[56]

As fears of greater destabilisation increased, Hussein asked Iraq for help. Israel's stance towards Iraq at this time is hard to fathom, but it is clear that Israel was very sensitive to any suggestion that Iraqi forces should enter Jordan. Israel's deep suspicion towards Iraq's motives and intentions existed because Iraq, which had taken an active part in the fighting in 1948, had never signed an armistice agreement with Israel.[57] Nicholls was aware of this sensitivity and suggested that if it became necessary to send Iraqi forces to aid Hussein, the operation should be carried out under absolute secrecy until the troops moved in and then should be swift and successful. Nicholls also assumed that the activists in the Israeli army might exert a strong influence on the government to seize the opportunity, while Jordan was encountering political confusion, to secure the Jordan river frontier. He thought that in Israeli eyes the situation was pretty grim and they might be tempted to improve their short-term position regardless of the subsequent consequences. He believed that Israel should be fully briefed once the operation started and that any Iraqi forces should be positioned at a safe distance away from the frontier. Nicholls also suggested that Israel should be reassured by the British government that hostile action against Israel would not be permitted, but that if Israel attacked Jordan, Britain would assist in Jordan's defence.[58]

In addition to the possibility of receiving Iraqi aid, the RAF regiment at Habbaniya was alerted to fly to Amman, and the armoured regiment at Aqaba moved closer to Amman. Selwyn Lloyd sent a message to Nasser, denying that the British government's policy aimed to isolate Egypt, and emphasising Britain's desire for closer co-operation with Egypt if the latter ceased its hostility towards Britain.[59]

The dust had barely settled when another major event took place in Jordan – the dismissal of Sir John Bagot Glubb. On 1 March, King Hussein decided to dismiss Lieutenant-General Glubb, Chief of the General Staff of the Arab Legion; Colonel W.M. Hutton, the Chief of Staff; and Colonel Sir Patrick Coghill, Director of General Intelligence. Glubb was escorted out of Jordan by air the following day.[60] The Jordanian Prime Minister told the British Ambassador to Amman, Sir Charles Duke, that Hussein had come to his office around noon and had produced an order for the immediate dismissal of Glubb.[61]

Hussein justified his action on the premise that he was obliged to do what he had considered to be essential for the 'preservation of the honour of the Kingdom'.[62] He added that if he had not taken these measures, the situation could have escalated, and added that as he felt a sense of danger it was imperative to eradicate it.[63] The British government was stunned by this sudden act.

The main question now facing the British government was whether the Jordanian government was willing to continue its close relationship with the United Kingdom or whether this incident marked a shift in Jordan's relations. Macmillan, like Eden, realised that there was no practical riposte that they could make.[64] Furthermore, there was always the danger that if Britain withdrew her subsidy, Jordan would look elsewhere for assistance, to countries like Egypt and Saudi Arabia, and would move even further from British influence. This fear clearly had some foundation; soon after Glubb's dismissal, Nasser announced that Egypt, Saudi Arabia and Syria had rallied together and were prepared to supersede Britain's assistance if it were withdrawn from Jordan. Egypt also invited Jordan to join its military pact with Saudi Arabia and Yemen.

Despite the anger and disappointment that the British government felt, they still had to consider the wider implications of their position in the region, especially at a time when their prestige in the area was in decline. Clearly, the British government could not afford to cut its close ties with Jordan or take any drastic step against the King which might draw him even closer to Egypt.

Israel viewed these events on its eastern border with great apprehension. For Israel the British influence in Jordan served as a restraining factor on Amman, even though it created the potential for an Anglo-Israeli war due to the special ties that existed between Britain and Jordan. The Israeli government therefore viewed the events with mounting anxiety as Israel was always keen to see the status quo preserved in Jordan. The Israeli Ambassador to Rome, Moshe Sasson, was told by his British counterpart that when Glubb was dismissed, Britain had the choice either to take a firm line or to be cautious in order not to lose Jordan totally. He explained that Britain had chosen the second option and had decided not to put the King in a difficult position. He added that he was aware that perhaps this decision was not to Israel's satisfaction but that it had led to positive results in that Hussein had the courage to announce that he would honour and keep his treaty with Britain.[65] In a discussion on 7 March with Wikely, from the British Consulate in Jerusalem, Colonel Haim Herzog said there was deep regret in Israel at the departure of Glubb and that his restraining influence would be greatly missed.[66] The grave mood in Israel was apparent to the British representatives in the region. Sir Charles Duke realised the growing tendency towards an aggressive mood among 'hot heads' in the West Bank, and warned that as a result of that development the Jordanian–Israeli border was now more sensitive than it had been for the last two years. He stressed that any Israeli manoeuvres close to the border, such as patrolling using live ammunition, could escalate the situation even further.[67]

At the same time as Glubb was dismissed, Selwyn Lloyd happened to be on tour of the Middle East. The events that transpired during March 1956 did not favour Britain's position in the area. Not only was Glubb dismissed; the ALPHA plan collapsed as well. In this respect March 1956 can be seen as a turning point for Britain in the region, as it was left without any clear policy regarding the Middle East.

EGYPT, ISRAEL AND THE WEST

The upheavals in Jordan and the strain in Anglo-Israeli relations were not the only important development in the first months of 1956. This period also saw growing tension and hostility along the Egyptian–Israeli border. In March and April 1956, the situation along Israel's southern border started to deteriorate after a relatively quiet period. One of the main disagreements was over patrolling on the demarcation line. During this period there was frequent shooting from the Egyptian side at the Israeli border police and the Israelis would then return fire. This action continued for hours, resulting in casualties and usually requiring the intervention of the UNTSO (UN Truce Supervision Organisation).[68]

It is evident that both parties contributed towards the instability along the border. Arab infiltration across the border and their violent activities against Israeli civilians and property could not go unnoticed. Israel, for its part, held the Arab governments responsible for these activities, regardless of their nature and motive. Israel could not tolerate such activities after the Gaza raid in February 1955, when the nature of hostilities changed and raids were organised on a larger scale by Egypt. One could hardly imagine that an Israeli government led by Ben-Gurion and assisted by his Chief of Staff, Moshe Dayan, would stand aside without taking action. As Dayan emphasised in his diary: 'The Israeli government could not, of course, remain indifferent to these actions and accept them with equanimity. It was clear that there would be no end to this terrorism as long as the Arab governments, particularly Egypt's, could harm Israel without endangering their countries and their armies'.[69] Furthermore, he stressed that Nasser had succeeded in placing the war within Israel's territory and that it would be a mistake for Israel to accept this. He believed that Israel should respond firmly in order to force the Arab countries to stop these terrorist activities. Dayan realised that it was impossible to defend and seal Israel's borders against every terrorist incident and therefore the only way to end them was to demonstrate to the Arab governments that they would have to pay a 'high price' for their actions.[70] As stated previously, it was clear that Dayan's motive was not just to retaliate in order to punish and to take revenge; he believed that retaliation would serve Israel's political aims by escalating the situation to a boiling point, thus providing Israel with both the opportunity and pretext to launch the preventive war which he favoured.

On 12 March, Israel complained to the Egyptian–Israeli Mixed Armistice Commission that there were Egyptian troops, including armoured vehicles and other offensive arms, in the Gaza-El-Arish area in contradiction to Article VIII of the GAA (General Armistice Agreements). In an attempt to bring about a calmer atmosphere along the border, Dag Hammarskjold, the UN Secretary-General, was asked by the Security Council on 4 April to visit the area and report on the situation, especially in regard to which parties had complied with the General Armistice Agreement.[71] The Secretary-General arrived on 10 April and went to Cairo. His primary objective was to obtain assurances from both sides that they would do their utmost to take greater responsibility to ensure that incidents along the border ceased.

The fact that the increasing unrest and hostilities brought about greater involvement of the UN machinery was not welcomed by Israel, whose leaders, including Ben-Gurion and even Sharett, did not trust the UN's ability to control the situation. When the armistice agreement between Israel and her neighbours had been signed in 1949 after the 1948 war, there had been great hope that not only would this safeguard Israel, but that it would also serve as a foundation for further peace treaties. However, seven years later Israel still faced a hostile Arab world which was not ready to recognise its existence.

Another cause of Israeli discontent was that Israel had often been condemned by the Security Council for its retaliation policy while the Arab governments were not criticised over the Fedayeen raids. The reason for this, in Israel's view, was that it was much easier to point a finger at a united military organisation under the authority of the Israeli government than to prove that there was a direct link between the Fedayeen activities and the Arab governments. This only added to the frustration among the Israeli government and public, and heightened resentment towards the UN. In addition, Ben-Gurion stressed that, although the armistice agreements had initially been a temporary solution, they were likely to stay for an extended period. He argued that it was therefore the responsibility of both sides to keep the peace along the border and that in any case the armistice agreements were between the Israeli and Arab governments and therefore did not involve the UN or any other non-Arab state. Ben-Gurion stressed that, according to the armistice agreements, the UN had a specific and limited role, and that with all respect for the UN as an instrument for world peace, the UN could not act as Israel's spokesman. He believed that if the UN could not force the other side to comply with the armistice agreement then Israel should do it itself. He also argued that the UN was trying to make the armistice agreement biased towards one side, and added that whenever there was a breach of the armistice agreement by Egypt it was ignored.[72]

General Burns, Chief of Staff of UNTSO and Commander of the United Nations Emergency Force, had the hard task of trying to reduce tensions. He therefore tried to convince the Israeli authorities that they should not patrol along the demarcation line, and he frequently asked them, especially Dayan, to patrol further away. Dayan refused to do so and told Burns that if the Arabs were led to believe that they could make Israeli forces stay away from the demarcation line, their attitude would become bolder and more aggressive.[73] Dayan's answer represented the common belief in Israel at the time, that any sign of compromise or softness by Israel towards its Arab neighbours, and lack of military response, would be interpreted as a sign of weakness. It is important to emphasise this, in order to understand the philosophy and mechanism of Israel's defence and foreign policy. Any suggestion that came from a 'foreign' body was met with suspicion. This came from a constant, deep feeling of isolation and vulnerability. The Israeli authorities also made it clear that it was within their rights to move their troops anywhere they wanted. Burns tried to convince the authorities in Israel that although legally they had the right to do so, 'it was not always sensible to insist on one's right to the limit', but his advice fell on deaf ears.[74] In a remarkably perceptive analysis of Israeli society, Burns noted in his memoirs that, in a country where young people spent the majority of their most formative years in an atmosphere in which military virtues were given the highest value and where the Arabs were always seen as the enemy, there was little inclination to solve disputes by negotiations via outside parties. Furthermore, the *Sabra* and the Israelis who had come to Israel as young children were in a difficult situation, completely surrounded by hostile neighbours, precluded from travel abroad by lack of money, and therefore with no concern for the world outside Israel or its opinion. 'And so, born of the success of the campaigns of 1948 and 1956, there is a certain arrogance, an inability to see that Israel should yield anything for peace, an inability to compromise.'[75]

The UN in any case lacked the power to enforce the armistice agreement on either side. Colonel Ely, Burns' liaison officer in Cairo, informed P. Murry of the British embassy in Cairo in March 1956, that UNTSO was working to investigate the incidents rather than to prevent them. He admitted that the UN machinery had little chance of preventing incidents in the Gaza area where, in the view of Colonel Bay (the American chairman of the Mixed Armistice Commission), the Egyptian troops were out of hand and would shoot at anything on the Israeli side. He recognised that this behaviour was partly because the local forces in Gaza were comprised mainly of Palestinians, and noted on 22 March that their recent behaviour 'is absolutely asking for a Jewish reprisal raid'.[76] Between 7 and 11 April, further incidents occurred along the Egyptian–Israeli border. One of the most horrific was on 11 April when a Fedayeen group fired into a synagogue at an agricultural boarding school in Shafir killing six pupils and wounding two others.[77]

In an attempt to restore dialogue between Egypt and Israel, and to test the chances of a new peace initiative as well as to increase the role of the UN as mediator, the UN Secretary-General, Dag Hammarskjold, was sent to the region. But he managed to achieve only a limited relaxation of tensions along the border. On 17 April, Ben-Gurion signed on behalf of the Israeli government an order which prohibited IDF forces from firing across the armistice line, and forbade any crossing of the border for any purpose. On 19 April, Hammerskjold announced that he had obtained a similar promise from Egypt.[78] He therefore managed to achieve a limited ceasefire and to obtain promises from Jordan, Egypt and Israel that they would take all possible measures to prevent infiltration across the border.[79] Although he succeeded in achieving some of his aims, there were nevertheless still more questions which had to be resolved. For example, though the Israelis and Egyptians had agreed to the establishment of an UN observation post on each side of the border, with the UN to patrol between them, the observers did not have complete freedom of movement, especially on the Israeli side. Furthermore, the agreement did not include a mutual withdrawal of armed forces on both sides of the demarcation line.

In the area around El-Auja, in particular, there was no progress.[80] Ben-Gurion argued that the Israeli presence in El-Auja was essential to its security and that therefore there would be no withdrawal without an indication that Egypt intended to change its policy.[81] Despite this, Sir John Nicholls stated in a letter to Shuckburgh in May his belief that, in view of Israel's lack of confidence in the Arabs' motives and its suspicion of any intermediate measure calculated to produce a temporary improvement without getting to the root of the matter, it was very much to Israel's credit that it had shown itself relatively co-operative in dealing with Hammarskjold. He was also aware that, although Israel desperately wanted peace on its frontiers, the Israeli government was worried that this relaxation might ease the Western powers' urgency to take crucial decisions regarding their Middle Eastern policy. Although the Ambassador stressed that he did not believe that the Israeli government welcomed frontier incidents as a means of keeping public opinion at home up to scratch, he felt that the three serious incidents that had taken place since the ceasefire were not entirely unwelcomed by the Israeli government.[82]

THE ASWAN DAM AND THE NATIONALISATION OF THE SUEZ CANAL

At the same time there was growing uncertainty over the US–Anglo-Egyptian co-operation over the Aswan Dam project. When Nasser came to power the Egyptian government had put the Aswan Dam project high on the agenda. Such a large undertaking raised the question of finance for the project and the obvious source was the World Bank. By the end of 1955, the World Bank declared that it found the project satisfactory from an economic and technical point of view. At the same time, Egypt negotiated with the British Treasury to accelerate the release of £150 million which was owed to the Egyptians from the end of the Second World War and was being held in a blocked account in the Bank of England.[83] On 2 December, the World Bank granted the Egyptian government $20 million to defray the foreign exchange costs of the initial stages of the Dam. In addition, in the light of the ALPHA plan, the US and British governments announced that they were willing to grant Egypt $56 million and $14 million respectively, subject to legislative approval.[84] However, Nasser's antagonistic attitude towards the West and his lack of co-operation over ALPHA disturbed the British and American governments, and they also began to doubt Nasser's ability to pay off the loan. This concern led to objections by the Senate Appropriations Committee regarding the US contribution and its conclusion that none of the funds for Egypt should be used for the Aswan Dam project.[85] The River Nile being the lifeblood of Egypt, this was an issue of the greatest importance. Furthermore, when Eugene Black, the President of the World Bank, went to Cairo to present Nasser with a final offer, the latter gave him a series of counter-proposals about the loan which were unacceptable to the financing authorities. Nasser had realised that by accepting the Western loan on Western terms he would bind Egypt to the West for a considerable period, and therefore sought to renegotiate. This convinced Dulles and Eisenhower that he was not interested in serious controls over the project.[86]

Consequently, on 19 July, Dulles told the Egyptian Ambassador, Ahmed Hussein, that the US government had decided to withdraw their offer to finance the Aswan Dam. This move came as a surprise to the British government, as Dulles had neither consulted nor informed them previously of his intention. 'It came as a shock', Macmillan wrote later, 'when we heard that, on 19 July, Dulles had bluntly told the Egyptian Ambassador, Ahmed Hussein, that the United States had decided to withdraw their support from the scheme.'[87] Two days later, the United Kingdom followed the United States and announced its own withdrawal from the project. The decision was a relief for the British government as its own financial situation hardly allowed it to take on such a huge financial burden.

Nasser, who attached great importance to the Aswan Dam project, did not remain idle. On 26 July he nationalised the Suez Canal Company and took over operation of the canal. That day, he announced in a speech that he intended to use a large part of the Suez Canal Company's income to fund the building of the Dam. This act came as a massive shock to the British government and confirmed their worst suspicions of Nasser. Anthony Eden, who heard the news while attending a dinner party with Nuri, the Iraqi leader, was totally devastated. 'I had no doubt', he wrote in his memoirs, 'how Nasser's deed would be read from Agadir to Karachi.'[88] He believed that failure to keep the Canal as an international waterway would inevitably lead to the loss of all British assets in the region, and that it was therefore urgent that immediate action should be taken by France, Britain and the United States.[89] The legal status of the Suez Canal was determined by two instruments: the concession granted to the company by the Egyptian government in 1856, which ran for 99 years from the date of the opening of the Canal to traffic, and by the convention signed in 1888, between Great Britain, Germany, Austria, Hungary, Spain,

France, Italy, The Netherlands, Russia and Turkey.[90] Moreover, two years prior to the nationalisation, the Egyptian government had also acknowledged that the company was an international enterprise and as such would continue to manage the Suez Canal. Legally, Nasser could nationalise the Canal if he paid compensation to the previous owners, but his promises to utilise the revenue from the Canal to pay for the Dam made it apparent that he had no intention of paying compensation.

Nasser's action endangered Britain's position in the Arab world and the British government was quick to react; on 28 July the Bank of England and the commercial banks were given authority to block the current Egyptian sterling balances in London. The funds and assets of the Suez Canal Company in London were protected against Egyptian expropriation and all exports of arms and military materials were banned. The crisis also had a grave impact on Britain's finances; it endangered the position of the pound, especially in view of the fact that a large amount of transferable sterling was held by Arab countries and oil companies. The pound thus presented an obvious target if these groups decided that it was vulnerable. This position would obviously worsen if the Canal or the communications lines were interrupted, as it would mean that Britain would have to buy her oil in dollars, thereby losing all her profit from supplying oil.[91] Being aware of the grave consequences of an oil crisis, the possibility of military action crossed Eden's mind. He felt that economic and political pressure alone would not be enough to re-establish international control over the Canal and therefore from the beginning of the crisis he considered that 'We had to prepare to back our remonstrances with military actions.'[92] Anthony Eden also hoped that the US government would stand by them and support military action against Nasser. However, the British government and Foreign Office officials were worried about the effect such an action might have on Anglo-American relations if the United States would not support them.[93]

The French position was similar to that of the British. The French were anxious to take military action against Nasser because of their vulnerable position in North Africa, and their belief that toppling Nasser would solve their problems in Algeria. Unlike the British government, the French government enjoyed an overwhelming majority at home in support of such action, and were determined to prove that the European powers could act without the United States' participation. They also believed that the United States should stand by them regardless of the situation. It is important to note that, although France and Britain did not share the same outlook on many issues in the Middle East as their interests lay in different areas of the region, they were both eager to seek a quick solution to the crisis, which would secure their position and revenue. As the French Foreign Minister said on 29 July to Selwyn Lloyd 'One successful battle in Egypt, would be worth ten in Africa.'[94]

These common concerns brought the French and the British closer and they soon began to proceed with military planning. The Chief of the French navy arrived in London on 29 July for consultations with the British military commanders. He stated his government's readiness to co-operate with the British under their command and that they would also make land and air forces available.[95] As a result, Operation 'Musketeer' came into being. Its aim was to secure international administration and control of the Canal, as well as replacing Nasser's regime by another more friendly towards the West.[96]

The American position differed from both the French and the British. Washington held that the West should only employ peaceful channels, and sought diplomatic means in order to put Egypt under pressure to operate the Canal efficiently and meet her international obligations. President Eisenhower noted in his memoirs, 'much as we valued our friendship with France ... we could not encourage the unjustified domination of a small nation by foreign armies.'[97]

On 16 August, a conference of the Suez Canal users opened at Lancaster House in London but ended without any concrete results. It is evident from the records that the details of the US position were not very clear, but it is also quite obvious that Eisenhower and Dulles viewed the dispute from a distinctly different angle to that of the French or the British governments, and calculated its significance against the wider background of the Cold War. They feared that military action against an Arab country, especially Egypt, might have severe repercussions on the Western position in the region which was already fragile. President Eisenhower tried to convey his view to Eden. 'For my part,' the President stressed, 'I cannot over-emphasize the strength of my conviction that some method must be attempted before action such as you contemplate should be undertaken. Moreover, initial military success might be easy, but the eventual price might become far too heavy.'[98] In his memoirs, he noted that, 'Above all there must be no grounds for our several peoples to believe that anyone was using the canal difficulty as an excuse to proceed forcibly against Nasser.'[99] The British and French governments, however, were determined to pursue military action.

ISRAEL AND THE SUEZ CRISIS

At the same time, a new element came into the picture of the Suez crisis – Israel. The Israelis already had a close relationship with France, and the ties between them had been consolidated during 1956. Shimon Peres, the General Director of the Defence Ministry and the architect of Franco-Israeli relations, had already convinced Ben-Gurion by the end of May 1956 that Peres should hold a meeting with Maurice Bourges-Maunoury, the French Minister of National Defence, to discuss closer military co-operation with France and to have an unwritten pact with the French against Nasser. Ben-Gurion had some reservations but knew that this was a unique opportunity to secure a close ally like France, and to ensure the continuance of French arms. Peres and Dayan were convinced that Israel should ally itself closely with the French and in a meeting between Ben-Gurion and Dayan on 10 June, Ben-Gurion agreed to further negotiations with the French, even if it meant an agreement or an understanding that in the future they might have to embark on a joint Franco-Israeli military operation.[100] Further discussion took place on 23 June at a meeting in Vermer, a small town 15 kilometres south of Paris, which resulted in an agreement that was close to being an alliance between Israel and France.[101] France thus had a potential ally which it could call upon to take joint action.

The likelihood of Israel joining with France in a military strike was also heightened by another major political event in June 1956 – the resignation of Moshe Sharett, Israel's Foreign Minister and former Prime Minister. Sharett and Ben-Gurion were divided over a number of major issues: Israel's attitude towards the Arab–Israeli dispute and the question of preventive war; the degree to which Western powers and worldwide public opinion should be considered in Israel's decision-making process; and the respective roles of the Foreign Minister and Defence Ministry in making decisions on Israel's foreign policy. Ben-Gurion believed that the Defence Ministry should take precedence over the Foreign Minister and should not have to consult him, and he warned Sharett that if he found that the Foreign Ministry was intervening in defence matters, he (Ben-Gurion) would have to resign.[102] The arguments between the two were bound to lead to an explosion and it came in the early summer of 1956 when Mapai was looking for a new General-Secretary. Sharett ironically suggested that he should take the position. Ben-Gurion, who desired a firmer policy, was not going to lose the opportunity to oust Sharett and threatened to resign if Sharett would not. On 17 June, Sharett announced he would resign on the following day, and Golda Meir replaced him.

Sharett believed that Meir suffered from an inferiority complex because she had not completed secondary education and thus did not have the qualifications a Foreign Minister needed.[103] However, for Ben-Gurion the way was now open for him to pursue his own policy. He could move forward without encountering any obstacles, as Meir was a great admirer of his. However, the biggest explosion was yet to come. Ben-Gurion pointed out in one of his speeches that the effort to gain arms from France had been fruitless until June 1956 (when Sharett resigned).[104] This comment only added more fuel to the tense relations between the two, as this was an accusation that Sharett, who always felt frustrated and bitter at the way Ben-Gurion treated him, could not accept.

Sharett's resignation caused concern in both London and Washington. In a letter to Lloyd on 20 June, Sir John Nicholls expressed the view that Sharett's resignation marked a turning point in the brief history of Israel. He observed that Ben-Gurion was now free to pursue his policy and that Meir, who shared his beliefs, could not be counted upon to exercise a more moderate influence. Nicholls believed that in these circumstances they must be prepared for some unwelcome changes.[105] Meanwhile, Israel consolidated its relationship with the French.

After the nationalisation of the Suez Canal, the French government very quickly wanted to ascertain whether the Israelis would be willing to commit themselves to a joint operation, but they only approached them formally on 18 September 1956.[106] Further discussions about military co-operation between Israel and France took place on 23 September. The most important negotiations, however, took place on 30 September between the Israeli delegation, including Golda Meir, now the Israeli Foreign Minister, and the French delegation in St Germain (though it was actually at Colonel Louis Magin's house in Paris). This marked a turning point in the involvement of Israel in the Suez Affair. The primary question the French raised was whether Israel would participate in an attack on Egypt, if the British government decided against military action. The French representatives suggested that in such circumstances they would assist Israel, both politically and militarily.[107] In spite of the fact that Israel had good reason to overthrow Nasser, Ben-Gurion hesitated. He was aware of the far-reaching political implications that such an event might create. For example, the possibility that Washington might declare an arms embargo on Israel, and the likelihood of Soviet assistance to Egypt were very serious consequences to consider.

Still, Israel had solid reasons for wanting to oust Nasser. After the arms deal agreement between Egypt and Czechoslovakia in 1955, the

Israelis viewed with great anxiety the large quantities and the high quality of the modern arms being delivered to Egypt. These weapons clearly threatened to alter the balance of arms in the region and increased the possibility of an attack on Israel. Furthermore, the Egyptians had blockaded the Straits of Tiran and did not allow Israeli ships to pass through. In September 1955, Egypt announced that the naval blockade on Israel was to become even tighter and that all aircraft wishing to fly through or over the Straits of Tiran would have to confirm their intentions 72 hours in advance. No Israeli aircraft would be permitted to fly over the Straits and this severed Israel's only air corridor with Africa.[108] There was no sign that diplomacy would help to alleviate the situation. Indeed, the United States and Britain had agreed not to bring the question of Israel's passage through the Tiran Straits and Suez Canal to the London Conference.[109] Thus war appeared to be the only way to remove this Egyptian stranglehold.

However, Ben-Gurion was cautious about engaging solely in a French–Israeli venture as he was concerned about France's ability to operate without the British. He believed that only the British could provide Israel with sufficient air power to defend itself from bombing by the Egyptian Air Force with its own advanced Soviet aircraft.[110] In his view, therefore, it was essential that Britain should participate in any operation against Nasser. However, this raised the crucial question of whether the British government would co-operate with Israel even if this meant that Britain would have to defend Israel against possible Jordanian or Iraqi attack.[111]

At the same time, British defence circles were themselves considering the overall implications of any Israeli intervention or any hostility that might result between Israel and its neighbours during a Suez operation. The British commanders were aware that Israel might use the situation to attack Egypt or Jordan, which would place Britain in a serious dilemma. They were aware that Israel aimed to eliminate Egyptian power and to expand its own eastern frontier to the natural border provided by the River Jordan, the Dead Sea and Vadi Arava (the land between the Dead Sea and Eilat).[112] The Chiefs of Staff and the British commanders assessed that it would be of great assistance to their operation if Israel arranged a practice mobilisation a few days prior to the Musketeer operation. But, although such a contribution could be beneficial from a military point of view, the British commanders considered that the political implications for the British position in Jordan and Iraq, and the possibility that they would have to reinforce their forces in the Persian Gulf, made the scheme impractical.[113] Therefore, they concluded that it was very important in their view 'to avoid the appearance of any collusion with the Israelis'.[114]

Already, in the past, the possibility of Israeli military action against Egypt had been tentatively discussed between Lloyd and the Israeli Ambassador. In a formal introductory discussion with Elath on 29 December 1955, Lloyd said that on such a solemn occasion it was not customary to 'talk business'. However, he was curious to know the mood of the Israeli public in regard to the new situation created in the region by the Czech–Egyptian arms deal and had wondered if those who favoured a preventive war had got stronger. Elath said that if such a movement existed in Israel, Britain more than any other country was to be blamed, because of its appeasement policy towards Nasser and its refusal to supply adequate arms to Israel. Selwyn Lloyd had then asked the Ambassador if Israel would ever embark upon a military operation against Egypt, and enquired as to the time involved and whether the Israeli forces would then withdraw back to their territory. Elath assumed that it would take approximately five days and asked the Foreign Secretary if this was the sort of operation he wanted, to which Selwyn Lloyd replied that it was a hard question, as one had to consider the political implications, such as the behaviour of the Soviet Union and the possibility that Jordan might join Egypt. His answer therefore was that they did not want to participate in such an operation. Elath's own interpretation of this curious discussion was that Lloyd was genuine and was not trying to set a trap or to get confirmation that Israel was preparing a preventive war.[115] This discussion can only be found in Israeli documents, not in British or American sources. We can assume that this letter from MAHAV (the US Department within the Israeli Foreign Office) addressed to Washington and Paris followed a letter from Elath to the Israeli Foreign Office. Lloyd's questions did not raise any special reaction in Israel, and it does not seem that Lloyd's comment indicated any special wish for close military co-operation between Israel and Britain; any such assumption would be too far-reaching. However, one could speculate that in view of Anglo-Israeli relations at the time the British government was always puzzled by the intentions of the Israeli government and tried to find out what was 'cooking' within Ben-Gurion's government. It seems that, although such an operation could serve British interests, this was a one-off remark which did not indicate any far-reaching plans or any change in the British attitude towards Israel. Certainly, in late 1956, the British government had no desire to co-operate with the Israelis. Their response to the French idea of an association with Israel was that they would only be willing to ally with it on condition that Israel launched an attack on the Egyptian army in Sinai. Ben-Gurion was totally opposed to this suggestion because it increased his fears that the British intended to leave the 'dirty work' to

Israel. This anxiety was influenced not only by his perpetual suspicion of Britain, but also by the background of events that occurred between Israel and Jordan in September–October 1956.

The Israeli government had long suspected that Britain would delight in witnessing a permanent quarrel between Israel and Jordan, because this would keep the Jordanians in constant fear and thus persuade them to preserve their links with Britain.[116] Dayan, too, shared the view that since the dismissal of Glubb, the British government wanted to prove to Jordan that Britain was the only country the latter could rely on for support against Israel.[117] These Israeli assumptions were wrong, for in fact the dispute between Israel and Jordan only served to add difficulties for Britain, as it increased the influence of the pro-Nasserist element within Jordan which posed a major threat to Hussein's leadership. However, these assumptions serve to highlight Israel's mistrust and apprehension regarding Britain.

THE QALQILYA OPERATION

Anglo-Israeli relations deteriorated alarmingly during the early autumn as a result of the frequent Israeli reprisal raids against Jordan during September–October 1956. Until the autumn of 1956 the internal events in Jordan had not had any effect on Israel's security. General Enab, who replaced General Glubb, did his best to prevent the Fedayeen from crossing into Israel. However, around this time, Israeli intelligence obtained some telegrams revealing that more Fedayeen groups were going to be sent from Syria to Jordan.[118] This coincided with the nomination of Abu Anwar as Head of the Arab Legion. He did not control the border as rigorously as his predecessor had done and there was therefore an increase in Fedayeen activities from Jordan into Israel. The Israeli government thus decided to strike back.

On 11 September, Israeli military forces crossed the demarcation line into Jordan, aiming to destroy Rahwa police station. The forces attacked the police station and completely destroyed it.[119] Further escalations along the Jordanian–Israeli border led to further Israeli responses. On 23 September an Israeli archaeological congress, which had gathered at Ramat-Rachel excavation south of Jerusalem, was fired on by a Jordanian soldier and heavy casualties resulted. The senior Jordanian delegation to the Israeli–Jordanian Mixed Armistice Committee explained that the soldier was suddenly overcome by madness and was taken to hospital for examination.[120] The spiral of violence did not stop and Israeli forces crossed the border into Jordan once again on the night of 25/26 September, attacking and demolishing the Sharafa police post, one kilometre south-east of the village of Hussan.[121]

Ben-Gurion was worried that the situation in Jordan was deteriorating and he suspected that there was a plan regarding Jordan's future, which he gathered was aimed at reducing Soviet influence. In a discussion on 3 October with the American Ambassador to Tel-Aviv, Edward Lawson, Ben-Gurion expressed his concern about the possibility of Iraqi forces entering Jordan and being stationed along Israel's eastern frontier. He also told Lawson that he was worried about rumours suggesting that Jordan should be united with Iraq in some form or another and the idea of giving the West Bank an independent status. (It is not clear what the basis was for Ben-Gurion's assumptions, whether it was his own suspicions or intelligence reports, as access to many of the relevant documents in the Ben-Gurion archive is restricted.) Ben-Gurion warned the Ambassador that if Israel's interests were not taken into consideration, it might take action against Jordan, even though this might increase the influence of pro-Egyptian elements.[122] It is clear, however, that tensions along Israel's eastern border ran high. The major conflagration between Israel and Jordan occurred on the night of the Qalqilya raid. On 9 October, two Israeli farm labourers were killed and their bodies mutilated by Fedayeen in Moshav Even-Yehuda (near the town of Nethanya). The Israeli government held the Jordanian government responsible for these brutal murders and hit back.

On the night of 10/11 October a substantial Israeli force attacked Qalqilya police station following an artillery bombardment. However, the Israeli force came under fierce attack by the Arab Legion, resulting in many Israeli casualties. In order to help the evacuation of the Israeli unit, an additional force was sent in, but they also faced heavy fire. The numbers of casualties grew from one minute to the next and the whole affair became a total disaster when an armoured vehicle carrying Israeli casualties turned over in the middle of a Jordanian post. Finally, at dawn, the Israeli force returned to Israel with heavy losses.[123]

King Hussein was alarmed at this escalation of the fighting and contacted General Sir Charles Keightley, the Commander-in-Chief of British forces in the Middle East, on 11 October, suggesting that under the circumstances he thought that it would be advisable to invoke the Anglo-Jordanian defence treaty. However, the British government refused to take such a step.[124] They were worried about the constant hostility along the Israel–Jordan border and a possible Israeli attack on Jordan, which would place them in the position of having to honour the Anglo-Jordan treaty.[125] The Qalqilya operation placed the British government in a delicate dilemma. In his memoirs, Macmillan referred to the incident, saying that on 12 October the British government was forced to warn Israel that, in the event of a serious attack against Jordan, Britain would be bound to come to the assistance of its ally if Hussein invoked the treaty.[126] Eden, in his memoirs, referred to such a possibility and described it as 'a nightmare which could only too easily come true'.[127] Eden emphasised that the British government therefore had to do all they could to prevent such a situation.[128]

This caution and hesitation was also evident in the Foreign Office's response to the King's requests. Hussein was in a shaky state and told Sir Charles Duke on 13 October that it seemed that an Israeli attack on Jordan was imminent. He again asked for British assistance, especially the strengthening of the RAF presence in Jordan. In addition, the King called for consultations with representatives from the Headquarters of MEAF (Middle East Air Force) in order to organise air cover for Jordan in case of an Israeli attack, and expressed his wish to announce publicly that Jordan would receive support from the RAF. Duke, in turn, reminded the King that the recent attacks on Israeli civilians, such as the killing of the two labourers near Even-Yehuda, gave Israel sufficient *raison d'être* to build up a case against Jordan. Nevertheless, the Ambassador urged the Foreign Office to take steps to enhance the King's position and prove that Britain would keep her promise to help Jordan.[129]

Duke believed that Jordan was faced with the most acute military threat from Israel since 1948, and although he acknowledged the objections against a British aerial demonstration in Jordan, including the risk that Israel might use the opportunity to create a serious incident with the RAF, he believed that some firm action was urgently needed. Duke had already argued on 11 October that the Israeli behaviour was obstinate, that the Israeli government constantly ignored British condemnation of the reprisal actions, and therefore that it was time to show the Israelis that Britain 'meant business' and demonstrate clearly that an Israeli attack on Jordan would be met by a firm British military response. He thought that such a threat would 'deter the hot heads and strengthen the moderates in Israel'.[130] Furthermore, it would boost the morale of the Jordanian government and could help Hussein to resist pressure for desperate measures from the extreme and irresponsible elements.[131]

However, despite the nature of the Israeli attack, the Foreign Office had great reservations about complying with Hussein's requests. The Foreign Office stressed to Duke on 14 October that it was not in British interests to take harsh measures and to treat a raid as if it were war. Furthermore, it was argued that Hussein, by his own actions, such as the dismissal of Glubb, had reduced the efficiency of the Arab

Legion.[132] The Foreign Office was aware of the possibility that the deployment of the RAF against Israel might result in an Israeli attack on British airfields in Cyprus and Jordan as well as the destruction of the Jordanian army. Therefore in the Foreign Office's view, if Jordan had to choose between a raid, even a very heavy one, followed by Israeli withdrawal or British intervention followed by war, the first option was better.[133] As a gesture of British commitment towards Jordan, a squadron of Hunters was sent from Cyprus to Jordan, but the British government refused to comply with Hussein's request to station further RAF units in Jordan. The Ambassador had to inform the King that in Britain's view an Israeli attack was not imminent, and that, although Israel might strike again, the pattern of her raids was inconsistent.[134]

Meanwhile, the British representatives in Israel tried to do their best to calm the Israeli government and also to analyse the present Israeli mood. On the night of the Qalqilya raid, the British Consul in Jerusalem was informed of the Israeli attack and of Hussein's request for RAF assistance. Hussein made a personal appeal to the British Consul in Jerusalem to do what was possible to call off the Israeli attack, saying that the RAF's assistance had been requested and that if the fighting would not stop then a grave situation in which Britons and Israelis were fighting each other might occur.[135] In a discussion on 11 October between Higgins of the British embassy in Tel-Aviv and Avrham Ofer of the Ministry for Foreign Affairs, the latter admitted that if the Israeli government wanted they could resist public pressure for raids, but stated that at the present moment the Israeli government did not believe that it was necessary to resist such pressure because they were convinced that the Jordanian authorities were responsible for the border incidents, and that the only way of deterring the attacks was by hitting back hard. A more complicated picture was described by one of the Israeli officials in the British and Commonwealth division of the Israeli Foreign Office. He said that the Israeli government did not believe that the recent raids were effective but they had no alternative, and added that the Foreign Office had little to say because 'they were merely civilians'.[136] This line emphasises once again the limited power the Foreign Ministry had on Ben-Gurion and on defence policy, and the degree to which they were excluded.

Taking into account the nature of Anglo-Israeli relations at the time, the British government had very little influence upon the Israeli decision-makers. As Eden explained, 'Our relations with Israel were not close or intimate.'[137] He believed that the best channel for exercising a moderating influence on Israel was through the French. Eden therefore asked the French government to do their utmost to make it clear to Israel that an attack on Jordan would have to be resisted by the British. Eden believed that failure to carry out Britain's commitment might have a fatal impact on its position in the region, but on the other hand to act would be a disaster for Western unity.[138]

As far as Anglo-Israeli relations were concerned the Qalqilya incident and its aftermath demonstrated two main points: the British hesitation to invoke the Anglo-Jordanian treaty and its anxiety to avoid even the slightest possibility of direct military confrontation with Israel, and, more significantly, the poor state of Anglo-Israeli relations at the time. The fact was that the deep-rooted suspicion and mistrust on both sides prevented the British government from more frank talks with the Israeli government, and necessitated using the French as a mediator in the hope that the Israelis would be willing to show some goodwill towards French pledges.

From the Israeli point of view: *The Qalqilya operation represented the end of an era.* It was clear that the policy of reprisals had not achieved its aims. The failure at Qalqilya, where 18 soldiers were killed and 40–50 wounded, demonstrated beyond doubt that this kind of military action would not solve the problem. As revealed in Dayan's diary, the operation also aroused a great deal of criticism and the chief commanders of the IDF had to face up to the fact that these actions were fruitless.[139] Dayan was left with the view that only a massive action could provide an answer to the problem.

But the question remains: why did Israel decide to undertake such a large-scale raid at a time when it desperately wanted to secure British participation in the Suez campaign? According to Bar-On, Israel was faced with a problem regarding retaliation against Jordan because it knew that by retaliating it would strengthen the radical elements within Jordan and those who favoured the entrance of Iraqi troops.[140] Moreover, even Dayan was aware that it would be better to avoid taking military action: 'We wanted', Dayan wrote in his diary, 'to avoid any military action, at least until the Security Council finished [its] session', but he justified the operation on the grounds that the killing of two Jewish workers on 9 October could not be tolerated.[141] Ben-Gurion, in his diary, confirmed that this was the Israeli government approach: '*More and more I do not intend to take any action against Jordan or Egypt because I do not want to give Eden any excuse not to join the action against Egypt*'.[142] As all the evidence demonstrates, Ben-Gurion and Dayan were aware that this was a crucial time for Israel and that it must calculate its policy very carefully. The question therefore is how can we explain the Israeli decision to launch such an operation which appears totally contrary to Israel's interests. Can we assume that the killing of two Jewish workers was the cause of it and, even if the answer is yes, does it explain the level of retaliation?

Another reason might be that the raid was an attempt to warn Britain against any plan to induce moving Iraqi forces into Jordan, and to demonstrate that such a plan would be confronted with a massive Israeli response. Some explanation can be found in Dayan's comments at the time: 'Unless the waters are come in unto the soul' (this is the biblical translation for the phrase Dayan used, which could also be translated as 'unless the situation is unbearable').[143] This comment was made in his diary after the Israeli Cabinet decided, at its meeting on 7 October, *not* to embark on any operation until 22 October. Dayan indicated by these words that, although aware that it was in Israel's best interest to show some restraint, he believed that if faced with further serious escalation along the border, it would be compelled, even at this crucial time, to exercise its 'iron fist'. We might therefore assume that following the murder of the Jewish workers, in addition to the anxiety over the possibility of an Iraqi intervention in Jordan, he felt he had no alternative but to seize the opportunity to launch the operation.

In an interview the author held with Yehoshafat Harkabi, the latter stated that he could not comment on the reasons for that operation because at the time he was in the United States. Harkabi tried to explain that, although immense force was used, it was not exceptional or significant. He also added that a comparison between the scale of the Fedayeen activities and that of the Israeli operation could not be made because the Fedayeen operated in a guerrilla-type manner which normally worked on a small scale, while the IDF was a regular force with heavy machinery and used an entirely different form of offensive.[144] In an interview with Mordechai Bar-On, formerly Dayan's military secretary, the latter remarked that it was difficult to know the real motive behind the Qalqilya operation, but added that he could accept the theory that the objective was to deter Jordan and Britain from their plan to send Iraqi forces into Jordan.[145] The question remains open, as most of the documents relating to this issue remain closed to most researchers. (Unfortunately most of the IDF documents are closed to the ordinary researcher.)

The Qalqilya operation demonstrated to the British that Israel was willing to take a firm line if it suspected that its interests were in danger. Even so, the British government announced on the day after Qalqilya that Iraqi troops would be stationed in Jordan in order to protect the King during the forthcoming elections. The Israeli government was furious about this decision, which was supported by the British, especially since Iraq had not signed any armistice agreement with Israel. The possibility that Israel might further escalate the situation aroused concern among the British government, who were already apprehensive that Israel would take action against Jordan if the latter appeared to fall into Egyptian control.[146] The possibility of Israel intervening if Iraqi forces entered Jordan was also considered, and although they thought this unlikely, it was nonetheless a possibility, particularly in the light of Qalqilya.

Golda Meir expressed Israel's anxiety over Britain's decision to support the entry of Iraqi troops into Jordan, and on 14 October told Westlake of the British embassy in Tel-Aviv that Israel regarded such a move as a breach of the status quo, arguing that, in Israel's view, the British government should consult them prior to such a move.[147] She also made clear to the British representative that the Jordanian government had nothing to fear from Israel as long as Jordan did not provoke any incidents, and argued against the assumption that there was an alternative to Egyptian intervention in Jordan. Golda Meir maintained that the British assumption, that Iraqi entry into Jordan was better for Israel, was not necessarily true, because if Egyptian troops went to Jordan, at least the Israeli government could react without the risk of confronting British forces.[148] Finally, in the face of this pressure, the British requested that the Iraqis refrain from entering Jordan, probably because they did not want to increase the possibility of Israeli action against Jordan or against the Iraqi forces. Moreover, King Hussein himself rejected the suggestion, a rejection which can be understood on the grounds that he did not want to appear to be a tool of the West, especially during an election period.

This tense atmosphere between Israel and Britain was hardly the right background for negotiations between the two, but, despite the suspicious attitude on both sides, negotiations concerning a combined military action against Egypt proceeded. Ben-Gurion's main fear was that Israel would find itself alone doing the 'dirty work' for France and Britain, while the latter two forces withdrew from the plan. Consequently, from Israel's point of view any plan of campaign had to be constructed in such a way that the first move by Israel would be perceived as just another raid, and should the other partners choose not to participate, Israel could withdraw. According to Yuval Neheman, then Deputy of the IDF Intelligence Staff, during his talks with General Challe, he led the negotiations towards the idea that French military action should come as a response to the Israeli invasion. Challe then 'thought' of the idea of Anglo-French intervention in order to separate the forces and secure the neutrality and safety of the Canal.[149]

The main obstacle at this stage lay in Britain's hesitation about co-operation with the Israelis, and equally with Ben-Gurion, who did not trust the British government and especially the Foreign Office.

Therefore there was a need for a meeting between France, Britain and Israel to overcome this hostility. For the British and Israeli governments, in particular, this was an uneasy task, bearing in mind their controversial background and their clash over the possible Iraqi entrance into Jordan which overshadowed relations between the two.

These tensions inevitably influenced the atmosphere at the meeting at Sèvres held on 22 October, at which Ben-Gurion's suspicious attitude towards Britain clearly emerged. Ben-Gurion bluntly told Selwyn Lloyd that he had no reason to believe in anything the British Prime Minister said.[150] Faced with this statement, Lloyd then had the difficult task of explaining to the Israeli government that open co-operation in a military operation might endanger the British position in the Arab countries and the traffic of oil, and thus the collusion had to remain secret.[151] He succeeded, however, only in creating ill-feelings among the Israelis, as Dayan wrote in his diary: 'the British Foreign Minister's behaviour had an antagonistic appearance. All his behaviour expressed revulsion.'[152] He thought that Lloyd's tactic was 'more like bargaining with small merchants'.[153] However, Dayan still tried to point out to Ben-Gurion that it was a significant opportunity, and argued that Israel should provide the excuse the British wanted by initiating an operation against Egypt. If Israel refused to do it, he believed, she would lose a historic opportunity.

Dayan also believed that the French air force was adequate to protect Israel from an Egyptian attack on its cities. He was surprised and disappointed when the French told him that if Israel was attacked by Egypt they would not come to Israel's assistance. However, the French government agreed to send their squadrons to Israel.[154] Surprisingly enough, co-operation on that level exceeded all expectations; Colonel Prederges (Commander of the French air force sent to Israel) suggested that his pilots be permitted to join direct bombardment of the Egyptian convoy which had withdrawn from Sinai. The Israelis asked for French assistance to destroy Egyptian aircraft in Luxor; they would provide the French with aerial photographs, and French F-84 bombers would attack the airfield.[155]

Finally, despite all the differences and difficulties between the British and the Israelis, Ben-Gurion agreed to co-operate on the basis that Israel would provide the excuse the British demanded. It was Dayan who succeeded in convincing him by putting forward the suggestion that in order to avoid the possibility that Israel might start a war and then be left alone, Israeli paratroops should jump into the Mitla mountain pass without immediately starting an overland operation and in that way it could always appear to be another raid. There was also a compromise with regard to the gap between the Israeli attack and the first allied air strike; it was shortened from 72 hours to 48 hours.

For Ben-Gurion, the primary objective of the Israeli attack on Egypt was to gain freedom of passage in the Straits of Tiran. In part his interest flowed from historical reasons, for in biblical times this had been the Isle of Yotvata, a self-governing Jewish community. It therefore aroused deep feelings in Ben-Gurion, who was especially interested in that period and felt emotionally close to those events. Moreover, Sharm el Sheikh, the southern point on Sinai, controlled the entrance to the Gulf of Aqaba. In 1950, Egypt acquired from Saudi Arabia two small islands, Tiran and Snapir, which were located in the narrow Straits. Egypt blockaded the passage of Israeli ships through the Straits and Israel's aim was therefore to capture Sharm el Sheikh in order to obtain free passage through the Straits. Sharm el Sheikh and the Straits of Tiran were therefore important for Israel because they would enable it to develop its southern port, Eilat. These aims had special significance for Ben-Gurion as he had a vision of Eilat as the future bridge between Israel and Africa and Asia. He also wanted to occupy Sinai because of the economic benefits to be gained from its oilfields.[156] Ben-Gurion was also aware of the significance for Israel of this unique opportunity to co-operate with other powers and not to have to stand alone against the Egyptians. This fact affected Ben-Gurion deeply, especially since Israel was going to co-operate with Britain led by Prime Minister Anthony Eden. Ben-Gurion and the Israeli decisions-makers saw Eden as a great friend of the Arabs, and to co-operate with him was therefore viewed as a special political victory.[157] He also hoped that the situation would provide Israel with a significant opportunity to gain recognition of its existence and position in the Middle East. Ben-Gurion told the French Ambassador to Israel about his own wild plan to reorganise the Middle East: toppling Nasser; dividing Jordan; annexing the West Bank and giving the eastern part to Iraq provided it made peace with Israel and settled the refugees within its country with the aid of American money. Also, Lebanon would be divided, and part of it would be given to Syria, while another part up to the Litani river would go to Israel; the rest would become a Lebanese Christian state.[158]

The British Ambassador in Tel-Aviv, Sir John Nicholls, had no idea of the Sèvres agreement and when he met Ben-Gurion on 26 October, he told him that the Israeli government was wrong to mistrust the British government, and as proof of this he told Ben-Gurion that Her Majesty's Government had decided to get rid of Nasser. To his surprise Ben-Gurion told him that he had already been informed of the decision.[159] On the same day, the British Ambassador informed his government that there was an indication that the previous night there had been a substantial call-up accompanied by considerable military activity in the Beer-Sheva district, but, 'despite recent incidents on the Egyptian border I do not believe that these moves are connected with preparation to launch a reprisal, the most likely explanation is I think a build up in the south perhaps in Eilath to counter the risk of Egyptian incursion to Jordan.'[160] He believed that the immediate cause was probably the announcement of the establishment of the Jordanian–Egyptian Joint Staff Organisation.[161]

The United States, who found itself excluded by its allies, suspected that the British were going to take some action. Their feeling of unease increased on 15 October, when they received information about the Israeli mobilisation. Eisenhower's memoirs indicate the extent to which the Americans were cut off from events, as they thought the reports of mobilisation were linked to Ben-Gurion's plan to seize Jordan and that he might have hoped to use the pre-election period (in the United States), believing that the President would do nothing to offend his voters who supported Israel.[162]

A big shock for the US government and the rest of the world came on 29 October with the news of an Israeli military attack – not on Jordan, as was expected, but on Egypt. An even bigger shock for the Americans and the rest of the world was yet to come.

NOTES

1. Mordechai Bar-on, *Sharei A'za, Medinut H'chuz Vehabithon shel Medinhat Israel 1955–1957* [The Gates of Gaza – Israel's Defence and Foreign Policy 1955–1957], (Tel-Aviv: Am-Oved, 1992). See also E.L.M. Burns, *Between Arab and Israeli* (London: Harrap & Co., 1962), p. 188.
2. Bar-On, *Sharei A'za*, pp. 76-7.
3. Moshe Sharett, *Yoman Ishi* [Personal Diary] (Tel-Aviv: Ma'ariv, 1978), Vol. 5, January 1955, p. 1328.
4. Ibid., 11 January 1956, p. 1307.
5. Ibid.
6. Ibid., 28 July 1956, p. 1519.
7. Ibid., 27 December 1956, p. 1318.
8. Ibid., 28 June 1956, pp. 1518–9.
9. David Ben-Gurion, *Yehud Veichud* [Singularity and Mission] (Tel-Aviv: Ma'archot, 1971:1982), p. 323.
10. Moshe Dayan, *Diary of the Sinai Campaign* (New York: Harper and Row, 1966), p. 5.
11. PRO, FO371/113838/VR1017/190, Dixon (New York) to Lloyd, 22 December 1955.
12. PRO, FO371/121732/VR1074/20, Dixon to Lloyd, 9 January 1956.
13. PRO, FO371/121732/VR 1074/27, Dixon to Lloyd, 12 January 1956.
14. *Hansard*, Vol. 548, col. 163, 24 January 1956.
15. Ibid.

16. PRO, PREM11/1464/PM56/37, 25 February 1956.
17. PRO, FO371/121331/V192/280, Makins (Washington) to Foreign Office, 6 March 1956.
18. PRO, FO371/121329/V1192/234, Lloyd to Makins (Washington), 24 February 1956.
19. PRO, FO371/121820/VR1213/11, Laurence (Foreign Office) to Botton (Admiralty), 27 September 1956.
20. PRO, FO371/121357/VR1192/844, Foreign Office memorandum, 14 August 1956.
21. PRO, FO371/121351/VR1192/849, Kirkpatrick to Rose, 15 August 1956.
22. Ibid.
23. PRO, FO121805/VR1052/2, Shuckburgh, Foreign Office minute, 9 January 1956.
24. PRO, FO371/121722/VR1073/18, Ross (Foreign Office) to Tel-Aviv, No. 14, 19 January 1956.
25. ISA, HZ2467/8, Elath to Israeli Foreign Ministry, 22 January 1956.
26. PRO, FO371/121692/VR1011/1, Nicholls to Lloyd, 20 February 1956.
27. Ibid.
28. PRO, FO371/121233/V1054/27, Foreign Office to British embassy Tel-Aviv, 18 February 1956.
29. PRO, FO371/121233/V1054/31, Lloyd to Nicholls, 24 February 1956.
30. ISA, HZ329/1, MABAR to Israeli diplomats (no specification), 9 March 1956.
31. PRO, PREM11/1476/11464, 1 March 1956.
32. Ibid.
33. Selwyn Lloyd, *Suez – A Personal Account 1956* (London: Book Club Associates, 1978), p. 57.
34. Anthony Eden, *Full Circle* (London: Cassell, 1960), p. 331.
35. Harold Macmillan, *Riding the Storm, 1956–1959* (London: Macmillan, 1971), p. 90.
36. Ibid., p. 93.
37. PRO, FO371/118865/JE1053/56, Nicholls to Shuckburgh, 7 June 1956.
38. Ibid.
39. PRO, FO371/118863/JE1053/54, Nicholls to Shuckburgh, 15 June 1956.
40. PRO, FO371/115869/VR1076/106, No. 1262, Makins (Washington) to Lloyd, 1 June 1955.
41. PRO, FO371/118863/JE1053/54, Hadow (Foreign Office) minute, 15 June 1956.
42. PRO, FO371/115825/VE1051/8, Shuckburgh to Nicholls, 22 March 1955.
43. Keith Kyle, *Suez* (London: Weidenfeld & Nicolson, 1991), p. 90.
44. Eden, *Full Circle*, p. 344.
45. Uriel Dann, *King Hussein and the Challenge of Arab Radicalism, Jordan 1955–1967* (Oxford: Oxford University Press, 1989), p. 28.
46. *Hansard*, Vol. 548, col. 594, 30 January 1956, p. 594.
47. Kyle, *Suez*, p. 91.
48. Dann, *King Hussein*, p. 291.
49. PRO, FO371/121233/V1054/9, conference of Her Majesty's representatives in the Middle East, 3 January 1956.
50. Ibid.
51. Eden, *Full Circle*, pp. 344–5.
52. Ibid., p. 345.
53. *Hansard*, Vol. 548, col. 156, 1955–1956, 24 January 1956.
54. ISA, HZ408/15b, Israeli Foreign Office research department to Head of MABAR, 27 December 1955.
55. Ibid.
56. PRO, FO371/121723/VR1073/30, despatch No. 12, Nicholls to Lloyd, 23

January 1956.
57. PRO, FO371/121463/VJ1015/117, Nicholls to Lloyd, 10 January 1956.
58. Ibid.
59. Eden, *Full Circle*, pp. 345–6.
60. Dann, *King Hussein*, p. 31.
61. PRO, FO371/121540/VJ1201/8, Duke (Amman) to Foreign Office, No. 274, 1 March 1956.
62. Ibid.
63. Ibid.
64. Macmillan, *Riding the Storm*, p. 92.
65. ISA, HZ2530/5, Sasson (Rome) to Head of MABAR, Israeli Foreign Office, 16 March 1956.
66. PRO, FO371/121725/VR1073/98, No. 1030, Wikeley (Jerusalem) 7 March 1956.
67. PRO, FO371/121773/VR1091/49, Duke to Lloyd, 14 March 1956.
68. Burns, *Between Arab and Israeli*, p. 60.
69. Dayan, *Diary*, p. 8.
70. Dayan, Moshe, *Avnei Derech* [Story of my Life], (Tel-Aviv: Edanin/Jerusalem: Dvir), p. 187.
71. Burns, *Between Arab and Israeli*, p. 140.
72. Ben-Gurion, *Yehud Veichud*, p. 258.
73. Burns, *Between Arab and Israeli*, pp. 66–7.
74. Ibid., p. 67.
75. Ibid., p. 68.
76. PRO, FO371/121715/1072/62, Murry (Cairo) to Watson (Foreign Office), 22 March 1956.
77. These and other incidents and their shocking impact are illustrated in a typically dramatic way by Sharett in his personal diary, pp. 1391–2. See also Burns, *Between Arab and Israeli*, and Dayan, *Diary*, pp. 7–8.
78. Dayan, *Diary*, p. 18.
79. PRO, FO371/121740/VR1074/268, Rose (Foreign Office) minute, 16 May 1956.
80. Ibid.
81. PRO, FO371/121740/VR1074/246, Hammarskjold (UN) to Lloyd, 14 May 1956.
82. PRO, FO371/121727/VR1073/160, Nicholls to Shuckburgh, 2 May 1956.
83. Donald Cameron Watt, 'The High Dam at Aswan', in *Dams in Africa* (London: Frank Cass, 1968), p. 112.
84. Ibid., p. 115.
85. Dwight D. Eisenhower, *The White House Years: Waging Peace, 1956–1961* (London: Heineman, 1966), p. 32.
86. There are detailed accounts of the Aswan Dam crisis in various books: for further details see Kyle, *Suez*, *passim*.
87. Macmillan, *Riding the Storm*, p. 98.
88. Eden, *Full Circle*, p. 423.
89. Ibid. p. 424.
90. PRO, FO371/119189/JE14211/2258, Foreign Office Research Department to African Department, 19 May 1955.
91. Diane Kunz, 'The Importance of Having Money: The Economic Diplomacy of the Suez Crisis', in Wm Roger Louis and Roger Owen (eds), *Suez 1956: The Crisis and its Consequences* (Oxford: Clarendon Press, 1989), p. 219.
92. Eden, *Full Circle*, p. 427.
93. Anthony Nutting, *No End of a Lesson* (London: Constable, 1971), pp. 69–71.
94. PRO, FO371/121825/JE14211/124, record of conversation between Lloyd and Pineau, 29 July 1956.
95. PRO, FO371/119078/JE1421/36G, No. 558, Lloyd to Jebb (Paris), 30 July 1956.
96. PRO, CAB1321/3094/9/132/3, draft to Allied Commander-in-Chief, 4

September 1956.
97. Eisenhower, *The White House*, p. 53.
98. PRO, WO32/16109/JE142141/228, record of conversation between Dulles, Pineau and Lloyd, 5 October 1956.
99. Eisenhower, *The White House*, p. 666.
100. Michael Bar-Zohar, *Ben-Gurion* (Tel-Aviv: Am-Oved, 1977), p. 1138.
101. Bar-On, *Sharei A'za*, p. 204.
102. Sharett, *Yoman Ishi*, p. 1597.
103. Ibid., p. 112.
104. Bar-Zohar, *Ben-Gurion*, p. 1457.
105. PRO, FO371/121693/VR1015/17, Nicholls to Lloyd, 20 June 1956.
106. Bar-Zohar, *Ben-Gurion*, p. 1201.
107. Dayan, *Avnei Derech*, p. 234.
108. ISA, HZ232/9, Israeli Foreign Ministry survey on Arab boycott against Israel, 22 April 1956.
109. ISA, HZ2450/3, Elath to Israeli Foreign Ministry, 21 August 1956.
110. Bar-Zohar, *Ben-Gurion*, pp. 1236, 1240.
111. BGA, Ben-Gurion diary, 28 September 1956, p. 108.
112. PRO, DEFE6/37/JP(56)149, 27 September 1956.
113. PRO, DEFE 11/133/JP(56)153, 2 August 1956.
114. PRO, DEFE6/37/JP(56)149, 27 September 1956.
115. ISA, HZ193/1, MAHAV to Israeli embassy Washington, 2 January 1956.
116. ISA, HZ2595/2, Avner (London) to Israeli Foreign Ministry, 24 July 1956.
117. Dayan, *Avnei Derech*, p. 249.
118. Orna Almog interview with Mordechai Bar-On, Jerusalem summer 1989.
119. PRO, FO371/121718/VR1072/156, Wikely (Jerusalem) to Foreign Office, 20 September 1956.
120. PRO, FO371/121718/1072/158, Wikely to Lloyd, 24 September 1956.
121. PRO, FO371/121718/VR1072/163, Wikely to Lloyd, 27 September 1956.
122. ISA, HZ2409/18, Israeli Foreign Ministry to Elath, London, 3 October 1956.
123. Kyle, *Suez*, p. 292, and Mordechai Bar-On *Etgar Vetigra* [Challenge and Quarrel: The Road to Sinai] (Beer-Sheva: Ben-Gurion University, 1991), pp. 231–2.
124. Dayan, *Avnei Derech*, p. 249. See also ISA, HZ2453/10, Elath to MABAR 11 October 1956. For the British version of the same discussion see: PRO, FO371/121781/VR1091/317, Kirkpatrick minute, 11 October 1956, and also: FO371/121780/VR1091/298, Wikeley to Foreign Office, 11 October 1956.
125. The tension along the Jordanian–Israeli border was a constant worry for the British government, see Eden, *Full Circle*, pp. 512–13.
126. Macmillan, *Riding the Storm*, p. 147.
127. Eden, *Full Circle*, p. 512.
128. Ibid.
129. PRO, FO371/121781/VR1091/315, Duke to Lloyd, 13 October 1956.
130. PRO, FO371/121780/VR/1091/303, Duke to Lloyd, 11 October 1956.
131. Ibid.
132. PRO,FO371/121781/VR1091/315, Lloyd to Duke, 14 October 1956.
133. Ibid.
134. PRO, FO371/121780/VR1091/303, Duke to Foreign Office, No. 1448, 12 October 1956.
135. PRO, FO371/121780/VR1091/298, Wikeley to Foreign Office, No. 380, 11 October 1956.
136. PRO, FO371/121781/VR1091/334, British embassy Tel-Aviv to Foreign Office, 11 October 1956.
137. Eden, *Full Circle*, p. 512.

138. Ibid., p. 513.
139. Dayan, *Avnei Derech*, p. 247.
140. Almog interview with Bar-On, Jerusalem, summer 1989.
141. Dayan, *Avnei Derech*, p. 246.
142. BGA, Ben-Gurion diary, 6 October 1956, p. 136. The emphasis is not in the original document.
143. Bar-On, *Etgar Vetigra*, p. 520.
144. Orna Almog interview with Professor Yehoshafat Harkabi, Jerusalem winter 1993.
145. Almog interview with Bar-On.
146. PRO, FO371/12166/VR1022/17, Westlake (Tel-Aviv) to Foreign Office.
147. ISA, HZ329/9, MABAR to Elath London, 14 October 1956.
148. ISA, HZ329/2, MABAR to Israeli embassy London, 19 October 1956.
149. Yuval Neheman, 'Kesher Eim Ha-tzorfatim ve-Habritim Bmarechet Sinai' [Connections with the British and the French during the Suez Operation], *Ma'arachot*, 306–7, December 1986–January 1987, p. 33.
150. Lloyd, *Suez*, p. 183.
151. Ibid., p. 181.
152. Dayan, *Avnei Derech*, p. 257.
153. Ibid.
154. Ibid., p. 254.
155. Eliezer Cohen and Zvi Lavi, *Hashamim Eynam Ha-gvul* [The Sky is Not the Limit], (Tel-Aviv: Ma'ariv, 1990), p. 206.
156. Bar-Zohar, *Ben-Gurion*, p. 1247.
157. Ibid.
158. BGA, Ben-Gurion diary, 19 October 1956, p. 187.
159. BGA, Ben-Gurion diary, 26 October 1956, p. 172.
160. PRO, WO32/16709/129/AH/5705, Nicholls to Foreign Office, 26 October 1956.
161. Ibid.
162. Eisenhower, *The White House*, p. 56.

—5—
From the Sinai War to the Israeli Withdrawal, March 1957

THE CAMPAIGN

ONE MINUTE BEFORE 5 p.m. on 29 October Israeli parachute battalions were dropped near the Mitla pass. By 5.30 p.m. they were already advancing towards Colonel Parker's gravestone and by 7 p.m. an IDF spokesman announced that Israeli forces had secured positions west of Nakhl near the Suez Canal.[1] Towards dawn on 31 October, the Israelis waited nervously to see the French and British air bombardment on the Egyptian airfields. But at noon a cable from Yosef Nachmias, the Israeli Defence Ministry representative in Paris, explained that the British had decided to delay the bombing because their aircraft were facing strong anti-aircraft fire as well as hostile and highly manoeuvrable reconnaissance jets. This incident aroused Britain's suspicions that the Egyptians were being assisted by Soviet pilots and they therefore decided not to take the risk of attacking in daylight.[2] However, the real reason behind the delay, according to Bar-On, was that the military commanders were not consulted prior to the operation and they disputed the order to attack in daylight because they believed it was too risky and irrational.[3]

Ben-Gurion was furious, and all his suspicions and anger against the British government erupted.[4] His concern for the safety of the Israeli soldiers in the Mitla pass led him to ask Dayan to bring the troops back home. Dayan, though, did not share Ben-Gurion's concern and told him that such action was unnecessary and that the Mitla pass was very important as a passageway to Sharm el Sheikh.[5]

When the news of the Israeli attack reached Washington, the American government was taken completely by surprise. The main shock was the fact that Israel had attacked Egypt and not Jordan as the Americans assumed might happen. The Americans therefore supported the UN Security Council resolution of 30 October condemning Israel as an aggressor; they demanded an Israeli withdrawal from Sinai and called upon all member nations to refrain from the use or the threat of force. The greatest surprise was yet to come, namely Britain's refusal to support the American proposal for the UN to condemn Israel as an aggressor. The American administration was amazed to discover that the British Ambassador was 'completely unsympathetic, stating frankly that his government would not agree to any action whatsoever being taken against Israel'.[6] Furthermore, Britain and France used their veto in the UN for the first time in 11 years against this Security Council resolution.

For the first time in his career, Anthony Eden, seen by the Israelis as their sworn enemy, addressed the House of Commons in a speech supporting Israel. This speech on 31 October made it clear that the British government would not support the UN resolution of 30 October accusing Israel of being the aggressor. 'We felt', he said,' that we could not associate ourselves with this ... it certainly could not be said to meet in any way the guarantees for Israel's security.'[7] Further, he wrote to the American President that, although Israel might be accused of technical aggression, he and his colleagues thought Israel had a case for arguing that it was acting in self-defence against increasing pressure from some Arab countries, notably Egypt.[8] Selwyn Lloyd told Parliament that the British government could not support the resolution because it pronounced judgement against Israel, but he hedged his government's support by announcing that although his colleagues could sympathise with Israel's motives for such action, they did not condone it and thought Israel should withdraw as soon as a satisfactory settlement could be announced.[9] Furthermore, the British and French governments told the US administration that they had decided to present the Israeli and Egyptian governments with an ultimatum demanding their forces withdraw ten miles from the Suez Canal, and that if this requirement was not met within 12 hours British and French forces would intervene to ensure compliance.[10]

The Egyptian refusal to comply with the ultimatum gave the French and British the green light to start Operation Musketeer and on 31 October they started to bomb Egyptian airfields. A sense of relief spread among the Israelis who were terribly concerned that the British would not fulfil their role. However, there were some difficulties, due mainly to Britain delaying its operation, the increasing opposition that Eden's government faced at home, and also because they knew that they could not accelerate the operation for military reasons. The British could not ignore the experience of the Second World War and send in paratroops who would have to face Soviet heavy artillery, and thus the British military opposed such a move.

However, the real battle took place in the international arena where the Americans brought up all their heavy guns against the British and the French. The American position hardened as a result of the Soviet invasion of Hungary on 31 October, placing the Americans in a very delicate situation regarding their allies' invasion.

Almost from the beginning of the operation there was also increasing restlessness in Parliament and among the public. Hugh Gaitskell, the Labour leader and a great supporter of Israel, accused the government of a disastrous action which could have tragic consequences.[11] He went on to attack the government's decision to reject the American UN resolution on the grounds that it contained a condemnation of Israel. He thought the British government should put forward an alternative resolution excluding this, but retaining the other part of the resolution.[12] The Conservative Party was also accused by the Opposition of collusion with Israel, but Gaitskell expressed his belief that it was within Israel's true interests not to be associated with the occupation of the Canal.[13] On 3 November, Eden promised that Britain and France would ensure Israel's withdrawal and Selwyn Lloyd told Elath that for the sake of British public opinion it was very important that Britain should not be accused of collusion with Israel.[14] Selwyn Lloyd tried to deny any co-operation with Israel and argued that his government had no choice but to intervene. According to Lloyd, the purpose of the meeting held on 16 October in Paris between himself, Eden and Pineau was to discuss the development of the Suez crisis debate in the Security Council and the differences between the United States, France and Britain on the scope and function of the Suez Canal Users Association (SCUA). Lloyd mentioned that there were some discussions about possible Israeli intentions regarding the Suez crisis, but only on the basis of trying to find some formula for negotiations.[15] In his personal diary, Lloyd admitted there had been talks with Israeli officials, although he claimed that these had been of little significance.[16] It was clear that the British government wanted to avoid a situation where they might be suspected of any collusion whatsoever with the Israelis.

This attitude offended the Israeli government, who believed that it was Britain's intention to refute any accusation of co-operation with Israel in order to maintain its position in the Arab world. However, the Israeli government recognised that it was also in their own interests not to be associated with France and Britain. They acknowledged the fact that public opinion in Britain and in the United States made a distinction between the Israeli action and that of its allies. The Israeli government was aware that many in Britain were willing to accept Israel's motives for action but would condemn Israel if they suspected it had collaborated with Britain.[17] Hence, the Israeli government decided that the best line to adopt in order to deny the accusation of collusion was to emphasise that Anglo-Israeli relations prior to the operation had been strained. The delay in the dispatch of the

Anglo-French troops could be used to prove that there was no combined planning between Israel, France and Britain beforehand. Furthermore, Israel could stress that the Anglo-French operation saved Egypt and enabled Nasser to appear in the Arab world as a hero and to maintain his prestige.[18]

In this atmosphere, Eden and his colleagues tried to play the game to the end and delay the dispatch of their troops from Malta until the ultimatum to Egypt was presented. Meanwhile, Egypt blocked the Canal by sinking ships, while Syrian saboteurs blew up the oil pipelines running through their country from Iraq to the Mediterranean. The French, who were eager to pursue the operation, believed they could save the day if they advanced the troop landings, a manoeuvre that would achieve the rapid occupation of the Canal. The French therefore proposed to drop paratroops 36 hours earlier than planned into Port Said but the British rejected the idea. As a last attempt the French suggested that they would do this without British assistance but with the help of Israeli forces, but the British objected to this idea as well. Finally, on 5 November, hundreds of British paratroops landed on Gamil airfield west of Port Said on the Suez Canal and 500 French paratroops dropped to the south of Port Said.[19] The Israelis troops for their part completed most of their mission in 100 hours, apart from the capture of Sharm el Sheikh which was taken on 4 November, along with the seizure of the Straits of Tiran and Snapir. At that stage, Israel was willing to accept a ceasefire providing that Egypt did so too, and Golda Meir, Israel's Foreign Minister, approached the British and French Ambassadors to Israel and asked them whether their governments had any objection to a ceasefire. The Ambassadors did not understand the meaning of the question, because they had no idea of the complexity of the secret agreement, and agreed. On 4 November, Abba Eban, the Israeli Ambassador to the UN, announced that Israel was willing to accept the ceasefire.[20] The British and the French governments 'almost jumped out of their skins'.[21] They were aware that if the fighting stopped they would have no excuse for proceeding with Operation Musketeer. Ambassador Eban had therefore to withdraw his announcement and explained it as a 'misunderstanding'.[22] This event was a classic example of the lack of co-ordination and co-operation between the civil authorities and the military circles, in particular between the Foreign Ministry and the Defence Ministry. It applied especially to the Franco-Israeli relationship and highlighted the degree to which officials in higher positions in the Israeli and French Foreign Offices were excluded from the decision-making that took place.

However, as the fighting ended, the diplomatic battle began and the focus was now on the international arena. The Suez crisis was a test of Soviet intentions as well as of Soviet commitment to the Arab states. On 5 November, Marshal Bulganin sent a letter to the Prime Ministers of France, Britain and Israel, accusing them of being aggressors and creating instability in the region. The Soviet Prime Minister warned Israel that his government had already taken measures to put a stop to the fighting.[23] The Soviets also advised their Ambassador to Tel-Aviv to leave Israel immediately and return to Moscow.[24] The American President also sent a message to Ben-Gurion expressing his government's dissatisfaction with the Israeli action.[25] It was a clear indication that the crisis had gone beyond being a regional dispute and had became an international one. The ball was now in the Americans' court and they planned to put all the pressure they could on all the parties involved in order to achieve a withdrawal of British, French and Israeli forces. The most successful tool the United States could use was the financial stick. Developments proved it to be a very effective weapon. At the beginning of the crisis it seemed that the British economy would be able to overcome the difficulties that would arise. In September, the reserves had fallen by $57 million and in October by $84 million, but the Chancellor of the Exchequer, Harold Macmillan, was still confident that these figures were tolerable, believing that the Americans intended to back Britain.[26] It appears, however, that the Treasury had warned Macmillan for months of the devastating financial implications and grave consequences a military action without US support would have on Britain's financial position. Macmillan, who strongly supported a military intervention in Egypt, preferred not to inform the Cabinet or Eden of the full repercussions of the Treasury's clear warning that a military action without prior agreement with the United States might have a detrimental effect on the British economy. The harsh reality, however, hit the British government in November when at the critical moment they faced the full pressure of the United States, in both Washington and New York.[27]

The American government made it clear that it would maintain its objection to any loan from the International Monetary Fund[28] and rejected any mutual collaboration between the international oil companies until the Anglo-French troops left Egypt.[29]

Britain's financial situation had already worsened with the closure of the Canal in three ways. First, it had led to a run on sterling which endangered Britain's position, the lack of confidence in banking circles being caused by doubts about Britain's financial future; second, the loss of oil revenue and the prospect of losing some export markets for political reasons had affected Britain's standing; and third, fear that the loss of Suez had hit Britain's balance of payments.[30] Harold Macmillan, who was well aware of Britain's grave position, warned the Cabinet on 20 November that Britain might face a crucial choice over whether to 'mobilise all the financial resources in order to maintain the sterling/dollars rate at its present level or to let the rate find its own level with the possible consequences that sterling might cease to be an international currency'.[31] British hopes to gain American financial aid after the ceasefire were therefore blown to the wind and all the British pleas fell on deaf ears.

In the face of this grave situation, the British government decided on 3 December to withdraw their forces from the Canal. This was the chief reason behind the British withdrawal. As Selwyn Lloyd explained to Dulles, 'As a result of what we had been told by the US administration and particularly the threat to sterling we had agreed to withdraw our force from Port Said virtually without conditions.'[32]

The Israeli government however, was still euphoric after its swift triumph. On 7 November, Ben-Gurion addressed the Knesset declaring that Israel would never surrender to outside pressure. Excited by the Israeli victory he stated that the armistice agreement between Israel and Egypt had ceased to exist and Israel would not agree under any condition to the presence of outside forces on Israeli soil or in any of the territories Israel occupied.[33] The speech angered the American administration and added fuel to the ill-feelings the US government felt towards the Israeli government at the time. Herbert Hoover, the American Under-Secretary of State, told the Israeli Consul in Washington, Reuven Shiloah, that the situation in the Middle East was critical and could lead the free world into a dangerous position which the Soviets might manipulate in order to further their own purposes. If Israel, he added, continued to reject the UN resolution it would be accused of endangering world peace. He concluded that the Israeli refusal insulted the United States and public opinion, and warned that such an attitude might lead to the adoption of a series of measures against Israel, from both governmental and private sources.[34] This was followed by a cable from the American President to Ben-Gurion on 7 November, urging Israel to withdraw its forces and warning that the United States viewed the Israeli refusal to withdraw 'with great concern'.[35] From New York, Ambassador Eban at the UN added his fears to the sombre mood by warning the Israeli government on 7 November that 'the situation had become critical and severe and all the parties reached a consensus in favour of Israel's withdrawal', and that there 'should be no doubt about the great powers' intention to send an international force'.[36]

Israel's situation became more acute due to the American threat to impose sanctions on it if it did not withdraw from the Gaza strip and the Tiran Straits. Facing a grave situation, Ben-Gurion cabled

Eisenhower on 8 November, proclaiming Israel's willingness to withdraw from Sinai if a satisfactory arrangement could be found for UN forces to take over positions around the Suez Canal. On 14 November, the Israeli government approved the decision and, on 3 December, Israel began to evacuate its forces 30 miles from the Canal.[37] However, the US administration wanted to see a full Israeli withdrawal from Sinai with no prior conditions and was determined to impose sanctions on Israel if necessary. Accordingly, it was suggested by the State Department on 3 December that financial aid to Israel should be slowed down until further guidance from the White House was received. No formal suspension would be declared and the Israelis were to be told that in the current situation the United States would examine its aid programmes to the Middle East and therefore further delays must be expected.[38]

The situation confirmed Ben-Gurion's fears prior to the operation when he told his Cabinet that Israel would be under heavy pressure to withdraw from Sinai but that the only power that could force Israel to do so was the United States.[39] Furthermore, the Israeli Treasury viewed the situation with great concern and told Ben-Gurion that Israel could survive for only five months living on its reserves of food and fuel.[40] However, Israel still refused to withdraw from Gaza and from the Tiran Straits unless it received sufficient guarantees of free passage in the Gulf of Aqaba and assurances that Egypt would not be allowed to return to the Gaza Strip. The Israelis were eager to obtain US support, but the Americans, although aware that such assurances were a vital priority for Israel, were reluctant to give them any such guarantees.

The US administration believed that such assurances might cause irreparable damage to America's interests and position in the region. Although they had sympathy for Israel in principle, it was thought undesirable under the current circumstances to show such support.[41] The Israeli government tried, therefore, to convince Eisenhower and Dulles of Israel's need for security guarantees prior to its withdrawal from the Tiran Straits and the Gaza Strip. Golda Meir, Israel's Foreign Minister, met Dulles on 28 December and tried to convince him that Israel must get some international guarantees for free passage through the Tiran straits. Meir, in her memoirs, emphasised that it was a troubled time for Israel and that dealing with Dulles, 'a grey and cold man' who did not understand Israel's needs and was obsessed with the fear of global war, was a very difficult task.[42]

When Golda Meir met Dulles on 28 December, she asked him for US guarantees of freedom of passage through the Gulf of Aqaba as well as an assurance that Egypt would not return to the Gaza Strip. Dulles used the opportunity to explain his government's view and told Meir that the American attitude towards the Suez crisis was not a result of narrow-mindedness, but a response to the methods used by the aggressors. Although he showed understanding towards the difficult situation Britain, France and Israel were in, he thought it was wrong to try to solve it by force, a method which the United States could not support.[43] Dulles rejected Meir's argument that peace in the region could not be reached because of Arab hatred of Israel and their objection to Israel's existence. He believed the Israelis were to blame as well. If Arab hatred was the only problem, it would eventually decline. However, Israel's retaliatory policy added to the hostility the Arab states felt towards Israel.[44] Dulles believed that Israel should try to gain some sympathy from, or at least reach some degree of co-existence with, its neighbours. Unfortunately, Dulles added, there was no indication that Israeli leaders gave any thought to the problem.[45] In the same discussion, the Secretary of State noted that the President and he were confused because they could not understand how Israel saw its future in the long term as a small country surrounded by hostile ones.[46]

Dulles's analysis of Israel's policy *vis-à-vis* its Arab neighbours, and of Israel's position in the region, was very accurate. However, Israeli leaders at this stage were more concerned to ensure US support for their requests than to think of their future relationship with the Arab states. It was also a characteristic strand of Israeli belief and philosophy that the problem in the region could be solved only if the Western powers adopted the 'right' line, in other words a firm line against the Arabs.

Dulles also expressed his reservations about the activities of American Jews who held mass demonstrations in support of Israel. He told Eban that American Jewry was creating a situation in which the Arabs felt it was not safe for them to rely on the United States. Already in March 1956, he had made it clear that the President and he had decided to 'formulate our policies without reference to the effect on domestic policies'.[47] This case proved that although the Jewish lobby in the United States operated usefully, it had its limitations. The Israeli Ambassador to Washington, as well as many other Israeli leaders, viewed the demonstrations by American Jewry during the Sinai campaign as a tremendous contribution to Israel.[48] However, they overemphasised its impact and influence at this time, and one has to recognise the very limited effect it had upon American decision-makers during the crisis.

THE INTERNATIONAL IMPACT AND THE ANGLO-ISRAELI RELATIONSHIP

As the pressure mounted on the Israeli government, its leaders looked for sympathy and understanding elsewhere and were anxious to ensure Britain's support against American pressure in the hope that the joint action against Egypt might lead to Whitehall following a more pro-Israeli line.

It must be made clear, however, that the so-called 'collusion' between Britain and Israel during the Suez war did not bring any major change in the two countries' relationship. If we examine the nature of the co-operation and the attitude of each party to the other it would be hard to point to any considerable shift in their mutual aversion. The old suspicions still played a significant role. At an early stage of the crisis, Elath had told Lloyd on 3 November that the Israeli attitude to Britain was one of constant mistrust because Israel believed that the British government wanted to restore its position in the Arab world at Israel's expense. He added that its past experience gave Israel a strong basis for this belief.[49]

The Sinai operation did not give the Israelis any indication that a different wind blew from the British government. On the contrary, in the midst of the battles, Dayan told Ben-Gurion that a British warship stayed near to Sharm el Sheikh, which in his view was a threat to Israel. He asked Ben-Gurion whether he believed that the British might shell the Israeli force. 'The British', Ben-Gurion replied, 'I do not know, but about the Foreign Office I can believe anything.'[50] Moreover, there were some cases of 'negative co-operation', for example when the Israeli forces, trying to assist a wounded British pilot, were warned off by British combat fighters.[51] Furthermore, the British government watched French assistance to the Israeli forces with anxiety. Eden protested to Guy Mollet that on the night of 31 October, French aircraft were operating from Israeli airfields and that on the same night the French cruiser *George Leygues* shelled Rafah in direct support of Israeli operations there. The French naval staff also asked for the destroyer *Gazelle*, which was under British command, to assist the Israelis. The British Prime Minister tried to explain to his French colleagues that action of this sort was embarrassing and could not remain secret, and therefore he hoped that the French Prime Minister would see eye to eye with him and agree that it was in their common interest not to continue with actions of this kind. 'Nothing', he concluded, 'could do more harm to our role as peace makers than to be identified in this way with one of the two parties.'[52] This resentful and suspicious attitude was also evident in the Foreign Office's approach to the idea of an air corridor over Sinai and its refusal in December of the RAF's request for overflying rights over Sinai because of the political implications they might have. The Foreign Office believed that it would be especially embarrassing if RAF aircraft flew over the Straits of Tiran, implying that the British recognised the Israeli military occupation of the area. This might be interpreted in the Middle East and elsewhere as evidence of British 'collusion' with Israel.[53]

Britain also faced a dilemma regarding arms supply to Israel. As a result of the Sinai operation, the UN General Assembly passed a resolution banning arms shipments to the area of hostilities in the Middle East. Reilly of the Foreign Office informed Elath on 2 November that Israel would face a temporary ban on arms supplies, but stressed that the Foreign Office view was that it would not have a grave effect on Israel because of the large quantities of arms and equipment the latter had acquired during the Sinai operation.[54] The Foreign Office was unsure how to interpret the resolution because there was no clear definition of the term 'area of hostilities and whether it meant that Britain could supply Israel with arms'.[55] Furthermore, it was quite obvious that despite the embargo, Egypt would continue to be supplied by the Soviets. Ross, the Head of the Levant Department at the Foreign Office, suggested that if Britain could prove that Egypt and Syria had acquired arms since 2 November, then Britain could legitimately also supply Israel with military equipment.[56] However, for the time being Britain had to comply with the UN resolution and the Foreign Office had to inform the Israeli Ambassador on 28 December that they could not supply Israel with three Meteor night fighters or spares for the destroyers and aircraft.[57] Although on the surface it looked as if the Foreign Office stance was unsympathetic towards Israel, one has to sense the mood of the Foreign Office to realise that there was little option but to comply with the UN resolution, and it seems that the Foreign Office was aware that Israel was being discriminated against and sought ways to supply Israel with arms without breaching the UN resolution.

It is worthwhile emphasising this change of mood, as it contrasts with the previously unsympathetic Foreign Office attitude towards arms supply to Israel and thus reveals that there was some change in the Foreign Office's stance. In the past, prior to the Sinai war, the Foreign Office was not only quick to condemn every Israel retaliatory action but also suspended arms shipments to Israel as a result. It seems that finally there was more understanding of Israel's needs.

The Israeli government, however, saw British policy in a very different light. They were aware that, while Israel was subject to an arms embargo, its Arab neighbours were still being supplied with arms either by the Soviet Union or by Britain, and this meant that the mistrust towards the Foreign Office remained. The chief architect of Franco-Israeli relations, Shimon Peres, tried to use with the British the same old method that had worked so well with the French. When he met Sir Ivone Kirkpatrick, the Permanent Under-Secretary at the Foreign Office, on 3 December, he put forward the argument that the Soviets would continue to supply arms to Egypt and Israel had the right to accumulate weapons for its defence.[58] Nonetheless, the British government was not willing to change its mind and when Peres suggested to Kirkpatrick that the British could supply arms 'under the counter' from Cyprus, Kirkpatrick replied that he was opposed to 'black market transactions'.[59] The Israeli government, however, were reluctant to accept Britain's arguments and tried to persuade the British government that there were indirect ways to supply Israel with arms. On 28 December, Elath suggested to Ross that if the material could reach France, the Israelis would do the rest.[60] The same line was taken by Ben-Gurion who told Nicholls on 7 January that he was reluctant to accept the British argument because arms were still being shipped to the Middle East, but he knew the Foreign Office attitude and as long as they hoped to gain influence in one of the Arab countries they would maintain their hostile attitude towards Israel.[61]

It might have been that this grievance of the Israeli government and its representatives in London could have been minimised if the Foreign Office had informed Elath that this suspension of arms deliveries was temporary and that in due course, when the atmosphere changed or when there was clear proof that Egypt continued to obtain arms from the Soviets, the British government would be willing to reconsider Israel's request. It appears, however, that a lack of communication and close consultation on the British part gave the Israeli leaders a very negative picture of British policy towards Israel, when in fact at this stage there was actually more consideration and understanding than previously.

On 15 January 1957, the Israeli Ambassador told Ross that the main obstacle in establishing friendly relations between Israel and Britain was the latter's lack of a clear policy regarding the Middle East, based on its interests in the Arab countries, and that consequently Britain's policy towards Israel was to manoeuvre in such a way that their relationship would not harm its position *vis-à-vis* the Arabs.[62]

Elath's comment is interesting for in fact it indicated that the British had a very clear policy towards the Middle East. This was evident in the case of Israeli withdrawal, which put the British in a difficult position between preserving their interests in the Arab states and at the same time maintaining a 'normal' relationship with Israel. The

Foreign Office believed that Britain was heading towards a dangerous situation because, on the one hand, they thought that the Israeli demands were reasonable and believed that a constructive solution should be found in preference to a return to the old status quo, but, on the other hand, recognised that this would alienate Arab opinion.[63] Furthermore, the British were sympathetic towards Israeli needs, especially on the grounds that they had supported the Israeli cause over Suez which had after all been the justification for their action. Therefore a completely negative approach towards Israel's needs would reflect on Britain's own motives and actions. On the other hand, they assumed that the Arabs would obstruct any resumption of traffic through the Canal or movement of oil through the Canal or pipeline until Israel withdrew back to the armistice lines. Consequently, Britain could not tolerate a situation in which Israeli demands would obstruct free passage through the Canal or the flow of oil to the West.[64] Britain's main aim was a quick recovery of its economy, which greatly depended on a rapid clearance of the Canal, and this aim was clearly in the mind of the Foreign Office which believed that Britain's priority was to guarantee its oil supplies, maintain friendship with the Arabs, and therefore 'We need the friendship of the Arab states more than the friendship of Israel.'[65] Thus, the British government had to find a path which would not alienate Israel but, at the same time, would enable it to renew its relations with the Arab world and the United States. Deciding on the best line to take was not easy because they were left in the dark over American intentions.

The British government realised, at the start of 1957, that there were two options: either to make a formal demand of Israel, if possible with Britain's friends and allies, to withdraw immediately from the Gaza Strip and the Tiran Straits, or to press the United States to extend UN administration to the Gaza Strip. The first option they believed would appeal to the Arabs and would do something to restore Britain's position in the region, but it would offend Israel and increase its stubbornness. This course would also open the way for an Egyptian return to Gaza. The second option, therefore, seemed preferable.[66] The Foreign Office stressed that Britain would find herself in an acute dilemma if the UN passed a resolution, supported by the United States, calling for economic sanctions against Israel, because public opinion within Britain was very sympathetic towards Israel.[67] On the other hand, Britain could not afford to stand against the United States and risk further deterioration of its relations with them. Therefore the favoured strategy was a Canadian proposal suggesting that Israel should withdraw its forces provided that it received adequate security guarantees and that UN peacekeeping forces entered Sinai.[68]

Although both the American and the British governments believed that Israel had to withdraw its forces from the Gaza Strip and the Tiran Straits, they differed over the means to achieve this. The British view was much more sympathetic to Israel and this was quite significant because it was the first time since the establishment of Israel that Britain's stance *vis-à-vis* Israel was more friendly than that of the United States. The British government opposed the American threat to use economic sanctions against Israel if it would not comply with the UN resolution to withdraw from Sinai, and believed that Israel's rights of freedom of passage in the Tiran Straits and the Suez Canal should be granted prior to Israel's withdrawal.

One might argue that this favourable attitude reflected Britain's own needs in the region and its negative attitude towards Nasser, and could also reflect a traditional policy of freedom of the seas. Yet, although there is some truth in this argument, British motives in the period immediately after the Suez war also indicate some kind of limited breakthrough in Anglo-Israeli relations. This is not to say that from this moment onwards British policy in the Middle East underwent a dramatic shift, and that Britain perceived its traditional interests in the region very differently. Rather, it suggests that there was a subtle change in the relationship between the two countries. This change, however, should be seen as an integral part, and a continued development of Britain's role in the Middle East, in which the Suez war represented only one, admittedly important, episode. At the time, it was believed that the Suez affair marked the end of an era of British influence in the Middle East and that the Anglo-Israeli relationship had undergone a dramatic shift as a result of their co-operation in the war. Yet there is only limited truth in these assumptions. Britain's position was already weakened prior to the Suez crisis, and the affair only accelerated the inevitable process which did not end in October 1956. The Suez episode was part of a long process of British decline in the region and should also be seen in terms of the changing balance in the region as evidenced by the increased Soviet commitment to the region and the rise of strong pan-Arab feeling in the Middle East. It was a prolonged process which only reached its peak in the summer of 1958.

The change of attitude towards Israel can also be put down to the 'changing of the guard' in 10 Downing Street, resulting from the domestic crisis the Conservative Party faced due to Anthony Eden's resignation. The official reason for the Prime Minister's resignation was his health, but it was quite obvious that as a result of growing opposition at home he realised that it would be very difficult to continue in office. The Suez affair had made an important impact on the Conservative Party even though the government succeeded in maintaining its authority. On 11 January, Harold Macmillan was appointed Prime Minister. In his new Cabinet he retained Selwyn Lloyd as Foreign Secretary, explaining in his diary that he was keen to keep Lloyd since one head (Eden) was enough to be sacrificed for the Suez failure, especially as, in the public's eyes, Eden's illness might be viewed as a diplomatic one. 'Two [heads]', he wrote, 'was more than England's honour could support.'[69] The Israeli government welcomed this change for two reasons: first, it was seen as a victory for the right wing, the hardliners within the Conservative Party who had supported the Suez operation, and, second, most of the Israeli officials viewed Anthony Eden as a sworn enemy. The Israeli Ambassador to London believed that with Eden's resignation one of the greatest irritants to Israel had departed; the man who conceived and supported the idea of the Arab League, and the man who embodied the pro-Arab line among British decision-makers was a thing of the past.[70] The Israeli daily newspaper, *Ha'aretz*, shared a similar view and expressed the opinion that Eden's resignation proved that he was not a suitable successor to Winston Churchill; 'A weak person,' the paper wrote, 'who like every weak man wanted sometimes to prove he was able to take tough measures.'[71]

The Israelis certainly believed that the election of Harold Macmillan as Prime Minister in place of Anthony Eden contributed to the change in the Anglo-Israeli relationship. The Israeli Ambassador to London advised the Israeli Foreign Office that Macmillan understood Israel's needs for guarantees, although in a very diplomatic way he tried to disarm the Israelis by telling the Israeli Ambassador that it would be preferable for other countries (like Canada) to be directly involved in the negotiations on Israel's withdrawal rather than Britain, because of the latter's limited influence over the US government.[72] Later in his life, the Ambassador still believed that after Macmillan became Prime Minister, the Anglo-Israeli relationship improved because Macmillan was much more sympathetic to Israel's needs.[73] The question still unresolved is whether a change occurred because Macmillan had a more positive attitude towards Israel or whether it was simply that the dramatic events in the region had changed Britain's position and perceptions. It does seem obvious, however, that Macmillan took a more pro-American line than his predecessor and that this, combined with his very pragmatic outlook, maybe gave the Israeli officials the impression that he was more sympathetic and understanding towards Israeli needs.

THE ISRAELI WITHDRAWAL

It is important to emphasise, however, that in spite of the fact that the British government demonstrated greater understanding than previously towards Israel's position, the key player in solving the crisis was the United States. The rising importance of the United States in the Middle East was underlined when, on 5 January 1957, President Eisenhower announced a new doctrine for the Middle East designed to fill the existing vacuum in the region before the Soviet Union could do so. The Eisenhower doctrine demonstrated that the United States was now the leading Western power in the region, and that the British and French had to follow the US lead. The doctrine guaranteed US economic assistance and, if necessary, the use of military force in the region. The American approach was an indication that the traditional roles of France and Britain had come to an end and that the United States perceived that the Suez dispute had exceeded the boundaries of a regional conflict and become a Cold War issue. The doctrine also emphasised US intention to act unilaterally in the Middle East and its dominant role in the region.[74] It demonstrated that, whereas previously the United States was willing to see the British as the major guardians of Western investments in the region, they had now decided that they should take a more active role themselves. Although British influence in Jordan and Iraq remained, it became impossible for any future British government to take independent action without the co-operation of the United States. This new development would clearly became evident in the Jordanian crisis of July 1958.

Both the United Kingdom and Israel welcomed the American initiative although not with great enthusiasm. Ben-Gurion told Sir John Nicholls, on 7 January, that the Eisenhower doctrine would strengthen the Baghdad Pact and therefore there was little hope that British policy towards Israel would become more positive.[75] The British government generally welcomed the doctrine because they were eager to see additional American involvement in the region, but they had some reservations. As Harold Macmillan expressed it, 'the doctrine was a gallant effort to shut the stable door after the horse had bolted'.[76] He was also disappointed to learn that it did not alter American attitudes towards French and British action over Suez.[77]

At that stage it seemed that Israel had reached a dead end in its relations with the United States. The Suez crisis demonstrated the growing importance of the United States and the fact that it was now the leading Western power in the region and Britain and France had to follow its lead. As the leading power the American administration was determined to find a solution to the Suez crisis and to force Israel to withdraw at almost any cost. On 4 February, the American Ambassador to Israel, Edward Lawson, gave Ben-Gurion a letter from President Eisenhower warning Israel that if it continued to ignore international law it might damage the American–Israeli relationship.[78] However, just at the time when there seemed to be a total deadlock, Yacov Herzog, the Assistant Director-General (in charge of Economic Affairs) at the Ministry of Foreign Affairs, suggested that Israel should announce its willingness to withdraw provided satisfactory agreement could be reached with UN forces.[79] On 11 February, the US administration finally agreed to announce that the Gulf of Aqaba was an international waterway and that UN forces would be stationed in the Gaza Strip, a guarantee which the Israeli government had sought for some time. In further talks between Ambassador Eban and Dulles, on 26 February, the Israeli Ambassador asked the latter whether American ships would bring oil to Eilat and whether the United States would guarantee freedom of passage to Israel. Eban suggested that the UN should send a naval unit to be stationed in the Gulf of Aqaba until peace was signed between Israel and Egypt. In addition, he asked Dulles for a message from the American President to be sent to Ben-Gurion assuring him that any renewal of the Egyptian naval blockade on Israel would lead to a tough response by the 'free nations'.[80] Dulles was reluctant at that stage to give such a promise, for although he agreed on the issue of freedom of passage in principle, he still believed that Egypt had full rights in the Gaza Strip according to the 1949 armistice agreement.[81]

On 28 February, Canada formally proposed at the United Nations an Israeli withdrawal in return for which the UN Secretary-General would appoint a governor to Gaza who would co-operate with the UN forces commander. This would be a temporary arrangement, and a final settlement would then be the responsibility of the United Nations. It seemed that the deadlock was over.

On 1 March 1957, the Israeli government finally announced that it would withdraw its forces from the Gaza Strip and Sharm el Sheikh. The reasons for this change need to be addressed. One might assume that the threat of economic sanctions by the United States was in itself sufficient to prompt a change in Israeli policy. However, this does not offer a complete explanation for the decision, which is much more complicated. The fact that the French, Israel's greatest ally, supported the proposal tipped the balance.[82] The French realised that there was no prospect for a better solution and that it gave some security guarantees for Israel's freedom of passage through the Tiran Straits. Pineau made it clear to the Americans that the French had not pressured the Israelis to accept the arrangement because, while they thought the plan for Aqaba was good, the arrangement for Gaza seemed at best uncertain. The French also suggested to the American government that if Israeli ships were stopped, this would be an act of aggression and Israel would be entitled to invoke article 51 of the UN Charter, the right to self-defence.[83]

Ben-Gurion explained, in his diary on 10 March, that he realised at that stage there would be no more concessions to Israel and therefore Israel had to reconsider its position. France, he added, was the only ally Israel then had, but France alone would not, and could not, support Israel against the entire world. Ben-Gurion had some reservations about the Canadian proposal because he believed it was not the best way to guarantee Israel's freedom of passage and safeguard Israel against any Egyptian attempt to return to Gaza. However, he thought that if Israel refused the proposition it would face harsh consequences in the long term. Ben-Gurion was aware that if Israel faced economic sanctions, which would include an embargo on oil and arms, it might be extremely vulnerable to an Arab attack. Furthermore, Ben-Gurion realised that France would not 'punish' Israel, but the implications for Israel's future if it rejected the Canadian proposal would be total isolation from the United States and the UN.[84] Ben-Gurion claimed, however, that the sanctions were not the decisive factor behind Israel's withdrawal, although an oil embargo might have been detrimental to Israel's survival. The key factor was the danger that Israel might find itself in total isolation, bringing with it great danger. If, for example, Nasser attacked Israel one or two years later, Israel would be in an inferior position to the Arab countries because no country, including France, would supply it with arms. Ben-Gurion appreciated that France had its own essential interests, including those in northern Africa, and understood that it was unrealistic to expect France alone to supply arms to Israel when it was completely isolated. Without arms Israel would be helpless and defenceless, and therefore he concluded, 'I, as a private citizen, cannot take the responsibility that Israeli soldiers would be forced into a situation where they might be defeated', and 'Gaza was not important enough', he added, 'to warrant his taking such a risk.'[85]

Furthermore, Ben-Gurion realised the difficulties Israel might face if it occupied Gaza. He took into consideration the Palestinians' likely resentment of an Israeli occupation and the consequent danger that they would launch terrorist attacks against Israel. He knew that it might be impossible to suppress such attacks, as the French in North Africa and the British in Cyprus had discovered.[86] 'If I believed in miracles,' he told the Knesset on 28 October, 'I would pray that Gaza would be washed down into the sea.'[87] In any case, he added, Gaza was a problem and it would not be worthwhile endangering Israel's future because of it: ' I prefer to lose my "world" than to put Israel's existence and safety at risk.'[88] It was a very hard decision for Ben-Gurion to take but he, like other Israeli leaders, was guided by a fundamental belief in Israel's critical need for arms supplies and allies, and therefore advised his Cabinet to accept the Canadian proposal.

Ben-Gurion's decision to withdraw was challenged by one of his greatest supporters, Moshe Dayan, his Chief of Staff. Dayan objected to Ben-Gurion's strategy, which was to gain time while bargaining for land and security guarantees. He thought Israel should not withdraw from Sharm el Sheikh on the basis of international guarantees, because any assurance could not prevent their breach and therefore they were worthless. He advocated instead the Israeli annexation of Sharm el Sheikh, including a strip around the shore which would connect Eilat with the Straits of Tiran. He believed Israel should use the victory to its benefit and create a 'big Eilat' which would bring a fundamental change to the strategic and political balance in the Middle East. As for the Gaza Strip, he thought it should remain as a buffer zone because any other solution would carry the danger that Gaza might become a potential Fedayeen base.[89] Nonetheless, the Israeli government decided to withdraw its forces and on 1 March Golda Meir announced that Israel was willing to comply with the UN resolution.

The UN had a key role in thais scenario. The United Nations Emergency Force (UNEF) played an important task ensuring the withdrawal of all foreign forces on Egyptian territory. The overall task of the UNEF was to maintain order during and after the withdrawal of French, British and Israeli forces under the terms of the UN resolutions. UNEF forces were to be stationed in Port Said and Port Fuad, and had to secure the co-operation of the local authorities. In the final stage, the Anglo-French troops withdrew to a narrow part in the north part of Port Said and Port Fuad, close to the Canal entrance, and the UNEF had to take responsibility for the vulnerable positions outside this particular zone.

As for the Israeli withdrawal, the UN had to take control of Israeli positions in Sinai and in the Gaza Strip. Consequently, successive lines were designated behind which the Israeli forces would withdraw by certain times and dates. The main principle on which the UNEF operated was to prevent hostilities and to keep the Egyptian and Israeli forces as far apart as possible. In the Gaza Strip, the UNEF took up positions in the most vulnerable places, such as police stations and water pumping installations, and United Nations Relief and Works Agency (UNRWA) food stores were placed along the Gaza Strip).[90]

THE AFTERMATH

The Israeli decision to withdraw was a great relief to the British government, which longed to rebuild its position in the Middle East and restore the British economy. Against the background of a more favourable atmosphere between Israel and Britain, Israel tried to break the ice between the two countries by suggesting that they shared common interests in the Middle East. On 9 March, Elath told Watson, the Head of the African Department of the Foreign Office, that both countries wanted to see Nasser isolated. As for the rest of the Arab states, the Ambassador stated that the oil-producing countries had no common boundaries with Israel and had no Palestinian refugees within their borders, and therefore co-operation between Israel, western Europe, Britain and the oil-producing countries might be possible.[91] However, Watson was reluctant to agree with the Ambassador's analysis and warned him against false optimism because as long as Britain and the Western countries depended on Middle Eastern oil, which probably meant for the next 20 years, they would not be in a position to challenge Arab attitudes towards Israel. Hatred, he explained, was the one factor that united the Arab countries and neither Britain nor any other Western state could take any pro-Israeli action, which meant that the 'cold shoulder' stance towards Israel would continue. As for the oil-producing countries, Watson said they could not initiate even a token step towards Israel without risking their position in the Arab world.[92]

The Israeli government and its representatives in London were disappointed to learn that the Suez events had not brought the two countries closer, and the Israeli Consul, Gershon Avner, expressed his regret when he wrote on 27 March that, 'One can say that since 1920 there was no change in the British attitude towards Zionism, the only turnabout are the circumstances and the fact that Britain today cannot do much harm to Israel.'[93] However, despite the fact that Anglo-Israeli relations did not reach a significant breakthrough, Israel's overall position had changed remarkably as a result of the Suez war. From being a country with a fragile existence, with Fedayeen raids along the borders and financial challenges, it turned into a more confident, self-assured country. Israel had achieved a formidable military victory and, despite having to withdraw its forces, Israel's world position had changed. It was now seen as a strong country whose existence was no longer debatable. Israel achieved a relatively quiet period on its borders and it was no longer subjected to frequent Fedayeen activities on its southern border. The opening of the Tiran Straits created new horizons for Israel, and it could fulfil the dream of developing its southern port as an important gateway to African and Asian countries with whom it succeeded in establishing very impressive political and cultural links. Yet the Israelis did not benefit from their ties with Britain and France, because Suez increased the image of Israel as being part of the imperialist camp. Israel's relationship with its neighbours did not improve as a result of the war: on the contrary, Israeli leaders were as certain as ever of the continuance of the dispute, and the defeat of Egypt only enhanced Israel's belief that the only hope for bringing peace to the region was by gaining a military victory. Nasser, on the other hand, had strengthened his position in the Arab world more than ever, and his military defeat only enhanced his and the pro-Nasserite elements' hatred towards Israel and towards the West in general. The Franco-Israeli relationship reached its peak during and after the campaign. The main contribution Israel gained from this relationship was not necessarily in the military sphere but rather in the diplomatic and political one. France's friendship in the period from November 1956 up to the Israeli withdrawal was a tremendous asset for Israel.

While Israel's political and military achievements as a result of the Suez war were remarkable, for Britain the Suez war had more serious consequences. The Foreign Office realised that, for the time being, it was better to take a back seat while the wounds of the Suez experience healed. As early as November 1956 Sir Gladwyn Jebb, the British Ambassador in Paris, noted that 'Neither England nor France can any longer pursue any really independent policy and that they must therefore henceforward content themselves with being satellites of the United States, unless they prefer to be satellites of the Soviet Union.'[94] Sir John Nicholls also appreciated the different climate that arose in the Middle East after the Suez crisis and advised the Foreign Office in December that Britain should limit its efforts to gain a peace settlement because the Arabs refused to recognise Israel's existence and therefore 'one has to start from the assumption that no Arab state will be willing to settle with Israel'.[95] Nicholls also rejected the previous British suggestion of a land bridge between Egypt and Jordan (see Chapter 2) and argued that any attempt to try to achieve a settlement at the present time would be to 'run our heads against a brick wall'.[96] He concluded that it would be better to accept that under the current situation a satisfactory settlement was unobtainable and Britain's aim, for the time being, should be limited and focus on securing its interests to the best of its ability by other means until the prospect for such a settlement looked brighter.[97] This realisation was quite remarkable, especially if one remembers that Nicholls' view of Israel's behaviour was not very sympathetic, and that he had often adopted quite a harsh and critical view of Israel's actions.

This belief that it would be better not to hold high hopes and to take a secondary role was reiterated by the Foreign Office later in February 1957, and it was recognised that under these circumstances the best Britain could hope for in the region was a 'peaceful, prosperous and stable area which is well disposed towards the West and towards Britain in particular'.[98]

As for the Anglo-Israeli relationship, this should also be viewed as part of a long march with small steps being taken towards a closer relationship. The Suez episode and its aftermath therefore marked a minor adjustment towards a better and more friendly relationship. The affair contributed to the reduction of tension between the two countries and smoothed the path for the future. The succession of Harold Macmillan as Prime Minister also eased the way for the Israelis to place more trust in relations with Britain. In the denouement of the Suez affair the two countries faced a new situation in the region and worldwide. Yet this was only the prelude before the curtains rose on an even greater drama.

NOTES

1. Mordechai Bar-On *Etgar Vetigra* [Challenge and Quarrel: The Road to Sinai] (Beer-Sheva: Ben-Gurion Centre and Ben-Gurion University in the Negev, 1991), p. 298.
2. Ibid., p. 307.
3. Ibid.
4. Ibid.
5. Moshe Dayan, *Avnei Derech* [Story of My Life] (Tel-Aviv: Edanim/Jerusalem: Dvir , 1976), p. 278.
6. A[von] P[apers], 20/27/90, Eisenhower to Eden, 30 October 1956.
7. *Hansard*, Vol. 557, col. 1447, 31 October 1956.
8. PRO, PREM11/1105/T485/56, No. 5025, Macmillan to Eisenhower, 30 October 1956.
9. *Hansard*, Vol. 557, col. 1563, 31 October 1956.
10. PRO, PREM11/1105/320/10/56, Foreign Office to Tel-Aviv and Cairo, 31 October 1956.
11. *Hansard*, Vol. 557, col. 1454, 31 October 1956.
12. Ibid., p. 1460.
13. ISA, HZ332/8, Elath to Israeli Foreign Ministry, 3 November 1956.
14. PRO, FO800/730, Selwyn Lloyd paper on the Suez operation 1956–60, 29 March 1957.
15. Selwyn Lloyd, *Suez 1956 – A Personal Account* (London: Book Club Associates, 1978), pp. 247–50.
16. ISA, HZ2592/29, Elath to Meir, 4 November 1956.
17. ISA, HZ129/36, Israeli Foreign Ministry to Paris, 23 November 1956.
18. Bar-On, *Etgar Vetigra*, pp. 318–20.
19. Ibid., p. 322.
20. Hugh Thomas, *The Suez Affair* (London: Weidenfeld & Nicolson, 1967), p. 152.

See also Dayan, *Avnei Derech*, p. 181.
21. Bar-On, *Etgar Vetigra*, p. 323.
22. David Ben-Gurion, *Medinhat Israel Hamechudeshet* [The Revival of the State of Israel], Vol. 1 (Tel-Aviv: Am-Oved, 1969), p. 531.
23. Ibid., p. 532.
24. Harold Macmillan, *Riding the Storm 1956–1959* (London: Macmillan, 1971), p. 164.
25. Dwight D. Eisenhower, *The White House Years: Waging Peace 1956–1961*, (London: Heineman, 1966), p. 94.
26. Ibid., p. 163.
27. For full details on the economics of the Suez crisis see Lewis Johnman, 'Defending the Pound: The Economics of the Suez Crisis, 1956', in A. Gorst, L. Johnman and W. Scott Lucas (eds), *Post-War Britain: Themes and Perspectives, 1945–1964* (London: Pinter, 1989).
28. Ibid., p. 167.
29. PRO, FO371/120832/UES/1171/137(9), Ministry of Fuel and Power to Washington, 12 January 1957.
30. PRO, T236/4190/145/8, Hall (Treasury) to Macmillan, 28 November 1956.
31. PRO, CAB128/30, CM(56)85, 20 November 1956.
32. PRO, FO371/129327/ZP24/4/G, record of ministerial meeting in Paris, 9–15 December 1956.
33. Michael Bar-Zohar, *Ben-Gurion* (Tel-Aviv: Am-Oved, 1977), p. 1276. and see also David Ben-Gurion, *Yehud Veichud* [Singularity and Mission] (Tel-Aviv: Ma'arachot, 1971: 1982), pp. 269–70.
34. Ben-Gurion, *Medinhat* [1969] pp. 536–7.
35. Eisenhower, *The White House*, p. 94.
36. ISA, HZ2459/7, Eban to Ben-Gurion and Meir, urgent, 7 November 1956.
37. Bar-Zohar, *Ben-Gurion*, p. 1295.
38. *FRUS*, Vol. 16, 1955–57, memo from the Regional Director of the Office of European Operation, International Co-operation Administration (Seager) to the Deputy Director for Operation, International Co-operation Administration (Fitzgerald), pp. 1236–7, 3 December 1956.
39. Ben-Gurion, *Medinhat* [1969], p. 527.
40. Interview with Yaacov Herzog, *Jerusalem Post*, 8 October 1977, cited in Bar-Zohar, *Ben-Gurion*, p. 1294.
41. *FRUS*, Vol. 16, 1955–57, memo of a telephone conversation between the Israeli Ambassador (Eban) in New York and the Assistant Secretary of State for Near Eastern, South Asia and African Affairs (Rountree) in Washington, 30 December 1956.
42. Golda Meir, *Hayay* [My Life] (Tel-Aviv: Sifriat Ma'ariv, 1978), pp. 222–3.
43. ISA, HZ2459/7, Israeli embassy Washington to Israeli Foreign Ministry, 30 December 1956.
44. Ibid.
45. Ibid.
46. Ibid.
47. *FRUS*, Vol. 15 1955–57, memorandum of conversation at the State Department, 2 March 1956, p. 280.
48. Bar-Zohar, *Ben-Gurion*, p. 1283.
49. ISA, HZ332/8, Elath to Israeli Foreign Ministry, 3 November 1956.
50. Dayan, *Avnei Derech*, p. 320.
51. Bar-On, *Etgar Vetigra*, p. 320.
52. PRO, PREM11/1132/T507/56, Eden message to Mollet, No. 2366, 1 November 1956.

53. PRO, AIR20/9436, 1956–57, Suez Canal crisis: overflying, letter from Rose to Air Commander, 14 December 1956.
54. PRO, FO371/121358/V1192/1062, memorandum by Reilly, 2 November 1956.
55. PRO, FO371/121358/V1192/1061, memorandum by D.P. Reilly, 21 November 1956.
56. PRO, FO371/121359/V1192/1104, Ross minute, 10 December 1956.
57. PRO, FO371/121359/V1192/1102, Ross to Kirkpatrick and Dean, 28 December 1956.
58. PRO, FO371/121359/V1192/1075, Kirkpatrick minute, 3 December 1956.
59. PRO, FO371/121359/V1192/1075, Kirkpatrick minute, 3 December 1956.
60. PRO, FO371/121359/V1192/1102, Ross to Kirkpatrick and Dean, 28 December 1956.
61. Ben-Gurion Archive (BGA), Ben-Gurion diaries, 7 January 1957.
62. ISA, HZ331/8, Elath to MABAR, 4 January 1957.
63. PRO, FO371/128127/VR1081/137, Ross to Kirkpatrick, 15 January 1957.
64. PRO, FO371/128126/VR1081/7, Ross minute, 5 January 1957.
65. PRO, FO371/121238, Foreign Office to Hadow, 7 November 1956.
66. PRO, FO371/128126/VR1081/7, Ross minute, 5 January 1957.
67. PRO, FO371/128107/VR1052/8, Ross to Macmillan, 20 February 1957.
68. PRO, FO371/128137/VR 1081/286, immediate, No. 708, Dixon (New York) to Lloyd, 22 February 1957.
69. Macmillan, *Riding the Storm*, p.186.
70. ISA, HZ/329/9, Elath to MABAR, 11 January 1957.
71. *Ha'aratz*, 11 January 1957.
72. ISA, HZ2459/12, Israeli Foreign Ministry to Israeli embassy New York, 22 February 1957.
73. Orna Almog interview with Eliahu Elath, Jerusalem, summer 1988.
74. W. Scott Lucas, *Divided we Stand: Britain, the US and the Suez Crisis* (London: Hodder & Stoughton, 1988), p. 324. See also Keith Kyle, *Suez* (London: Weidenfeld & Nicolson, 1992), pp. 527–9.
75. BGA, Ben-Gurion diary, 7 January 1957.
76. Macmillan, *Riding the Storm*, p. 213.
77. Ibid., p. 214.
78. Ben-Gurion, *Medinhat* [1969], p. 547.
79. PRO, FO371/128137/VR1081/286, immediate, No. 708, Dixon (New York) to Lloyd, 22 February 1957.
80. ISA, HZ330/12, Herzog to Israeli Foreign Ministry, 26 February 1957.
81. For a wider account on the diplomatic negotiations see Kyle, *Suez*, pp. 535–40.
82. BGA, Ben-Gurion diary, 10 March 1957.
83. Ibid.
84. PRO, FO371/129327/ZP24/3G, record of conversation held in Paris, 9 March 1957.
85. BGA, Ben-Gurion diary, 10 March 1957.
86. Ben-Gurion, *Yehud Veichud* [1969], p. 527.
87. BGA, Ben-Gurion diary, 10 March 1957.
88. Dayan, *Avnei Derech*, p. 330.
89. E.L.M. Burns, *Between Arab and Israeli* (Institute for Palestine Studies, Beirut, 1969). The role of the UN is widely addressed in this book in chapters 16–18.
90. Ibid., p. 270.
91. ISA, HZ2331/8, Avner (Israeli Embassy London) to Scheneorson (MABAR), 9 March 1957.
92. Ibid.
93. ISA, HZ331/8, Avner to Maroz (Israeli Embassy London), 27 March 1957.

94. PRO, FO371/124431/WF1022/63, confidential, No. 426, Jebb to Lloyd, 17 November 1956.
95. PRO, FO371/121712/VR 1041/145, Nicholls to Rose, 5 December 1956.
96. Ibid.
97. Ibid.
98. PRO, FO371/127748/V1051/37, Ross minute, 15 February 1957.

—6—

Beyond Suez: The Israeli Withdrawal and the Search for a New Status Quo

SECURING FREE PASSAGE OF THE WATERWAYS

ON THE NIGHT OF 7/8 March 1957, the Israeli army completed its withdrawal from the Gaza Strip and Sharm el Sheikh. For the Israelis, the Suez crisis had come to an end, but there were, however, still many problems which both Israel and Britain had to overcome.

The Suez war had a very powerful impact on the region. It enhanced the existing opposition to the West, it increased the popularity of Nasser and marked a growing involvement of the Soviet Union in Middle Eastern affairs. This trend led to regional destabilisation, with upheavals among the more pro-Western regimes, thus causing grave anxiety to Britain, Israel and the United States. The Israeli government was anxious to ensure that the situation prior to Suez would not return. In particular, it wanted to protect its newly acquired right of free passage through the Tiran Straits, the Gulf of Aqaba and the Suez Canal, and to prevent the possibility of Egypt returning to the Gaza Strip. The UN resolution of 4 November called for the deployment of UN forces in the Gaza Strip, but the immediate developments following the Israeli withdrawal were not as simple as this process suggested. New problems emerged as Nasser announced in early March his intention to send a military governor and staff to Gaza, while, simultaneously, Cairo radio officially declared that Egypt would not permit Israeli ships free passage through the Tiran Straits.[1] This naturally caused concern in Israel and Prime Minister Ben-Gurion immediately complained to the United States about these serious developments. In an official letter to President Eisenhower on 13 March, he stressed that only a week after Israel had evacuated the Gaza Strip, it was already facing the danger that the status quo ante might be restored.[2] Ben-Gurion noted that Israel did not wish to take aggressive measures to change the situation, but that under certain circumstances it might have to resort to 'self-defence'.[3] He concluded his letter by expressing his hope that the Israeli people would not live to regret their decision to withdraw from Sinai.[4] Following this on, 18

March, Golda Meir, still in the United States, told Dulles and State Department officials that the Egyptian army now controlled the road between El-Arish and Gaza, and that Israel had information that Nasser planned to put his army into Gaza and then ask the UNEF to withdraw to the border. Meir said that all these developments would cause uproar in Israel if they became public, especially from those living along the southern border with Egypt.[5] On 2 April, Ben-Gurion also expressed his apprehension to the American Ambassador in Tel-Aviv, Edward Lawson, stating that his government was gravely concerned about what had happened in Gaza and that he suspected that Nasser's action enjoyed the support of the UN Secretary-General, Dag Hammarskjold.[6] He also said to Lawson, on 17 March, that he suspected that the dispatch of a military governor to Gaza enjoyed the support of the UN Secretary-General.[7] Mistrust towards the UN was also expressed by Meir in her talks with State Department officials. Meir dramatically warned that if Israel wanted it could take the Egyptian general and 'parade him through Tel-Aviv'.[8] Meir concluded, in her talks on 18 March, that Israel did not rely on the UN but on the United States.[9]

The fact that Israel's pleas were addressed to the United States was not accidental and derived from two reasons. First, that it was the United States who had put the biggest pressure on Israel to withdraw and had guaranteed freedom of passage to Israeli shipping in the Gulf of Aqaba through the Canal. Second, that the Israelis had little confidence in the UN and believed that only the United States had the power to ensure that the promises made to Israel prior to its withdrawal would be upheld. In addition, on 13 March, Ambassador Eban stressed the American responsibility to keep the promises made to Israel prior to its withdrawal. He said that Israel had taken a difficult and historic step in placing its hopes in the United States, and therefore it expected that they and the other nations who had urged it to withdraw from Sinai would help to uphold the UN resolution.[10] It seems, however, that Israel's anxiety in this respect was unfounded. According to the American records, Nasser had promised Hammarskjold at the end of March that no Egyptian troops would move into Gaza[11] and argued that it was in his own government's interest to prevent raids from Gaza into Israeli territory.[12] He also assured Hammarskjold that Egypt had no intention of moving into the Sharm el Sheikh area.[13]

Meanwhile, tensions also grew as a result of Nasser's announcement on 18 March that he would not allow Israeli ships through the Suez Canal until there was a settlement of the Arab refugee problem.[14] For Israel, free passage was not just a question of principle but was seen as vital for the development of its southern port of Eilat. Eilat had special significance for Israel's economy because it was the port nearest to East Africa, South Africa and the Far East. Furthermore, goods brought to Eilat from the East did not pass through the Suez Canal and thus were cheaper and avoided the risk of interference from Egypt.[15] Israeli diplomats in Washington and London were therefore quick to indicate that their government would not tolerate any act of discrimination and emphasised that any interference with the passage of Israeli shipping through Suez or the Gulf of Aqaba would be seen by Israel as an act of war.[16] Moreover, Gideon Rafael[17] said at the beginning of April that Israel would want to test the Egyptian attitude and would not let the matter rest.[18] The Israelis were therefore keen to publicise the passage of the US flag oil tanker *Kern Hills*, under charter to the Israeli government, which, in late March, entered the Gulf of Aqaba through the Straits of Tiran and discharged its cargo of oil at the port of Eilat.[19]

Britain and the United States feared that Israel might follow this by putting the matter of freedom of passage to test by sending one of its own ships to Eilat. This would place them in a delicate position. Apparently, a British correspondent in Cyprus was told by the Israeli Consul that the ship in question was the *Atlit*. It was thought that Israel's desire to send this ship to Eilat was natural and reasonable, although it was doubtful whether it was in Israel's interests to draw attention to the ship's passage by publicising it.[20] It was felt that if Israel went ahead and sent a ship the Egyptians would be bound to stop it. Britain would then be placed in a difficult and delicate position as Israel would probably complain to the UN and Britain would have to support Israel. However, at the same time, this would damage Britain's negotiations with the Egyptians over the future of the Canal. If Israel's complaint to the Security Council failed, a breach would have been made in the principle of non-discrimination, subject to the 13 October resolution, which was the basis for British negotiations with Egypt.[21]

Fortunately, in a conversation between Hammarskjold, Nasser and Egyptian Foreign Minister Fawzi in March that year, the Egyptian position proved to be much more flexible and forthcoming. The Egyptians assured the UN Secretary-General that they were closing their eyes to the Aqaba situation. Nonetheless, when Hammarskjold asked about the possible Egyptian reaction to Israeli ships proceeding through the Canal, Fawzi answered, 'Please forget you asked that question'.[22] Nasser's response was to state simply that Israeli ships would not be allowed to use the Canal; a decision he justified on the grounds that any Egyptian government permitting Israeli ships into Port Said or Ismailia would risk immediate sabotage of the Canal.[23] On the other hand, Nasser and Fawzi indicated that they had no objection to the matter being taken to the International Court and thus Israel's rights could be discussed without involving the Egyptians in any initiative.[24] However, just as an unwritten agreement on Israeli passage through the Gulf of Aqaba was reached with Egypt, further objections were raised by the Saudi government in the summer of 1957. On 7 June 1957, the Saudis complained to the State Department that they were concerned at the presence of Israeli warships in the Gulf of Aqaba.[25] However, in a discussion between Eban and State Department officials on 11 June, the Ambassador vigorously denied to his American counterpart the Saudis' accusation that Israeli warships were patrolling in the Gulf. The warships, he told the US Under-Secretary of State, had remained in Eilat save for a training trip sometime in May and were under instructions to keep out of Saudi waters. He also denied that Israel had any intention of interfering with Moslem pilgrims.[26] On 11 June, Eban told the State Department that the Saudis must know that they were not bombed as they claimed; Israel would be 'off its head', he told Dulles and Rountree, to do such a thing at a time when they were trying to develop the Gulf. He reassured them that Israel would respect territorial waters and asked that this message be conveyed to the Saudis.[27] The Saudis were clearly unconvinced and in a discussion between Azzam Pasha, the representative of King Saud, and Rountree, the Assistant Secretary for Near Eastern Affairs at the State Department, on 24 June, Pasha said that the King expressed his opposition and reservations about the new situation created in the Gulf and accused Israel of taking aggressive action in these waters. He said that an Israeli destroyer had sailed from Eilat heading towards the Arab town of Sheikhameed. The King also stated his grave concern over the fate of the holy places of Islam in the Arabian peninsula. He was afraid that, if Israeli shipping were allowed to use the Gulf of Aqaba, Arab pilgrims would be blocked from visiting those places.[28] Furthermore, Pasha emphasised that the King resented the benefits Israel had gained from its recent aggression. The Saudis did not want to bring the case to the International Court, but Saudi Arabia, together with Jordan, complained to the Security Council, saying that the traditional route for pilgrims in the Gulf area was no longer safe. The US administration was worried by this development, because if the matter was not settled it could damage Saudi–US relations and thereby the US position in the region.[29]

At the end of September, the Saudis also expressed their concern to British officials, and in a letter to the British embassy in Washington, they emphasised their objection to Israel's use of the Gulf, stressing that it was Arab waters.[30] Britain's attitude to the matter was based on the consideration that the Gulf of Aqaba must be regarded as high seas, i.e. waters that are not internal or territorial. The same consideration applied to the Straits of Tiran which could be used for international navigation between the two ports of the high seas under article 1794 of the draft article on the law of the sea drawn up by the UN International Law Committee.[31]

Yacov Zur, the Israeli Ambassador in Paris, had already informed the Israeli Foreign Ministry in July that, according to French sources, the State Department was anxious to solve the problem of the Gulf. The State Department, he continued, had pressed Saud not to associate with Nasser if he decided to prevent Israeli passage. Zur wrote to Jerusalem that his information was that the State Department was aware of Israel's great sensitivity on the matter and assumed that if Israeli rights to free passage were disturbed, Israel would immediately respond, a move which might bring the Soviets into the picture.[32]

While Israel still faced obstacles in the use of the Gulf of Aqaba, the British government was steaming ahead in an effort to resolve its differences with Egypt and to facilitate a quick solution of the Canal issue. The Israeli withdrawal from Sinai made possible the reopening of the Canal to shipping, but it had first to be cleared of the ships the Egyptians had sunk during the war as part of their blockade of the Canal. During the spring, the Suez Canal was steadily cleared of these obstacles, but there was still the question of the terms to be agreed between the Egyptian government and the nations using the Canal. Nasser said that the Canal would be operated by the Suez Canal Authority and that Egypt would be bound by the convention of 1888, and that therefore the dues should be paid to the company.[33] The British and the French governments, with the support of the United States, suggested that the dues should be paid to the UN or the International Bank.[34]

As revealed in Macmillan's memoirs, the intention of the British government was to keep the large sterling balances blocked in the No. 1 account and to persuade the Egyptians to accept payment of the dues in transferable sterling, which would be made available for each transaction. Negotiations in Basel between the Bank of England and the Bank of Egypt proved to be very successful and a plan for a special transferable sterling account to be opened for Canal dues and other outgoings in connection with shipping was agreed by the two parties.[35] The Canal was officially reopened on 10 April and British ships began to use the Canal again in mid-May, French ships in June.[36]

SECURING THE WESTERN OIL SUPPLY

Britain attached great importance to a quick solution of the Canal problem because its closure had severe financial consequences for Britain and it was in its interests to ensure that trade, and especially oil, flowed through the Canal as soon as possible. The Suez war highlighted the vulnerability of the oil supply from the Middle East in time of crisis, especially with the growth of Arab nationalism, and revealed the necessity of finding an alternative supply route. Both the American and the British governments were aware of this and at the Bermuda Conference in March 1957, Eisenhower and Macmillan discussed the issue in order to find a common policy towards Middle Eastern oil. The Bermuda Conference was also one of the first steps Macmillan took to restore better relations with the United States after the breach caused by the Suez crisis.[37]

Although the Suez crisis showed that Europe could obtain its oil from the American continent, it resulted in heavy financial difficulties, especially for the British economy whose companies traded in sterling. One of the lessons of Suez over the medium term was therefore that an alternative pipeline from the Persian Gulf to the Mediterranean coast was of immense importance. In addition, it was felt that the oil companies should be encouraged to ship oil in large tankers which could be navigated around the Cape of Good Hope.[38]

The main routes of oil supply were:

- *Iraq* – the main oilfields were at Kirkuk and Basra. The output from Kirkuk depended on conveyance by pipeline (Iraq Petroleum Company) across Syria to the Mediterranean coast. The main weakness here was that the pipeline traversed Syrian territory, whereas output from Basra was carried by tanker from the head of the Persian Gulf and therefore was much more secure.

- *Saudi Arabia* – Saudi oil (100 per cent under American control) output was carried by the Trans-Arabian pipeline (Tapline) across Jordan, Syria and Lebanon to Sidon. Although this line was not destroyed during the Suez campaign, its route through Syria also placed the Tapline in a vulnerable position.[39]

Iranian output was carried wholly by tankers and therefore was not affected by difficulties with the pipeline.

Taking into consideration that 70 per cent of the free world's oil reserves were in the Middle East, that by 1957 the region supplied approximately 80 per cent of the free world's oil requirements,[40] and that it was unlikely that increased supply of other sources of energy would be sufficient for the needs of western Europe, the US and British governments recognised the importance of joint efforts to ensure the flow of oil and, at the same time, saw the necessity of reducing Western dependence on the Middle Eastern transit countries.[41] The favoured alternative pipeline route suggested in a memorandum drawn up by the United States and Britain was one that would run through Iraq to Turkey and to the Mediterranean coast. The idea was that a large-capacity pipeline from Kirkuk to a deep-water terminal in Turkey would provide not only a very useful new outlet but also an insurance against disturbances by Syria and Egypt.[42] At the same time the British and the Americans believed that it was desirable to seek alternative sources outside the Middle East, such as Colombia, Venezuela and North Africa.[43]

A similar conclusion was reached at two conferences held in London on 18–19 March and 13–16 May, where the eight major oil companies decided on a pipeline system running from the Persian Gulf to the Mediterranean.[44] They also concluded that as long as the Middle East remained the main source of oil it was important to minimise the possibility of interruption to the flow of oil from the region. This could be achieved by restoring normal relations with Egypt, and, at the same time, further enhancing the prestige of Iraq and Saudi Arabia in the Arab world.[45] The United States and Britain, the State Department paper emphasised, should therefore aim to reduce the tension between Israel and its neighbours, as any further escalation of the dispute would jeopardise the safety of the oil supply, and Israel should be persuaded to take a less militant posture.[46] As for the British position in the region, the US administration believed it was of immense importance to reach some agreement with the Saudis and to solve the Burami dispute.[47] The Burami oasis consisted of eight villages whose inhabitants had managed to live without an alliance to any state but their allegiance was claimed by the ruler of Abu Dhabi and by the Sultan of Muscat, places where Britain held a 'special position', including responsibility for their foreign policy. It was hoped that if oil was discovered in that area, the concession would go to the Iraqi Petroleum Company. However, the Saudis were also keen to get their hands on any oil that might be found, meaning that any concession would go to ARAMCO and the British would lose possible revenue. Nasser had sided with King Saud on this issue and they attacked the British government for conducting a colonial-type relationship with the Gulf sheikdoms.[48] The Burami issue also became a bone of contention between the United States and Britain, because the US government was eager to support and promote King Saud as a counter to Nasser. When finally the Americans convinced the Saudis that the matter should be referred to international arbitration, the British arbitrator resigned and finally, on 26 October 1955, a British military force occupied the oasis.[49] Therefore a settlement of this issue was needed to ease Anglo-American co-operation over the regional oil issue.

POLITICAL AND STRATEGIC IMPACT ON BRITAIN'S POSITION IN THE REGION

By the spring of 1957, it seemed that the confusion and upheaval of Suez had finally passed. Despite the financial losses the British economy suffered as a result of the campaign, the country was on its way to recovery. The financial estimates for July–December 1957 showed a surplus of £167m; the balance of visible trade showed hardly any change compared with that of 1956, and an increase of £38 million appeared in the current account surplus as a result of a recovery in invisible earnings from oil in the second half of 1957.[50]

However, although the financial effects of the Suez crisis were mainly temporary, the political and strategic consequences were more painful and placed Britain in a difficult position. The repercussions of Suez radically affected Britain's military mobility in the region.[51] An air barrier was established from Syria to the Sudan, which restricted Britain's ability to reinforce and maintain the Arabian peninsula from the eastern Mediterranean.[52] The most direct air route to the Persian Gulf, East Africa and the Far East lay across the Middle East and therefore it was important that the UK enjoyed adequate overflying facilities. Under its formal agreements Britain enjoyed rights to overfly Iraq, Libya and Ethiopia and had ad hoc agreements with Turkey, Iran, Lebanon and Sudan. Prior to Suez, Britain had enjoyed overflying rights in Egypt under the Suez Base Agreement of 1954. However, the Egyptian and Syrian air corridors were closed after Suez. It was thought that overflying Israel could create some political problems, especially if the Israelis were to request in return the right to use Cyprus for unarmed planes.[53] Apart from the realisation that as a result of Suez the Persian Gulf now had a greater strategic importance, it is hard to demonstrate any other strategic or political change in British aims in the Middle East. The overall picture was still guided by the same traditional principles: securing the oil-producing countries, keeping the Baghdad Pact intact and preserving British influence in the region.

THE IMPACT OF THE SUEZ WAR ON ISRAEL

In spite of the fact that the period following Israeli withdrawal from Sinai led to continuing difficulties in Gaza and in the Gulf of Aqaba, the overall picture, after the initial period of complications, proved that the Suez operation had improved Israel's security and international standing, and that it was the only party involved in the operation to benefit from the war. It gave Israel a sense of security and brought peace to the southern border region now that Fedayeen activities had ceased. Israel's military victory contributed to a calmer atmosphere and a greater belief in Israel's ability to defend itself. Stability along the borders was increased and the risks of militant action reduced. As events were to show during 1957 and 1958, Israel's ability to restrain itself was far greater now than in the past. Israel's military triumph in Suez paved the way for a new era in Israel, a period in which it could concentrate more than ever on internal goals: building its internal strength, investing in science and higher education, and absorbing the mass Jewish immigration from North Africa and the Eastern bloc. In addition, it extended its relations with new countries and built a more positive image worldwide.

In assessing the consequences of Suez, Ben-Gurion told IDF commanders in December 1956 that Israel's victory had brought great benefits. First and foremost, he emphasised it had achieved freedom of passage through the Tiran Straits and was now able to develop the port of Eilat which was vital for Israel's future. He continued by saying that Israel had managed to achieve world recognition for its right of freedom of passage and also the right to use force in order to protect this freedom, and had thus opened the gate to Asia and Africa. He assured those soldiers who felt that they had fought in vain (because of Israel's decision to withdraw) that this was not true, because all the aims and achievements he mentioned could not have been accomplished without Israel's military victory.[54] Ben-Gurion concluded that the Sinai war was like 'lightning that rekindled the fires of inspiration in the Jewish people'.[55]

In analysing the Sinai war from this perspective, Ben-Gurion emphasised the importance of the Western powers and the newly emerging states in Africa and Asia. In one of his political essays, Ben-Gurion stressed the significance he attached to Israel's relations with, and position within, the wider world. He said that the global role of the great powers had not ended and that, although they were not in the same position as before, France and Britain were still great nations that had contributed greatly to civilisation. He believed that the United States, the one country that had pressured Israel to withdraw from Sinai, had changed its attitude towards Israel as a result of Suez. 'We must be aware', he stated, 'that Israel's security and strength depended not only on its military capacity, but to a large extent on its position in the international sphere.'[56] This emphasis is very important as it indicated Ben-Gurion's deep understanding that Israel's security could not solely rely on its armed forces. It had to improve its foreign relations and therefore it was of immense importance for it to establish its position worldwide. It was a belief that Ben-Gurion had always had, but as a result of the Suez crisis he stressed it more than ever.

Sir Francis Rundall, the new British Ambassador to Tel-Aviv, also noted the effect the Sinai war had on Israel's self-confidence. In a letter to Lloyd in January 1958, the Ambassador noted that its victory reduced its previous psychological necessity to take reprisal action whenever border incidents reached a certain level and had overall strengthened its confidence. Rundall went on to remark that, at the same time, the Suez campaign had forced Israel to realise its vulnerability to economic pressure, especially from the United States, and to become more aware of public opinion.

> The blinkered truculence of past years is being modified by the growing realisation that Israel must hence-forward face up to the progressively grimmer realisation of living in an area of active tension between East and West ... It is nevertheless clear to the Israeli government that they must count the risks of far greater repercussions than before to any trigger-happy initiative on their part.[57]

He also believed that the maintenance of the status quo in the region was of major interest to Israel.

As the dust settled on the Suez crisis, giving more security to Israel on its southern border, its decision-makers tried to widen its foreign relations with more countries. One of the main priorities on Israel's agenda after Suez was its relations with the Asian and African states. Ben-Gurion attached great importance to these and in his diary he emphasised their significance for Israel. He believed the African and Asian states were a rising force which one day could form the strongest political factor in the world.[58] The relations between Israel and African–Asian states, known as the 'Periphery Treaty', was one of Israel's main priorities during the 1950s and 1960s. Ben-Gurion saw great importance in these relations as an indirect strategy to gain friends in the peripheral region and a way to break out of isolation.[59] He believed that the importance of Africa and Asia would increase in the light of the Cold War, which was to a large degree a struggle between East and West in Asia and Africa, but noted that many of those African and Asian states that had recently gained independence did not wish to be closely associated with the Western powers who had previously been their oppressors. Here was an opportunity for Israel, a small nation which had also recently freed itself from British imperialism, to offer assistance and advice. The Suez affair had contributed to Israel's positive image, thereby enabling it to gain a special position with these countries.[60] Ben-Gurion believed that the friendship between Israel and the African and Asian states was based on common ground, for example they shared a fear of the pan-Arab movement. In addition, Israel had a unique way of life in the Kibbutzim, and its ability to absorb people from different cultures appealed to them.[61] Israel was willing to assist these countries in restoring their villages, in training their inhabitants to work in factories and in helping them with advances in agricultural and medical fields. A special department in the Israeli Foreign Ministry was set up to conduct activities in these countries.[62]

In their desire to build these relationships, the Israelis were willing to explore any possible channel that could help them broaden their contacts with countries in this region and sought British help to achieve this goal. Walter Eytan, the General Director of the Israeli Foreign Office, told Sir Francis Rundall on 27 July 1957, that Her Majesty's Government would be able to assist Israel in this matter, for example in its relations with Burma. He said that Israel had begun to establish good relations with that country, but then the Burmese had suddenly changed their attitude and he was suspicious that Britain was involved in this. Rundall thought that this was unlikely and considered rightly that it was symbolic of Israel's suspicions towards the United Kingdom.[63] In fact, the Foreign Office in London viewed Israel's relations with Asian and African countries quite favourably, because Israel's influence, as a pro-Western country, could work against that of communism and the pan-Arab movement. The advantage to Britain was that it helped Israel to find an outlet for trade, thus evading the Arab boycott. If the boycott succeeded in bringing Israel's economy to a standstill it would pose a danger to Middle East peace and therefore to Britain's interests. In addition, the Foreign Office hoped that the relationship between the African–Asian states and Israel would contribute to a reduction of Israeli feelings of isolation and claustrophobia.[64]

THE ARRIVAL OF SIR FRANCIS RUNDALL

Sir Francis Rundall, who succeeded Sir John Nicholls in April 1957, was quick to realise the bitterness the Israelis felt towards Her Majesty's

Government and even more so towards the Foreign Office. Rundall had previously served in the North American department at the Foreign Office and was Consul-General in New York prior to his appointment to Tel Aviv. There is nothing significant in his career that would explain why he adopted a more sympathetic view towards Israel than his predecessor, John Nicholls, although one can cautiously speculate that his experience in the United States might have influenced his views. One can also assume that the fact that Rundall served in a period when Israeli policy was much more cautious and less aggressive, enabled him to adopt a more understanding outlook.

In Rundall's first meeting with Ben-Gurion on 1 June, he faced the usual Israeli complaint about Britain's unfriendly and flawed attitude. After an initial expression of admiration for the British people and their way of life, Ben-Gurion said that the Foreign Office had not changed its attitude towards Israel since 1945. The Ambassador, in return, explained that Britain's interests in the region prevented it from adopting a more forthcoming attitude, and that the feelings of Her Majesty's Government towards Israel were sympathetic but reserved. He expressed his hope that no one still believed in the myth that the Foreign Office was anti-Israeli, emphasising that responsible officials must be realistic and that British policy in the region must be realistic, too. Ben-Gurion agreed but said this did not change the fact that British policy towards Israel was not particularly friendly. He went on to say that he fully appreciated the motives of British policy, but believed it was mistaken because their basic assumption that the attitude of the Arab states towards the West depended on Western behaviour towards Israel was wrong. Ben-Gurion said that the Arabs would follow whatever served their best interests, but that as long as Britain stuck to this assumption there was no hope of improvement in Anglo-Israeli relations. The Prime Minister argued that it was all very well to say that Britain was friendly towards Israel but could not express this warmth because of its need for oil, but that in twenty years time, when Britain's dependence on oil was reduced, it would be able to state its friendship towards Israel openly. Ben-Gurion concluded that for Israel, the next 20 years were of immense importance and it could not afford to wait until then.[65]

So although Sir Francis Rundall served in a different and quieter environment than his predecessor, Sir John Nicholls, he still faced the traditional difficulties of the Anglo-Israeli relationship. Rundall clearly realised the difficulty of the task before him, and was aware of the sensitivity of the Israelis. 'Israel', the Ambassador noted in August 1958, 'is a country where there is more happening per square mile than in any other country of comparable size, and its people are patently eager that one shall see, understand and above all approve of what their country is doing.'[66] In one of his first dispatches it was evident that Rundall clearly saw the strategic and political value of Israel in the likelihood of a new Middle Eastern crisis. He wrote, 'One can even speculate that the time could come when we should wish to be in closer collaboration with Israel, for example, if the Eisenhower doctrine would have failed and the Arabs would fall generally under Communist influence ... If this observation was accepted then the problem was how to maintain Britain's influence in Israel without facing repercussions in the Arab world.'[67] However, he continued, 'One has to be aware of the difficulties the Western powers might have in helping Israel,' because 'the blunders, that to the outside world wreck the good case they have built up, are to them merely the logical development as judged by their peculiar terms of references.'[68] 'One learns after a little time', Rundall concluded, 'to judge events in their local context; they make little sense otherwise.'[69] As for Anglo-Israeli relations, the Ambassador believed that Britain had enjoyed a short popularity during October 1956, but afterwards relations had gone back to their old pattern. He suggested that the Foreign Office should be more aware of the great suspicion among Israeli leaders of British motives. 'From Ben-Gurion onwards,' the Ambassador indicated, 'Britain was considered to be engaged in the appeasement of the Arabs at Israel's expense in order to restore its influence in the region, and the popular picture was of a friendly Israel trying to break through a closed British door.'[70] Ben-Gurion's remark to Rundall in July 1957 that 'My Ambassador to London is no more use than my Ambassador to Moscow!'[71] expressed the common view of many Israeli leaders about the nature of Anglo-Israeli relations, implying that they were merely formal without any real and meaningful co-operation.

Rundall thought that, in spite of all the consequences close relations with Israel could have on British interests in the region, it would be wise for Her Majesty's Government to retain some loose influence upon Israel which he justified with reference to political and economic arguments. Israel, Rundall wrote to Lloyd in August 1957, was an expanding market, and politically it was important to maintain some influence, especially in times of tension. 'Although', he continued, 'one might argue that British decline of power was balanced by American dominance, one has to remember that there could always be differences in view between the United States and Britain.'[72] Rundall believed that it was important not to let British influence in Israel sink any further, even though friendly relations with Israel contradicted other British interests in the region, 'Because, after all, Israel was the most democratic country in the Middle East, politically stable and anti-Communist and likely to remain Western in her way of life.'[73] Rundall believed that Britain still enjoyed respect and admiration in Israel for the institutions that had been established during the Mandate period. He warned that the generation who shared this admiration would not remain in power forever, and would soon be replaced by *Sabras* (native-born Israelis). The new generation, in the Ambassador's eyes, combined the aggressiveness of their parents with a complete indifference to outside opinion or advice.[74] Therefore, in Rundall's view, they should be watched and guided in the next twenty years, or else, 'Israel could become the Germany of the Middle East.'[75] Rundall's remark proved to be true to some degree, as Israel did become a state with a strong military capacity. It is also true that the Defence Ministry and the IDF had, and still have, a major influence upon Israel's foreign policy and its decision-making. However, one should bear in mind that, unlike in Britain, the IDF is an integral part of Israeli life and is not an establishment of professional soldiers. In a society where there is compulsory military conscription there is very little division between the IDF and civilians, hence the great influence it has upon decision-makers.

However, although the Ambassador recommended the Foreign Office to improve British relations with Israel there is no indication that the mood in Whitehall changed dramatically. Furthermore, the Foreign Office did not give up, even at that stage, its search for a frontier adjustment between Israel and its neighbours. The Suez crisis and its bitter consequences did not lessen the British desire to make further suggestions with regard to Israel's frontiers. In a parliamentary debate in the House of Commons on 14 March 1957, the Foreign Secretary addressed the problem of frontier adjustments between Israel and its neighbours, and suggested that the Arab states should receive a guarantee that Israel would not expand its territory, while Israel's right to exist would be assured. In addition, Lloyd said that a compromise should be reached on the Arab refugees and the frontier question because the current situation was, in his view, 'nonsense'. 'Anyone', he said, 'that had made his way from Tel-Aviv to Jerusalem must realise that there could not be a permanent peace with the present demarcation line.'[76] We can assume that the Foreign Secretary's comment referred to the Israeli frontiers as they were at the time. According to the Armistice lines of 1949, Israel's main cities were within very close range of its border and therefore put its citizens in a very vulnerable situation. From the north of Israel to the south it was only 300 miles.

Lloyd was careful not to specify the frontier adjustments he had in mind, thereby not repeating Eden's mistake of 1955. 'I think', he concluded, 'that both sides will have to realise that we shall not get peace unless Israel has a more sensible form of frontiers.'[77] Unusually, this speech did not seem to lead to any special reaction in Israel, and one can assume that it was due to Lloyd's deliberate lack of precision over potential border adjustments. This can be seen as an indication that right after the Suez crisis, when Britain was still licking its wounds, it was still trying to rebuild its relations with the Arab countries and had no real desire to get closer to Israel.

THE 'SHELL' CRISIS

Tension between Britain and Israel also arose during autumn 1957 because of the Shell oil company's decision to withdraw from Israel. Owing to the Egyptian ban on Israeli shipping and on any cargo destined for Israel using the Suez Canal, oil tankers were prohibited from reaching the Haifa refineries. Shell's decision was a blow to Israel's effort to strengthen its economy, especially in the face of growing Jewish immigration from the Eastern bloc and North Africa. Shell's formal excuse for leaving Israel was that it was not profitable. However, Israel had secret information which indicated that financial reasons were not the main cause. The Israeli Foreign Ministry informed Yacov Zur, the Israeli Ambassador to Paris, and Eliahu Elath, the Israeli Ambassador to London, on 3 September, that Israel had obtained a secret document, which proved that Shell made satisfactory profits in Israel and therefore confirmed Israel's suspicion that Shell's decision was not a result of purely financial considerations, but was taken under Arab pressure.[78] Previously, during July, the Foreign Office had been informed by Shell that Saudi Arabia had made a representation, tantamount to an ultimatum, ordering it to cease trade with Israel by July or otherwise the company would be asked to leave Saudi Arabia. While Shell's interests in Saudi Arabia were modest, they were nevertheless apprehensive that if they did not comply with these demands, this would result in a rescinding of their right to trade in Saudi Arabia, as well as the possible loss of business in other Arab countries. The decision to relinquish trade in Israel was thus concluded.[79] British Petroleum (BP) supported this decision and, shortly afterwards, they too decided to cease trading with Israel. They justified their action by stating that in recent years they had been 'chiselled and squeezed' by the Israelis. (The Shell company of Palestine was 50/50 Shell and BP but under Shell management.) Furthermore, the company stressed that this decision was not politically based and had been determined solely on financial and commercial grounds.[80]

As the co-operation of Arab countries was vital to the successful operation of oil companies in Britain, the Foreign Office decided that, in this instance, it would be more prudent to adopt a policy of non-intervention.[81] In July, Selwyn Lloyd expressed the British government's disappointment regarding the decision to withdraw from Israel and said that the important issue was not the short-term goals of the oil companies, and that his chief concern lay in addressing the question of how far Britain should proceed in submitting to Arab pressure. He concluded by stating that, although the government did not want to intervene or influence the companies' decision, he wanted them to be aware that it was the British government's express desire that a situation would not develop whereby Israel was starved of oil.[82]

Ever since the establishment of Israel and the Arab boycott imposed on it by its neighbours, Israel had lived under the threat that Western companies would give in to Arab pressure and cease commercial relations. For Israel, the prospect of a successful boycott threatened financial disaster to its economy, thereby jeopardising Israel's very existence. Therefore every Israeli government had done its utmost to ensure that the Arab boycott would end in failure. The Israeli government was willing to use all kinds of methods to fight the boycott, for example publicising worldwide the names of those companies that had abandoned the Israeli market as a result of Arab blackmail. This method proved to be quite effective, and those companies that abandoned Israel because of Arab pressure found themselves boycotted by Jews, especially in the United States.[83]

This case of the British oil companies appeared to be so important that, on 26 July, the Jewish Board of Deputies expressed its concern to the Foreign Office that BP and Shell's decision would encourage Arab states to act against Israel and sought to pressure the British government to advise the oil companies to reverse their decision.[84] When Golda Meir met Rundall on 15 July, she told him that Israel viewed Shell's decision very seriously, as the stoppage of oil was tantamount to declaring economic war against Israel. Meir argued that giving in to the Arab boycott and the blackmail of Nuri and Saud could damage Israel's economy and concluded by saying that a boycott of Israel by the major oil companies served as a reward for the Arabs' blackmail and aided their ambition to destroy Israel.[85] This point was also argued by Elath who told Lloyd, on 15 July, that in Israel's view the British government shared responsibility for the Shell company's actions, because Britain held shares in British Petroleum. The Ambassador was reluctant to accept Lloyd's explanation that the British government, despite its shares in British Petroleum, had not intervened in the company's affairs. Elath argued that it would have been different if the Shell decision had been taken purely on economic grounds, but it was clear that it was taken on political grounds and the Israeli government could only conclude that this policy was deliberately calculated to gain credit in the Arab world at Israel's expense.[86]

In Shell's case, it was not just a political issue, but also a very important economic matter, and it was in Israel's interests not to let Shell withdraw unless a satisfactory agreement, which assured the continuance of the flow of oil from Iran to Israel, could be reached. Shell's decision was seen by the Israeli government as another indication of the biased attitude of Her Majesty's Government towards Israel, because they believed that it was within the power of the British government to prevent Shell from leaving Israel.[87] The Israeli government was willing to allow the company to leave Israel quietly, providing it ensured that Israel would get the oil it needed from Iran in future years. In order to enable the negotiations to proceed in a calmer atmosphere, the Israeli government stopped the anti-Shell public campaign for a while in the hope that a satisfactory agreement could be found.

Negotiations with Shell, in November 1957, were not held directly by Israeli officials, but by a British Jew, Isaac Wolfson of General Universal Stores, and with French Jews acting as mediators. Israel was willing to subsidise the investment in the Haifa refinery as long as Shell promised to continue the flow of oil. Rundall believed that although Wolfson was a tough businessman he was a devoted Zionist and suspected that he was more on Israel's side than on Shell's and that he probably got 'full treatment by the locals as the saviour of Zion'.[88] He also argued that the government of Israel was being deliberately obstructive so that it could take both the distribution network and the refinery at a bargain price.[89] However, as public pressure was reduced Shell adopted a more stubborn line. Shell's suggestion of supplying oil from Venezuela did not satisfy Israel as this alternative was open to it without the company's assistance. Shell did not want to guarantee supply from Iran because it would provoke an immediate adverse reaction in the Arab states, of which Iran would be bound to take notice. The company, in turn, felt that Israel's reason for insisting on oil supplies from Iran was not merely economic, but also political.[90]

The negotiations were soon deadlocked because Shell was not willing to promise anything that could be seen by Israel as a satisfactory agreement. It was decided therefore that Israel would not allow the company to transfer any property as long as the flow of oil from Iran was not secured and to leave the solution to Shell. By late November, the company was eager to find some way out because its property in Israel was now out of use.[91] There were some voices at the Foreign Office like John Wright of the Economic Relations Department, who thought that if the British government could not speak publicly against the boycott, it at least could guide companies in private to stand against the boycott as long as possible. He warned against a surrender to Arab pressure because it would only encourage the Arab states to intensify their campaign and, at the same time, could further complicate Britain's relations with Israel. He concluded therefore that, 'it is time that we should stop adopting a wishy-washy attitude over the boycott question'.[92]

The Israeli government also sought to put pressure on the British government through its supporters in the Labour Party. When Hugh Gaitskell, leader of the Labour Party, and Aneurin Bevan discussed the problem with Macmillan in early August, the Prime Minister told them that Shell's decision was taken purely on financial grounds, and that even if Israel could give the company better terms, they were anxious to leave Israel. Gaitskell said that such a policy would strengthen the view that the real reason for Shell's withdrawal was not economic. He said that his party opposed the government policy of repairing the damage the Suez operation had caused Britain in the Arab world at Israel's expense and emphasised that the Labour Party believed that friendly relations between Israel and Britain should be one of the main pillars of British policy in the region.[93] Macmillan in reply said that there was a limit to the government's ability to persuade the company to supply Israel with oil. He told Bevan that he might think that Her Majesty's Government held a lot of cards but that in reality, 'they had a very difficult hand to play'.[94] Macmillan also rejected the accusation that the British government was aiming for a rapprochement with the Arabs at Israel's expense.[95] In a House of Commons debate on 2 August, Labour Party members also attacked the Shell decision and claimed that the government should share the responsibility for the company's actions and accused it of giving in to Arab pressure.[96] Israeli government pressure and that of the Labour Party came to nothing and, finally, in late 1958, the Pazit company of Israel bought the consolidated refinery from BP–Shell and it later became a government concern.[97]

The crisis over Shell proved to the Israeli government that it was necessary to build a pipeline which could guarantee Israel's oil supply against interruption and damage. The opening of the Gulf of Aqaba and the Straits of Tiran to Israeli shipping increased the rapid development of Eilat as a port and centre for unloading crude oil.[98] The Israeli government wanted to construct a 32-inch pipeline capable of handling about 400,000 barrels a day, at a cost of approximately $470 million.[99] Israel already had, by this time, some minor oilfields; in 1955 oil had been found at Heletz, and in 1957 an additional source at Bror

Chail near Heletz was discovered. However, these sources could not alone meet the increased demand for oil in Israel. Because of the boycott, Arab oil supplies to Israel were banned. Before Suez, Israel had reached an agreement with the Soviet government for an alternative oil supply. However, as a result of the Suez crisis, the Soviets unilaterally revoked this contract, which increased the importance of a pipeline from Eilat to Haifa. Following the Suez operation the Israeli government began laying the pipeline and on 15 April 1957, oil began to flow from Eilat to Beer-Sheva.

Israel's next project was to build an additional large pipeline from Eilat to Haifa. However, Israel's financial position meant that it could not carry out this enterprise alone and urgently needed assistance from foreign investors.[100] Israeli diplomats tried to attract finance by emphasising to the West the unique value Israel had due to its geographical position between Asia and Europe, which meant that it could offer an alternative to the traditional oil supply routes.[101] However, Israeli efforts to convince the British and American administrations were not successful. In a background paper prepared by the State Department in April 1957, the Department put forward its reservations about assisting the project, noting the uncertainty of the oil supply, although no objection was raised against private investment.[102] Dulles told Macmillan on 22 March that, in his view, no encouragement should be given to Israel's desire to export its oil and Macmillan fully agreed.[103] Indeed, the head of the African Department at the Foreign Office, Adam Watson, had already explained to Gershon Avner, the Israeli Consul, earlier that month that Israel could not be considered as an alternative source of oil supply by the British government because this would alienate the other oil-producing countries. Even if Iran supplied Israel with oil, the British government could not afford to risk negative reactions from Saudi Arabia and Iraq. He concluded that it was hard to overcome the hatred towards Israel in the Arab states, and though the Israeli proposal was attractive in the long term it was not valid under the present circumstances.[104]

The only country that offered almost unlimited assistance to Israel was France. Franco-Israeli relations remained as close as before Suez and co-operation between the states exceeded all expectations. Moreover, whereas before Suez the special relationship was secret, it could now be brought into the open. France backed Israel during the early months following the Suez war when there was a fear that the situation in Sinai might revert to its previous position. On 14 March, the French Defence Minister told the US chargé d'affaires that if the situation in Gaza deteriorated and Israel decided to reoccupy it, France would provide Israel with air cover in order to prevent possible action by Egypt's air force.[105] On the same day, Prime Minister Mollet wrote to Eisenhower to say that Egyptian actions in Gaza justified firm Israeli action in the matter.[106] France was also the only country that was willing to assist Israel with the pipeline project from Eilat to Haifa and to extend credit to Israel. On 6 April, the Quai d'Orsay announced the French government's readiness to co-operate with the project and to provide $115 million, in addition to a $30 million loan for wheat and medical equipment.[107] In a new year message to Israel, Mollet promised Israel that it could count on French support to obtain the peace it deserved.[108] Franco-Israeli co-operation extended to all areas; high-ranking delegations visited Israel, and France and Israel carried out combined military exercises,[109] as well as co-operating in research into advanced combat methods.[110]

Anglo-Israeli relations, although calmer than in the pre-Suez period, had not undergone any significant change in the immediate post-Suez era. Britain was still licking its post-Suez wounds and trying to re-establish its position in the Middle East. Both Israel and Britain would have to get past obstacles and upheavals before they could embark on a new path. The crisis over Shell's withdrawal from Israel proved that suspicion and bitterness towards the British government still existed in Israel. The arrival of the new British Ambassador, Sir Francis Rundall, at Tel-Aviv, was one of the few positive aspects in Anglo-Israeli relations. He was to become an understanding friend of Israel at the Foreign Office, but this did not immediately alter the overall pattern of the relationship.

The Suez war improved Israel's internal and external position, and its relationship with its main ally, France, became even closer. Israel managed to establish itself as a respectable nation and showed growing maturity in its stand towards its Arab neighbours. Still, Israel's flexibility and maturity were put to the test yet again during the spring and the autumn of 1958 when the status quo was challenged once more.

NOTES

1. *FRUS*, Vol. 17, 1955–57, Ben-Gurion to Eisenhower, 13 March 1957, pp. 410–11; see also PRO, FO371/128140/VR1081/403, Rose (Levant Department) minute, 2 April 1957.
2. Ibid., *FRUS*, pp. 410–11.
3. Ibid., p. 411, and PRO, FO371/128146/VR1083/118, Makins (New York) to Lloyd, 13 March 1957.
4. PRO, FO371/128147/VR1083/73, Foreign Office minute, 9 April 1957.
5. *FRUS*, Vol. 17, 1955–57, memorandum of conversation, State Department, 18 March 1957, pp. 433–4.

6. Ibid., telegram from the embassy in Israel to the State Department, 17 March 1957, p. 429.
7. *FRUS*, Vol.13, 1955–57, telegram from the American embassy in Israel to the State Department, 17 March 1957, p. 429.
8. Ibid., memorandum of a conversation, State Department, 18 March 1957, p. 441.
9. Ibid., p. 434.
10. *FRUS*, Vol. 13, 1955–57, memorandum of a conversation, State Department 13 March 1957, p. 407.
11. Ibid., memorandum of a conversation, State Department, 29 March 1957, p. 489.
12. Ibid.
13. Ibid.
14. PRO, FO371/128140/VR1081/403, Rose (Levant Department), minute, 2 April 1957. See also *FRUS*, Vol. 17, 1955–57, memorandum of a conversation, State Department, 18 March 1957, p. 434.
15. PRO, FO371/128141/VR1081/428, Laurence minute, 8 May 1957.
16. PRO, FO371/128140/VR1081/403, Rose minute, 4 February 1958. See also various discussions between Israeli officials and State Department officials, for example *FRUS*, Vol. 17, 1955–57, memo of conversation, State Department, 2 April 1957, p. 509.
17. Gideon Rafael was Head of Middle East and United Nations Affairs at the Israeli Foreign Office during the mid-1950s, and Israeli Ambassador to Belgium 1957–60.
18. *FRUS*, Vol. 17, 1955–57, State Department memorandum, 2 April 1957, p. 509.
19. Ibid., memorandum of record by the Chairman of the Joint Chiefs of Staff, 19 April 1957, p. 557.
20. PRO, FO371/128141/VR1081/431, No. 2340, Ross to Washington, 24 May 1957.
21. PRO, FO371/128139/VR1081/366, Beely (Foreign Office) minute, 8 March 1957. p. 475.
22. *FRUS*, Vol. 17, 1955–57, telegram from the mission at the United Nations to the State Department, 28 March 1957, p. 477.
23. Ibid., p. 479.
24. Ibid., pp. 479–80.
25. *FRUS*, Vol. 17, 1955–57, Rountree memorandum to Herter, 7 June 1956, p. 634.
26. Ibid., 11 June 1957.
27. Ibid., p. 635.
28. *FRUS*, Vol. 17, memorandum from the Assistant Secretary of State for Near Eastern Affairs to the Secretary of State, 24 June 1957, p. 657.
29. Ibid.
30. PRO, FO371/128142/VR1081/469, British embassy Washington to Levant Department, 23 September 1957.
31. PRO, FO371/128142/VR1081/454, Lloyd to Macmillan, 2 July 1957.
32. ISA, HZ 330/14, MABAR (Jerusalem) to Avner (London), 19 July 1957.
33. Dwight D. Eisenhower, *The White House Years: Waging Peace 1956–1961*, (London: Heineman, 1966), p. 192.
34. Harold Macmillan, *Riding the Storm 1956–1959* (London: Macmillan, 1971), p. 230.
35. Ibid., pp. 233–4.
36. Roger Owen, 'The Economic Consequences of the Suez Crisis for Egypt', in Wm Roger Louis and Roger Owen (eds), *Suez 1956: The Crisis and its Consequences* (Oxford: Clarendon Press, 1989), p. 365.
37. For further information on the Bermuda Conference see Macmillan, *Riding the Storm*, pp. 240–3, and Eisenhower, *The White House*, pp. 241–5.

38. PRO, CAB134/2341/O.M.E.(58)10, official committee on Middle East oil, note by the Ministry of Power and Ministry of Transport and Civil Aviation, 4 April 1958.
39. PRO, FO371/133881/V1533/3, Middle East–Mediterranean group, problems of Middle Eastern oil, part 1, April 1958.
40. PRO, FO371/133880/V1532/2, Foreign Office minute, Middle East oil pipelines, 17 January 1958.
41. PRO, FO371/127202/UES1171/56, Caccia (Washington) to Lloyd, 13 March 1957, and *FRUS*, Vol. 12, 1955–57, guarantees for maintenance of Middle East oil through pipelines (Agreed US–UK paper), 16 March 1957, pp. 460–1.
42. *FRUS*, Vol. 12, 1955–57, oil pipelines in the Middle East, background paper prepared in the State Department, 19 April 1957, p. 515.
43. Ibid., memorandum from the Assistant Secretary of State for Near Eastern Affairs, 13 April 1957, pp. 501–2.
44. PRO, FO371/127204/UES1171/90, Falle (Foreign Office), minute, 3 April 1957.
45. *FRUS*, Vol. 12, 1955–57, memorandum from the Assistant Secretary of State for Near Eastern Affairs, to the Acting Secretary of State, 13 April 1957, p. 499.
46. Ibid., p. 500.
47. Ibid., memorandum from the Deputy Under-Secretary of State for Administration, 20 June 1957, pp. 548–9.
48. Keith Kyle, *Suez* (London: Weidenfeld & Nicolson, 1992), p. 69.
49. Ibid., p. 100.
50. PRO, T236/4604/OF252/043, Bailey (Treasury) minute, 10 March 1958.
51. PRO, DEFE5/75/COS(57)96, command organisation in the Middle East and Arabian Peninsula, 24 April 1957.
52. Ibid.
53. PRO, CAB 34/2340, note for the Prime Minister's Commonwealth tour, and FO371/115921/VR1266/8, Laurence (Levant Department) minute, 25 November 1957.
54. David Ben-Gurion, *Yehud Veichud* [Singularity and Mission] (Tel-Aviv: Ma'arachot, 1971: 1982), pp. 296–7.
55. Ibid., p. 302.
56. Ibid., p. 318. Emphasis is added.
57. PRO, FO371/134267/VR1014/1, Rundall to Lloyd, 6 January 1958.
58. BGA, Ben-Gurion diary, no specific date, 1958.
59. Ben-Gurion, *Yehud Veichud*, pp. 331–5.
60. Ibid., pp. 330–1.
61. Ibid., pp. 332–3.
62. Gideon Rafael, *Besod Leumim* [Destination Peace] (Jerusalem: Edanim, 1981), p. 817.
63. FO371/128107/VR1052/19, Rundall to Lloyd, 27 July 1957.
64. PRO, FO371/134286/VR1051/66, Tesh (Foreign Office) minute, 12 November 1958.
65. ISA, HZ331/8, MABAR to London, 12 June 1957. The same discussion appears in the British and the Israeli documents; for the British version see: PRO, FO371/128107/VR1052/14, Rundall to Lloyd, 11 June 1957.
66. PRO, FO371/128087/VR1015/10, Rundall to Lloyd, 1 August 1957.
67. Ibid.
68. Ibid.
69. Ibid.
70. Ibid.
71. PRO, FO371/128087/VR1015/10, Rundall to Lloyd, 1 August 1957.
72. Ibid.
73. Ibid.

74. Ibid.
75. Ibid.
76. *Hansard*, Vol. 566, col. 1330, 14 March 1957.
77. *Hansard*, Vol. 556, col. 1330, 14 March 1957.
78. ISA, HZ334/11, 25 November 1957, and HZ328/9, MABAR to London, 3 September 1957.
79. PRO, FO371/128201/VR1533/6, Falle (Foreign Office) minute, 15 July 1957.
80. PRO, FO371/128201/VR1533/21, record of conversation between Selwyn Lloyd and the directors of BP and Shell, Lloyd to Rundall, 29 July 1957.
81. PRO, FO371/128201/VR1533/6, Falle (Foreign Office) minute, 15 July 1957.
82. PRO, FO371/128201/VR1533/21, Lloyd to Rundall, 29 July 1957.
83. ISA, HZ232/9, the file includes correspondence from various dates on the subject of the Arab boycott; see for example survey by the Israeli Foreign Office, 22 April 1956.
84. PRO, FO 371/128201/VR1533/20, Jewish Board of Deputies to Lloyd, 26 July 1957.
85. ISA, HZ331/8, MABAR to London, 15 July 1957.
86. ISA, HZ325/9, Elath to Meir, 15 July 1957.
87. PRO, FO371/128181/VR115/40, Chadwick (Head of Economic Relations Department) minute, 7 August 1957.
88. PRO, FO371/127213/UES1171/282, Rundall to Beely, 4 November 1957.
89. Ibid.
90. PRO, FO127214/UE1171/325, Sir Paul Gore Booth, Deputy Under-Secretary of State, 2 November 1957.
91. ISA, HZ334/11, Bartur (Head of Economic Division) to Zur (Paris) and Elath (London), 25 November 1957.
92. PRO, FO371/134336/VR1151/7, Wright (Foreign Office) minute, 29 January 1958.
93. ISA, HZ325/9, Elath to Israeli Foreign Office, 9 August 1957.
94. PRO, FO371/128107/VR1052/20, 1 August 1957.
95. ISA, HZ325/9, Israeli embassy London to Jerusalem, 9 August 1957.
96. *Hansard*, Vol. 574, cols 1738–1754, 2 August 1957.
97. Benjamin Shwadran, *The Middle East, Oil and the Great Powers* (Jerusalem: Israel Universities Press, 1973), p. 457.
98. Ibid.
99. *FRUS*, Vol. 12, 1955–57, oil pipelines in the Middle East, paper prepared by the State Department, 19 April 1957, p. 517.
100. Schwadran, *The Middle East*, pp. 454–5.
101. ISA, HZ325/9, Bartur to Zur (Paris), 20 November 1956.
102. *FRUS*, Vol. 12, 1955–57, oil pipelines in the Middle East, 19 March 1957, p. 515.
103. PRO, PREM11/1838/B.C.(P)2, 22 March 1957.
104. ISA, HZ331/8, Avner (London) to Shenerson, Head of MABAR, 9 March 1957.
105. *FRUS*, Vol. 17, 1955–57, Mollet to Eisenhower, 14 March 1957, pp. 415–16. For further information on French policy after Suez see: PRO, FO371/127728. On the French attitude towards Israel see, for example, PRO, FO371/127728/V10317/7, Young (Paris) to Foreign Office, 28 March 1957.
106. *FRUS*, Vol. 17, 1955–57, Mollet to Eisenhower, 14 March 1957, pp. 415–16.
107. Michael Bar-Zohar, *Gesher Al Hayyam Hatichon* [Bridge Over the Mediterranean] (Tel-Aviv: Am-Hassefer, 1964), p. 180.
108. PRO, FO371/128093/VR10317/3 Nicholls to Lloyd, 4 February 1957.
109. Bar-Zohar, *Gesher Al Hayyam Hatichon*, p. 188.
110. Ibid., p. 189.

—7—
Before the Storm: From the Jordanian Crisis to the Lebanese Turbulence, April 1957–June 1958

'Out of the north an evil shall break forth.' (Jeremiah 1: 14)

THE IMPACT OF THE GROWTH OF ARAB NATIONALISM ON ANGLO-ISRAELI RELATIONS

THE SUEZ AFFAIR left a strong impact on the Middle East and consequently the period following Suez was marked by upheavals and destabilisation in the Arab world. Nasserism and Pan-Arabism became popular among young Arabs and spread quickly through the region, consequently causing difficulties for the more conservative states.

The first country to be subjected to an upsurge in Arab nationalism was Jordan. The internal unrest in Jordan reached a peak during April 1957, when army officers led by the Chief of Staff, General Abu-Nuwar, attempted, with Syrian assistance, to organise a coup against Hussein with the object of removing him from power. Hussein's problems had begun at the end of 1956 when he faced increasing opposition to his leadership from Said Suleiman Nabulsi, the Prime Minister, who wanted greater co-operation with Nasser. In an attempt to reduce criticism, the King, in late December, asked the British to terminate the Anglo-Jordanian treaty, while the Nabulsi government reached an agreement with Egypt, Syria and Saudi Arabia for financial help and alternatives to British assistance. This agreement would be for ten years and was to take effect from the date of the exchange of instruments of ratification in Cairo.[1] Macmillan and his government were advised by their Ambassador in Amman that, in view of public feeling in Jordan, the British government would gain sympathy if they agreed to replace the treaty with a new arrangement. This could involve a general withdrawal of British troops, apart from the RAF, while leaving behind certain military installations which Jordan would agree to maintain.[2] As the old agreement held minimal strategic importance to Britain, especially since the signing of the

Baghdad Pact which involved expensive commitments, and in view of the cost of subsidising Jordan, the British government was willing to start negotiations about the termination of the treaty as soon as possible.[3] However, although the King saw that it was in his interests to terminate the treaty, he was also aware of the vulnerability of his position which could best be guaranteed by British forces, and saw that once they withdrew he would be at the mercy of Nabulsi and his allies. Nevertheless, on 12 February 1957, an agreement was reached by which the two countries agreed to the cancellation of the treaty as of 1 March.[4]

The shift of the Nabulsi government away from a pro-Western policy was made even more evident when, on 4 April, the Prime Minister announced the government's decision to establish relations with the Soviet Union.[5] A few days later, on 13 April, the Nabulsi government went even further and began an attempted coup d'état against Hussein. The faction that aimed to remove Hussein was a group of officers on the Egyptian model who had first met in early April at an establishment called the 'Gundenia', with Nabulsi and Abu-Nuwar also attending the meeting. The second meeting took place during the afternoon and evening of 13 April and most of the Nabulsi government attended.[6] Their aim was to force the King to abdicate, and to declare Jordan a republic. Contingency plans were made to ensure that the coup would not fail due to either Iraqi or Israeli intervention.[7] Apparently, however, Abu-Nuwar and some of his associates decided to warn the King that the government would be reformed by Nabulsi, and Hussein was thus prepared for the challenge.[8] When the Commander of the First Armoured Car Regiment ordered his men to take action against Hussein, they refused to obey. Then on 14 April, there was nearly a clash with a Syrian regiment already in Jordan, which had started marching on Irbid. After some fighting at Zerqa, Hussein arrested Abu-Nuwar and other civilians, and General Ali Hiyani, who was faithful to the King, succeeded Abu-Nuwar as Chief of Staff.[9] The King subsequently took strong measures to ensure his own safety and placed the police and security forces under army command. He abolished all political parties and declared martial law. In addition, a day and night curfew was declared in Amman, the old city of Jerusalem, Nablus, Ramallah and Irbid.[10] On 26 April, 500 leading left-wing and communist activists were arrested by the army, and Suleiman Toukan, the Defence Minister, was sworn in as military governor of Jordan. The following day, a military court was set up to try all cases arising out of the political crisis.[11] Hussein, aware of his sensitive position, asked the United States for aid. The US administration was keen to give firm backing to the King and in a measure of support dispatched the Sixth Fleet to the eastern Mediterranean.[12]

The situation in Jordan also caused concern in Britain. On 14 April, the British Ambassador to the United States, Sir Harold Caccia, on instructions from the Foreign Office, asked about the possible US reaction to British intervention if the need should arise. The Ambassador stated to the Acting Secretary of State, Christian Herter, that, in Selwyn Lloyd's view, Hussein's cry for help was an act of desperation. Herter replied that because the situation in Jordan at the moment was so fluid it was difficult to have an accurate picture of Hussein's position.[13] In addition, there were growing concerns about Israel's reaction if the status quo in Jordan changed. The Foreign Office's Levant Department itself expressed a similar concern that a change in the status quo might lead to renewed Arab–Israeli fighting.[14] The State Department, aware of the great sensitivity of Israel to events in Jordan, was quick to warn Israel against military intervention in the event of Iraqi assistance. Meanwhile, Nuri el-Said emphasised to Sir Michael Wright, the British Ambassador to Iraq, the importance of preventing Israeli retaliation if Iraqi forces had to come to Hussein's aid, and stressed that Britain and the United States should warn Israel against interfering.[15] Dulles therefore told Eban, on 24 April, that precipitous action by Israel in this case could be the one thing that would unite the Arab world.[16] The US Ambassador to Israel, Lawson, also conveyed the US position in this matter and warned Israel against military action if events in Jordan deteriorated. The State Department wanted to assure Israel that the United States was fully aware of her position on the question of Iraqi forces stationed in Jordan, but felt that the Iraqi forces would only enter Jordan to maintain the status quo. Given that this aim accorded with Israel's interests, the latter therefore should not oppose such an action and should instead exercise restraint.[17] On 18 April, Lawson informed the State Department that he had conveyed the US position to Ben-Gurion and that the Prime Minister had only asked him how close to the River Jordan the Iraqi forces proposed to come.[18]

In a further discussion between Golda Meir and Lawson on 19 April, the Foreign Minister assured the Ambassador that, although Israel would like to keep out of the dispute and had no wish to become involved in Jordan's upheavals, it would conduct its policy according to the general impact on Israel's position. Israel would watch the Iraqi movements carefully and would not tolerate any escalation of tensions on its own eastern border resulting from the internal instability in Jordan. Meir then assured Lawson that Israel had no intention of taking action as long as the status quo was maintained.[19] Eban also told Dulles that the Israeli government would avoid anything that might play into Nasser's hands[20] and suggested that it was important to avoid giving the impression that the United States had warned Israel.[21] Although Jordan became quieter, it was only a matter of time before further trouble erupted.

THE IMPACT OF THE EISENHOWER DOCTRINE

In addition to acting swiftly over Jordan, the United States also adopted a more general role in the region. In an attempt to broaden US support and reduce Soviet influence, Eisenhower sent James Richard, a Democrat from South Carolina and former chairman of the Senate Committee of Foreign Affairs, as a special envoy in order to find an effective method of co-operating with countries in the region to ensure their security and their economic progress. He was authorised to determine which countries wished to co-operate in this effort and to make commitments for US aid under the auspices of the Eisenhower doctrine.[22] He subsequently visited several Middle Eastern countries, among them Israel.

The Israeli government generally welcomed this initiative, but had some reservations and was cautious about openly announcing their support. The positive side of the doctrine, in Ben-Gurion's view, was the fact that it would decrease Israel's isolation.[23] The main disadvantage was that it did not state the United States' commitment to military assistance for any country in the region, and this meant that Israel would not be guaranteed this automatically.[24] Ben-Gurion told Richard, at their meeting on 4 May, that Israel was a small country and that in the event of an Arab attack, the granting of American military aid, even if provided immediately, could be too late. In Richard's meeting with the Israeli Finance Minister, Levi Eshkol, and Golda Meir, the two ministers expressed Israel's support for the West, and Meir, in a typically dramatic manner, compared Israel's firm opposition to communism with Jewish resistance to Hitler. Israel had no choice, she said, but to 'live or die with the free world'.[25] She repeated Ben-Gurion's line that the doctrine had little value unless it gave Israel almost automatic help.[26] The second reason for the Israeli government's caution in accepting the doctrine was the effect that such an announcement could have on the flow of Jewish immigrants from communist countries. It was a major concern to the Israeli government that the possibility of these Jews emigrating to Israel should not be jeopardised. Soviet Jewry and the Jews in the Eastern bloc were one of the main factors that influenced Israel's policy towards the USSR. Israel, therefore, tried to minimise confrontation with the Soviets, despite the latter's hostile attitude. The Israeli government did not want to jeopardise the fragile link it still had with Soviet Jewry, mainly through the Israeli embassy in Moscow. Once again it was clear that the freedom of Jews to emigrate to Israel was seen as one of the major considerations of Israeli foreign policy.

THE SYRIAN CRISIS

Events in the summer of 1957 showed, however, that the recent Western efforts to get more countries into their camp had not been successful; on the contrary, Britain and the United States faced a growing challenge to their supremacy, particularly from Syria.

In 1957, the situation in Syria rapidly deteriorated and there were indications of growing Soviet penetration. Since 1955, Syria had been dominated by a group of extreme Arab nationalist army officers and civilians whose chief common denominator was hatred of 'Western imperialism'.[27] Two key positions in the coalition government were held by members of the extremist Socialist Renaissance Party and while, officially, the Communist Party had no part in the government, its influence in both government and army was beyond question.[28] From what is now known of the communist movement in the Arab world, especially in Syria, it was a small grouping of the semi-educated from various minorities. The United States and Britain watched developments in Syria with concern, bearing in mind past examples of Soviet intervention, such as the seizing of power in eastern Europe (e.g. Hungary in 1947 and Czechoslovakia in 1948). Further involvement of the Soviets appeared in March when an important contract for Syria's first oil refinery was awarded to the Czechoslovak Techno-Export Company and this was followed by a left-wing victory in the May by-elections.[29]

Syrian resentment towards the West had already grown into open hostility in the spring of 1957, after it became clear that Richard's tour was resulting in the shaping of a Middle Eastern alliance hostile to them, and this antagonism became worse as a result of US assistance to Jordan during the April crisis.[30] Anthony Nutting, the Deputy Under-Secretary of State at the Foreign Office, held a meeting with the Syrian Prime Minister on 27 April which left Nutting with the impression that the situation was grim and that Syria was on its way to becoming a Soviet satellite. He told Ian Scott from the British embassy in Beirut that the Prime Minister was rude and very anti-Western. The Syrian Prime Minister opposed Nutting's suggestion that Syria obtain aid from the United States in order to balance the help from the

Soviets, because he asserted that US assistance implied treaty commitments even if not specifically stated.[31] Selwyn Lloyd told the Israeli Ambassador in London, on 29 April, that Britain felt grave anxiety about the situation in Syria and that the Syrian authorities wanted to reach an agreement with the Soviets.[32]

Events, however, came to a head in August. On 6 August, the Syrian Defence Minister, Khalid al-Azm, signed an extensive technical and economic agreement with the Soviet Union in Moscow, and on 17 August, the Commander-in-Chief, Nizam al-Din, retired without any explanation and was replaced by Afif al-Bizri, who was known for his sympathetic attitude towards the Soviet Union.[33] US–Syrian relations reached their lowest level in August, not simply because of the pro-Soviet tilt in Damascus, but also because of the Syrian decision to expel three American diplomats who were accused of plotting against the Syrian government, a plot which they claimed was conducted by the United States in league with Syrian, Jordanian and Lebanese officers.[34] On 12 August, the Syrians surrounded the US embassy in Damascus with armed security forces.[35]

The developments in Syria caused great concern for her neighbours – Iraq, Turkey and Israel – and to Britain and the United States. In a State Department memorandum from the Assistant Secretary of State for the Middle East, on 13 August, it was recommended that the United States should protest to the Syrian government about radio and newspaper attacks on them and the expulsion of their diplomats.[36] Subsequently, on 14 August, William Rountree met the Syrian chargé d'affaires, Mamun Haumi, and protested against Syrian actions towards the United States over the past few days. He explained to Haumi that the US government had declared Ambassador Zeinddine and Second Secretary Zakria *personae non gratae* and expressed the desire that the Ambassador should not return to the United States.[37] The expulsion of the American diplomats, combined with the appointment of al-Bizri, brought Washington and London closer together over policy in the region. Dulles confirmed to Caccia that he viewed the threat of communism in Syria very seriously and that it might justify US support for covert action by Syria's neighbours.[38]

The deterioration of the situation caused grave concern in Britain, particularly over the future of the oil pipeline that ran through Syria. The pipeline could handle some 25 million tons of oil a year from Iraq and a further 12 million from Saudi Arabia. It was feared that if Syria became heavily influenced by the Soviets they would try to sabotage the flow of oil through the pipeline. If the Soviets failed to convince the Syrian government, the former might try instead to do so through Syrian extremist groups within the army or with the help of members of the Communist Party.[39] In his diary, Macmillan revealed the dilemma his government faced: on the one hand the British government wanted to prevent further Soviet involvement in Syria, but, on the other, they did not wish to take action which could damage the flow of oil. Macmillan believed that if the pipeline was cut for a long time it could threaten Iraq's position and stability.[40] Because of the Suez experience, he wanted to be sure that if his government took such a risk the United States would stay the course. 'We could not again', he wrote, 'be pushed forwards by Dulles with some attractive plan and then left in the lurch.'[41]

The question was what would be the best method of dealing with the crisis: a military intervention or standing aside and watching the Syrians become a sort of Soviet satellite. At the very beginning of the crisis, during July and to some degree still during August, it seemed that the United States would do something to prevent the drift in Syria. By early autumn 1957, there was still no change in the Syrian situation and Dulles told the British Ambassador to the United Nations, Sir Pearson Dixon, on 17 September, that the deterioration in the situation had to be halted and that he agreed with the British assumption that neither Jordan nor the Lebanon would be able to protect themselves against a communist Syria. The Ambassador's impression, however, was that, in spite of Dulles' intention to stop Soviet influence spreading in Syria, the Secretary of State did not have a clear idea about the best method of achieving this. Dulles also told the Ambassador that he thought that, if no action were taken by the West, Turkey or Israel would take the initiative, although the Ambassador doubted whether the Secretary was convinced of his theory.[42]

Contrary to their policy during the Suez crisis, and as a result of the Eisenhower doctrine, the US government tried to take some measures to tackle the problem. They moved the Sixth Fleet to a position where it could exert US naval power if necessary and kept in close touch with the British government. In fact, it brought about the establishment of the Syrian Working Group, which aimed to co-ordinate diplomatic, military and intelligence activities.[43] In addition, Loy Henderson, the Deputy Under-Secretary of State for Administration, was sent to Ankara, where he met King Hussein, the Crown Prince of Iraq and King Faisal. Although there was a general agreement as to the gravity of the situation in Syria, there was no consensus about what action should be taken.[44]

The British government agreed with the United States that it appeared as if Syria was to become a base for military and subversive activities designed to destroy the independence of other countries in the area.[45] However, Macmillan did not think that the best method was to show the 'iron fist' of the United States. In a letter to Dulles on 23 August, he outlined the delicate position Britain and the United States faced in dealing with Syria. He wrote that, on the one hand, they could not afford to allow Syria to become a Soviet satellite, but that, on the other hand, any action they might take could have grave consequences. Macmillan noted that the British government could not ignore the control that Syria had over the pipeline. 'For the moment,' he concluded, 'I am sure that the West should not take the lead in opposition.'[46] Macmillan felt that if the Americans undertook a successful operation then they should be supported and welcomed, but that ,on the other hand, the United States should not be stimulated to do something 'which (if goes off half-cocked) will be fatal'.[47] According to Eisenhower, Macmillan thought that the one positive result of the crisis would be the realisation among the Arab states that communism and not Israel was their mortal enemy.[48]

The best solution to the crisis seemed to be to encourage neighbouring states such as Turkey and Iraq to take the initiative. They were very concerned about the possibility of Syria's close association with the Soviets. However, it appeared that Turkey was the only country willing to take some action, as a Soviet presence in Syria would outflank the Baghdad Pact and threaten Turkey's rear. The Iraqi government, on the other hand, was too frightened to take any initiative against Syria. On 21 July, the Iraqi Acting Secretary for Foreign Affairs, Ali Mumtaz, told Richard Beaumont, the British Chargé d'Affaires in Baghdad, that there was no possibility of Iraqi military action and that Iraq did not want to give the Syrians any excuse to sever the pipeline. The Iraqi Prime Minister also wrote a letter emphasising this point,[49] and Nuri told Sir Michael Wright, on 11 September, that any action against Syria could be dangerous and might lead to a process of collapse in the Middle East that would favour communism.[50] The Iraqis were also worried about possible Israeli action and urged the British government to put pressure on Israel to stay on the sidelines. In addition, they wanted to avoid a situation in which the West would take action that could be seen as anti-Arab and pro-Israeli.[51] Nuri told Wright that it was important to spike Nasser's assertion that the West was acting in the interests of Israel, and urged the United States and the UK to announce a statement on the situation in Syria, while being careful to divorce the statement from the problem of Israel.[52]

One of the main concerns of the British government, the US administration and regional countries such as Iraq was to make sure that Israel held back and demonstrated a policy of restraint. The fear was that if Israel took action against Syria it would play into Syrian and Soviet hands, rally the other Arab countries around Syria and weaken the position of countries like Jordan, Lebanon and Iraq.[53] The situation in Syria, however, caused grave concern in Israel not only because it meant that Syria was heading towards a more extreme nationalist policy, but also because it provided the Soviets with a greater hold on the region close to the Israeli border. The Israeli government tried to emphasise, in Washington and in London, the danger that the situation in Syria posed to the region as a whole and not just to Israel, stressing that Soviet penetration was not just a regional danger but also a global threat.[54] The British government and the US administration tried their best to restrain the Israeli government from taking military action. Macmillan wrote to Dulles on 23 August that the British government had urged caution on Israel and would continue to do so.[55] Fortunately, Ben-Gurion assured Baxter, the counsellor at the US embassy in Tel-Aviv, that Israel had no intention of causing trouble in Syria and expressed warm regard for Dulles' desire to exchange views on Syria.[56] While he told Baxter that it was impossible to distinguish between Syria and the Soviets, and expressed his fears that the weapons the Syrians had obtained from the Soviets would ultimately be used against Israel, he also promised that Israel would not take action against Syria and would not provide an excuse for a Soviet attack on Israel through Syria.[57]

Israel made these assurances in the hope that the West would take action to stop Syria drifting any further towards the Soviet Union. Reuven Siloah, Michael Comay and Yacov Herzog of the Israeli Foreign Ministry told Loy Henderson, on 28 August, that every day of delay increased the danger of the threat posed by Syria.[58] Reuven Siloah, Minister at the Israeli embassy in Washington, said that one could draw an analogy with Egypt in 1955 when the West made an attempt to play down the significance of the Czech arms deal, and he observed that it was Israel's belief that Syria might be more easily turned into a Soviet satellite than Egypt because there was already an indigenous communist movement. 'Unless something was done to halt it,' he warned, 'there was a possibility of another Hungary.'[59] Although this scenario was not likely, it was an example of the way the Israelis used the fear of communism to manipulate the West.

While Ben-Gurion promised that his government would not take any action that would jeopardise the situation, there was still great apprehension in London and Washington about the possibility of a desperate act by Israel if the situation deteriorated further. Against this background we can understand the close discussions between Eban and Dulles and the British attempt to keep in contact with the Israelis on this matter. It was Francis Rundall who, on 27 August, suggested the need for close consultation with Israel as a means of preventing a sense of isolation in Israel which might drive her to take military action.[60] The Foreign Office agreed with this analysis and Michael Rose, in a Foreign Office minute of 27 August, recommended acceptance of Rundall's suggestion as a means of reassuring Israel that the British government would not allow Syria's neighbours to acquiesce in the new situation. He emphasised that it would also enable Britain and the United States to place more restraint on Israel, thus influencing it to move away from using its military power.[61] However, he warned against giving any impression that Britain was siding with Israel, which would embarrass Britain's Arab friends.[62] The Israeli government also approached the British embassy in Turkey in order to gather more information on developments in Syria. The Israeli Chargé d'Affaires called on the Head of the Chancery on 27 August, and asked for news of what action Britain, the United States and Turkey might take, stating that his government was 'in complete darkness' and very anxious.[63] Alon, the Israeli Chargé d'Affaires, said that in Israel's view it would be a mistake to adopt a soft option; on the contrary, what was needed was firm action.[64]

When Ambassador Eban met Dulles on 12 September, he carried a message from Ben-Gurion expressing the official Israeli line that the situation in Syria was a matter of concern not only to Israel but to the whole region, and stressed that 'Israel would need steady nerves to live in the Middle East during the days ahead'.[65] Elath, meanwhile, assured Lloyd that Israel was determined to avoid steps that could only serve Egyptian and Syrian aims.[66]

In a conversation between Rundall and Comay on 26 September, the latter emphasised that there was still a danger to Jordan and Iraq in the future, but that Israel would remain on the sidelines and appreciated the importance of keeping tensions to a minimum. He said that Israel accepted the American thesis that they must offer no provocation and basically agreed with the US position, although they considered the tone Eisenhower and Dulles used against Syria to be too mild.[67]

It is clear that the Israeli government wanted to see military action against Syria but it also hoped that this might be the right time to try to obtain a specific security guarantee from the United States. A letter from Ben-Gurion to Dulles, on 31 October, was an attempt to proceed along these lines by emphasising the danger to the region. Ben-Gurion stressed his hope that, with the rise of tensions, the United States might see fit to reconsider its relations with Israel and enter into some special agreement or alliance. He tried to emphasise that the situation in Syria was not irreversible and that everything depended on the US reaction.[68] Dulles' reply to Ben-Gurion, on 12 November, was a repetition of the standard US policy towards Israel. In his letter the Secretary of State assured Ben-Gurion that the United States had indicated to the Soviets their interest in maintaining the independence and integrity of all the states in the region, including Israel. However, he was inclined to accept Ben-Gurion's suggestions and stressed that the US administration continued to believe that the Israeli armed forces should retain their military superiority and capability to deal with any threat that might arise from within the region. Dulles wrote that Israel's membership of the United Nations and the strength of US forces provided Israel with sufficient protection against external attack and were a better defence than rearmament.[69] When Edward Lawson, the American Ambassador to Israel, delivered the message to Ben-Gurion, the latter was disappointed that Dulles' views did not indicate any change in US policy. He told Siloah and Comay, 'it is very general'[70] and, according to Bar-Zohar, Ben-Gurion's biographer, the Prime Minister said that it was a 'typical' Dulles letter.[71]

Although the United States considered the possibility of a covert operation, in the end no action was taken against the Syrians. It seems that Nasser's intervention at Latkia in northern Syria, through the landing of Egyptian troops, removed the immediate danger of a communist coup, and this, combined with the lack of co-operation from Iraq, Jordan and the Lebanon, caused the United States to cancel their plan.[72] Loy Henderson concluded that, with the exception of the Turks, the capacity and readiness of Syria's neighbouring countries to take military action in the event of border difficulties seemed to be slight.[73] It seems also that the Israeli government realised that the chances of its neighbours co-operating with the West in a joint military action were slim.

The crisis was important as it demonstrated the great dependency of both Israel and Britain on the United States, and their inability to take independent action. Furthermore, the crisis showed the lack of a unified will in the Arab world to combine against communism, and that fear existed in Riyadh, Amman and Baghdad about the possible implications of any military intervention for their fragile regimes. The events in Syria also showed the growing Israeli concern and wariness about the Soviet threat and the effect of the Cold War on the region. Although it might be argued that Israel played on the West's fears of increased Soviet involvement in the region in order to pressure the West and especially the United States to take action in Syria, one should also realise that Israel's fear of the Soviets was genuine.

THE SOVIET UNION'S PENETRATION AND ISRAELI POLICY

The increasing Soviet influence in the region was one of the major topics at a meeting of Israeli diplomats in Europe. At this meeting in Paris, held in February 1958, the diplomats acknowledged the fact that the Soviet Union had become to some extent Israel's neighbour. Meir said that she had no reason to believe that the Soviets had changed their attitude towards Israel, and that in her view they would not hesitate to destroy the state of Israel. She believed, however, that, despite the difficulties that existed between the two countries, Israel should keep all communication lines with the Soviet Union open.[74] Discussions between the Soviet Foreign Minister, Andrei Gromyko, and Meir, on 30 September 1957, had clearly revealed the hostile attitude Moscow had adopted towards Israel and made it obvious that there was little prospect of better relations between the two countries. Gromyko accused Israel, at this meeting, of adopting an aggressive policy which might lead to dangerous developments and warned that a continuation of Israel's present policy might endanger it.[75] Meir had replied that the Soviet government's policy did not help to further the cause of peace, emphasising that Israel was willing to meet the Arab leaders at any time in order to sign a peace agreement. Gromyko said that this was the way to reach peace, and argued that the Arab countries had the same right as Israel to obtain arms for their security.[76] He said that the Israeli government had adopted an aggressive attitude towards the Arabs states, as was evident during the Sinai war, and it would not be forgotten easily by 'peace-loving countries'.[77] However, the Israeli government did not want to attack the Soviets publicly. Israel preferred to prevent further deterioration in the relationship and reach some accommodation with the Soviets, if only for the sake of Soviet Jewry.

GUILDHALL REVISITED

In the light of the situation in Syria, Nuri el-Said was eager to convince Britain and the United States to launch a new initiative which would provide some formula for an Arab–Israeli settlement, in particular a solution to the refugee problem and a frontier adjustment.[78] During the Bermuda Conference, Eisenhower and Macmillan had already stressed the need for an Arab–Israeli settlement. However, the two had agreed that in the current situation in the Middle East it was hard to foresee how a general peace settlement between Israel and its neighbours could be achieved in the near future because the Arabs were divided and Israel was confident and in no mood for concessions.[79] Therefore, it was impossible to provide a formula of agreement under which the Arabs and the Israelis could live happily together, although the Foreign Office still believed that it was possible for a settlement to be negotiated with a third party exercising pressure on one side. The Foreign Office recognised that Britain was not in a position to put pressure on either side, but the United States on the other hand could pressurise Israel. With some obvious regret, the Foreign Office doubted whether the United States would want to exercise its power to put pressure on Israel, a step that would have been welcomed by Her Majesty's Government.[80] Hence, it is clear that the Suez war had not led to any fundamental change in British policy *vis-à-vis* the Arab–Israeli conflict, nor to a new era in Anglo-Israeli relations. This was also evident if one analysed British policy in other areas, for instance arms supply or trade and economic relations. The only effect Suez had on British decision-makers was the realisation that in conducting their policy in the region, the British government was not the leading player and had to rely heavily on the United States. However, this realisation did not prevent the British Foreign Secretary, Selwyn Lloyd, from addressing the issue of a comprehensive peace settlement and from again offering advice on the matter.

In October 1957, the British embassy in Washington prepared a draft proposal on the Arab–Israeli situation, stating that the main problems in the region were those of the refugee and border questions. A just settlement, the proposal suggested, should accord recognition of the right of repatriation for the Arab refugees who desired it, and should make adequate provision for the compensation and resettlement of those who chose not to return. The proposal also put forward a suggestion for the reshaping of the frontiers along the lines of the old Guildhall plan.[81] However, the proposal was not welcomed by the State Department. In a covering memorandum to Dulles, sent on 22 November, Rountree advised against US participation in such a statement, because it would alienate Israel and gain no support from the Arabs. In his view, the Arab states might perceive it as another attempt to score points in the face of Soviet success in the area, and this could provoke a belligerent reaction as the proposal would be seen as attempting to put pressure on them. Moreover, he doubted the wisdom of the United States forming a close association with the British whose reputation in the region had not yet been restored.[82] In a meeting between Dulles, Rountree, Lloyd and Sir Harold Caccia on 22 November, Rountree stated that the draft statement was a departure from US policy. He said that the offer to permit all refugees who desired to return to do so, and, at the same time, to seek frontier modification based on a compromise between the 1947 resolution and the present frontiers, was more far-reaching than any previous US suggestion and unacceptable.[83]

It is easy to imagine Israel's reaction to the proposal when it got a hint of the suggested plan. Israel's worst suspicions of the British government were confirmed, adding more bitterness to the already complicated relations between the two countries. All the attempts of the British Ambassadors to Israel and of the Foreign Office officials to convince Israel that Britain was not one-sided and did not aim to sacrifice Israel's interests appeared merely as a deception. It is not clear how the Israelis were informed of the British proposal, but the Israeli embassy in Washington reported, on 28 October, that Willie Morris, the First Secretary at the British embassy in Washington, had appeared at the State Department and handed over a proposal for a joint US–UK statement on the Middle East, which was almost a repetition of the 'Guildhall plan'. According to the Israeli embassy, the State Department was surprised and passed it on with some caution to Dulles, who read it and 'jumped out of his skin'.[84] When Dulles asked Lloyd, who was on a visit to the United States, for an explanation, the latter said that it was an idea put together by some experts in the Foreign Office, but that if the Secretary opposed it it would be better to forget it.[85] We cannot possibly say whether the Israeli description of Dulles' reaction completely corresponded with the real version, but it was evident that Dulles did not appreciate or approve of the British suggestion. Dulles said to Lloyd and British officials on 25 October that there had been a similar statement in 1955, which had no results, and that, in his view, the Arab world was gradually becoming more concerned with the communist threat than with the Palestinian issue. Selwyn Lloyd reluctantly agreed that the time was not right for such an initiative.[86] Already in an earlier discussion, on 22 October, Lloyd had admitted to Dulles that the statement did not address the most important aspects of the Palestinian issue, which were the increasing dangers of Israel's immigration policy.[87]

Israeli fears were reinforced by another event, for Nuri's visit to the United States in December highlighted once more the unsolved problem of the two main issues – frontiers and refugees – and also the question of Jewish immigration to Israel. Nuri's main aim was to gain the support of the British and US administrations for a Palestinian settlement based on the 1947 UN resolution. Nuri argued that, if the refugees were settled along the lines of the resolution, 70 per cent of them could return to their homes.[88] He tried to play the card of the dangers of the Cold War and the benefits the Soviets had gained as a result of the Arab–Israeli wars, and said that the United States could get Israel to co-operate if they wanted to.[89] 'To listen only to Ben-Gurion,' he said, 'will help only Russia.'[90] However, Nuri failed to convince Dulles of the logic of his suggestion. Dulles' response was that Nuri's policy meant that in order to solve one problem they would have to create another one, because the areas previously settled by Palestinians were now populated by Jewish people and '500,000 Jewish people could not be driven into the sea'.[91] Dulles also told Nuri that the number of refugees had grown since 1947, and concluded that in any case, 'The clock could not be turned back.'[92]

Nuri's visit to Washington raised concern among Israeli decision-makers that they might be forced to agree to concessions if the United States was willing to fall in with Nuri's plan. In a meeting on 10 December, Elath warned Michael Hadow and Lloyd against any attempt to renew any plan which would lead to major changes to the frontiers. He said that any attempt to implement the latter would face strong resistance from Israel and that any party that tried to impose it would have to use force. However, the Ambassador continued, if their view was only theoretical then they must be aware that it could only increase Israel's suspicion of Britain.[93] Lloyd replied that, in the Guildhall speech, Eden had only meant that there should be a mutual frontier arrangement, but he was reluctant to answer the Ambassador's query about whether Lloyd's explanation of the Guildhall plan was the formal opinion of Her Majesty's Government. Lloyd also accused Israel of being too sensitive and that it showed a lack of appreciation of Britain. Elath responded by stating that Israel would be very happy if Anglo-Israeli relations were based on genuine friendship and understanding. He emphasised that Israel had great respect for the British people and their democracy. The Jews honoured Balfour's memory and everyone in Britain who had helped them establish their state. Israel was the only country, he said, that, in spite of all the troubles Britain had caused it, was not anti-British, but British policy towards Israel was discriminatory, for instance its arms policy. The Ambassador stressed that Lloyd was not in a position to be disappointed with Israel, as one could not forget that it was Britain who had, over the years, adopted a policy that had occasionally placed Israel's existence in danger. Furthermore, a speech by the British Foreign Secretary at the House of Commons, on 20 February 1958, renewed the belief among Israeli decision-makers that the spirit of 'Guildhallism' was still alive. In his statement Lloyd addressed the question of Israeli frontiers, emphasising that the permanent frontiers between Israel and its neighbours must be a matter of negotiation and that a peace settlement would require a compromise. His suggestion was challenged by Hugh Gaitskell, who argued that there was a difference between mutual frontier adjustment and a proposal which, by its very nature, involved the cession by Israel of a substantial amount of territory.[94] Lloyd in response argued that a guarantee of Israel's existing frontiers would be resented by all its Arab neighbours and added that Sir Anthony Eden's Guildhall speech was misunderstood.[95] Selwyn Lloyd's speech aroused anger and frustration in Israel. Rundall wrote to Hadow, the Head of the Levant Department, to explain that Lloyd's speech was a blow to his latest efforts to convince the editors and writers of local Israeli newspapers to go over the Guildhall speech again and see that it was not inveterately anti-Israeli.[96] In a discussion with Walter Eytan on 28 February, Rundall expressed his distress over the Israeli press and government's attitude to the issue and complained that his explanations had fallen on deaf ears. Eytan replied that it would be helpful if someone in authority in Britain could state publicly that the Guildhall speech did not imply the cession of sizeable bits of Israel's territory. Rundall replied that Lloyd's speech aimed to point out that any settlement between Israel and its neighbours would require mutual compromise. The Ambassador, in desperation, concluded that, 'It [the Guildhall speech] remained, to my mind unnecessarily, the big point of friction in Anglo-Israeli relations.'[97]

In a discussion between Lloyd and Elath later in spring 1958, the Ambassador emphasised again that there were no anti-British feelings in Israel, but that there was a feeling against the British government and, in particular, against the Foreign Secretary, because of Guildhall.[98] Lloyd responded by noting that for every military item Britain supplied to Israel, the Soviets could supply the Arabs with ten times as much, and added that it was better that Hussein should receive supplies from the West rather than from the Soviets. Lloyd complained that Israel was always quick to send its 'arrows' against Britain when it felt injustice was being done, but did not adopt the same policy towards the United States. The Ambassador replied that, concerning the issue of arms supply, in Israel's view there was no advantage in the West supplying arms to Hussein; as for the accusation that Israel did not complain to the United States when it felt its interests were not taken into consideration, this was not true. His government defended Israel's interests against any country that pursued a policy that might jeopardise its interests, including the United States.[99]

Rundall was aware of the great sensitivity in Israel towards Britain's approach and thought that as long as Israel believed that the Foreign Office adhered to the Guildhall plan, suspicion between Britain and Israel would remain. 'The suspicion was so deep rooted', Rundall wrote on 2 December, 'that it can create misunderstanding between the two countries.' He also warned against an imposed settlement on Israel. 'Here, [in Israel]', Rundall wrote, 'impose is the operative word. It could be done but only if the UN were prepared to use sanctions which would bring Israel to a standstill.'[100] The Ambassador doubted whether, in a relatively calm period, the American public would support such a measure, or whether the American administration would have the courage to do so. If the imposition of a settlement was ruled out, then the prospect for a settlement was very slight. Rundall also warned that if Israel, with its 'endemic sense of claustrophobia and isolation', found itself pressured, it might be tempted to desert its relatively restrained policy and return to its old behaviour and rely on its military strength to reach a solution.[101]

Against this background, Nuri's initiative came to nothing. It was decided at the Foreign Office that Nuri should be presented with the disadvantages of his plan. He should be told that the implementation of the 1947 resolution would cause Jordan the loss of more territory than Israel would give in return, and he should be made aware that an Arab Palestinian state would probably be dominated by pro-communist extremists.[102]

UNITY AND DIVISION

However, there were yet more upheavals for the Israeli government to be concerned about. On 1 February 1958, Egypt and Syria announced their agreement to form a union known as the 'United Arab Republic' (UAR). The union created a new state with one government and constitution. It was, however, decided that the laws in Syria and Egypt would remain effective unless they were changed and that any international agreement which either country had signed prior to the new establishment would remain in force.[103] The idea of a Union had been proposed by the Syrian government as early as 1956, but had initially received little response from Nasser, who supported the idea but was not ready at the time to act upon it. However, as a result of Suez and the US attempts to curb Egypt's influence in neighbouring states, Nasser increasingly favoured the idea. At the same time, Syria was facing unrest and growing divisions between the army, civilians and the political parties. This led to greater support for a Union with Egypt, which was welcomed as the best solution to Syrian problems. Under the Union, the Communist Party was banned, which also increased the Union's popularity with right-wing circles.

It was assumed by the IDF intelligence branch that the Union was likely to bring an escalation of the Arab–Israel dispute because Syria and Egypt would probably highlight Israel's existence as an obstacle to achieving an even wider geographical pan-Arab union.[104] A survey by the Israeli Foreign Ministry emphasised that, despite Nasser's desire for Egyptian non-alignment in order to preserve its neutrality, in his battle against the West Nasser saw the Soviets as natural allies. Moreover, Egypt's dependence on the Soviets was likely to grow if it obtained financial aid in addition to arms supplies from that source.[105] In this environment the regional states might find themselves in a difficult position and seek to make some move to reduce Nasser's influence in the area. The obvious way to do this was by pressing the West to take some initiative with regard to the Arab–Israeli question, a situation which could place Israel in an unfavourable position. There was also the danger that neighbouring countries, especially Jordan, could be coerced into joining the Union in order to create a large territorial entity.[106] As for the economic implications of the Union, an Israeli army intelligence report estimated that the benefits to both countries, especially for Syria, were few. There was the prospect that it might bring Egypt a possible advantage if some of its inhabitants were moved to Syria, but that would be at the expense of Syrian farmers. The report concluded that the Union would provide Syria with a new market for its wheat but would not bring it the hard currency that it needed in order to honour its commitments to the Soviets, and in any case economic relief would be only temporary.[107]

It could be said that the common response in Israel, Washington and London to the Union was one of caution. Lloyd told the French Ambassador in London, on 3 February, that the best tactic was to let the internal difficulties work themselves out. 'Middle East politics', Lloyd said, 'was like a game of tennis in which the only way of scoring was by waiting for the opponent to serve double faults.'[108] For Britain, the main concern was the consequences the Union might have on oil supplies. In the short term the likelihood of change was small. However, in the long term much would depend on the constitutional changes arising from the Union and how they would affect the Iraqi Petroleum Company and the Tapline agreement with Syria. Nasser, in any case, would be in a stronger position than before because he would now have both the pipeline and the Canal under his control.[109] Although the mood in Britain was one of caution, the Union was not welcomed and the Foreign Office concluded on 4 February that, 'In present circumstances any successful move towards greater Arab unity would be a disaster from the point of view of British interests, since it could only be carried out under Nasser's leadership.'[110] The British Ambassador to Lebanon viewed the event as 'momentous' in Middle Eastern affairs and argued that, although there were historical and geographical difficulties in the way of unity, the move engendered great sympathy among many Arabs.[111] After some consideration, Her Majesty's Government decided to give *de facto* but not *de jure* recognition to the Union. The British reservation about giving *de jure* recognition was explained on the basis of uncertainty over the stability and permanence of the UAR.[112]

The regional Baghdad Pact members, who were at this time engaged in a Pact meeting, were caught by surprise at the news of the establishment of the UAR. The Iraqi delegation, in a desperate mood, raised doubts over whether their government and other regional states had the ability to stop similar events taking place in other countries. They realised that the slogan of Arab unity appealed to many Arabs and that it was hard to stem the tide. Dulles, who was attending the meeting, suggested that there was a need for an Arab initiative, but thought that Iraq should first wait and see the reaction in other Arab states. He said that it would be better if a common policy between Iraq, Saudi Arabia and Jordan could be worked out.[113]

Due to their growing fear of Nasser and his dominance in the region, Jordan and Iraq announced, on 14 February, the creation of a union between their states to be known as the Arab Federation. The two unions were different not just from their political standpoint but also in their nature. Whereas the UAR aimed to blend the two nations into one, the Arab Federation intended to create a federal entity which still maintained the separate national and political identities of the two member states. According to its constitution, the Federation would be responsible for security, foreign affairs and currency, and a new parliament, in addition to those currently in existence in Iraq and Jordan, would be set up.[114] Faisal was to be the president of the Federation and Hussein his deputy and chief commander of the Federation forces in Jordan.

The UAR demonstrated the extensive division in the Arab world by quickly launching into an attack on the Federation. Already, on 13 February, Radio Damascus condemned the effort to establish a Hashemite federation, saying there was a world of difference between a natural union (UAR) and an artificial one like the Hashemite federation. But on 14 February, Nasser blessed the Federation.[115] According to a secret survey prepared by the research department at the Israeli Foreign Office, Nasser initially welcomed the Hashemite federation because he believed that Jordan and Iraq would not be able to create a viable entity in practice, and that even if they did succeed he would appear in the Arab world as a leader willing to encouraged any Arab union, even if it was against him. In addition, it was assumed that Nasser blessed the Federation because he hoped that it could lead to increasing destabilisation in Iraq, which was basically better off and stronger without Jordan. According to the Israeli report, Nasser hoped that relations between Iraq and Jordan would deteriorate as a result of competition between the two leaders for influence over the Federation.[116] Despite Nasser's 'blessing' of the new grouping, the Egyptian and Syrian newspapers attacked the Federation, and the Egyptian newspaper *ELSHAB* commented that Israel welcomed the union between Iraq and Jordan.[117] It did not take long for Nasser to change his tune. On 26 February, he now attacked the Federation, saying that 'The Arab people would finish the traitor.' Cairo newspapers explained that Nasser had attacked the Federation because the Iraqi Foreign Minister had argued that the UAR was established under compulsion, an accusation that was in turn denounced by Iraqi radio on 28 February.[118]

Britain welcomed the Arab Federation and, in a House of Commons debate on 20 February, Selwyn Lloyd said that it seemed to be a natural grouping designed to bring a more prosperous and better future to the people of the two countries and expressed his belief that the new union would not bring more tension or greater risk of war.[119]

The announcement of the Arab Federation presented Israel with greater difficulties. In their meeting in Paris in February 1958, Golda Meir and the Israeli diplomats addressed these issues, recognising the different environment in which Israel operated and the need for greater caution in the initiation of military operations against its neighbours. Assessing the Western response to the Federation, Elath informed his colleagues that there were some in Britain who saw the Arab Federation as the fulfilment of Lawrence of Arabia's dream, and stated that the support for the Federation in Britain was shared by both parties and therefore it could hardly be expected that the Labour Party would help Israel on this issue as it had in the case of the Guildhall speech. The Ambassador said that if Israel declared its opposition to the Federation then it might offend the Labour Party as well as friends in the Conservative Party and they might conclude that Israel was like a 'lump in the throat'.[120] He thought it would be better if Israel did not take a clear stand against the Federation, especially in view of Britain's inability since Suez to take independent action without first consulting the United States. Moshe Sasson, the Israeli Ambassador to Italy, thought that the move towards unity in the Arab world was a revolutionary and historical act, and that the two unions should be seen as complementing each other. He stated that until the Union and the Federation united they would compete between themselves at Israel's expense. He said that the fact that the Federation was established 15 days after the creation of the UAR gave the impression that the West was working behind the scenes, and this impression would increase the Federation's need to take a more hostile line against Israel. Israel, he said, should not take any initiative as it could not adopt the Western position vis-à-vis the Federation because it was a factor in the region and Israel's outlook therefore was different. Yacov Zur, the Israeli Ambassador in Paris, stated that the French were confused, and felt they could not do much, especially because the United States was not willing to take any initiative. Furthermore, the French felt unable to assist because of their position in North Africa, which had put France in the 'prosecution dock'.[121] Meir said that Israel realised that the West did not like to listen to Israel's suggestions because they also had to consider their own interests in the region and, in particular, wanted to protect their oil supply.[122]

In general, the Israeli government was in favour of division in the Arab world as a means of reducing the possibility of a combined attack against it. However, although the two unions demonstrated a great disunity, the current divisions, unlike those of the past, were not welcomed by the Israeli government. This different outlook arose for a number of reasons. First, the Soviet penetration in the region placed Israel in a more complex position and limited its freedom of action. Second, the position of the pro-Western states in the region was more vulnerable than it had been before Suez, and it was evident that the West, and especially the United States, was unwilling to exercise its military power to defend them. Under these circumstances any Israeli military action would not only alienate the Arabs but might offend the West and bring the Soviets onto the scene. The Foreign Minister and the diplomats present at the meeting agreed that, despite the division and rivalries in the Arab world, an Israeli action against either one of the unions would bring the other to its assistance. Chaim Yahil summed up the consensus by observing that Israel's former belief that any division in the Arab world was in Israel's favour was no longer valid.[123]

From Israel's point of view the Arab Federation posed a greater threat than the UAR. While the UAR did not create, at least in the short term, a new situation or problem, the Arab Federation could directly affect Israel's security and defence position. The Arab Federation posed a threat to Israel because Iraq had no armistice agreement with it and, although Israel was in a more confident mood than in 1956, it was still anxious about Iraqi intervention in Jordan. The best way forward in Meir's view was to emphasise that, for Israel, the two unions threatened its security situation and that Israel should maintain its right to act if Iraq entered Jordan.[124] Still, she speculated, there might be one advantage for Israel from the Arab Federation; if the formal border between Jordan and Iraq ceased to exist it might increase the possibility of a transfer of Palestinian refugees from Jordan to Iraq.[125] In further discussions in Paris, Gideon Rafael said that the IDF's view was that if the Iraqis entered the West Bank, Israel would not be able to call all its military forces to meet the Iraqis, as such an incident also raised the danger that the UAR might enter the scene. Therefore Israel should not permit the entrance of Iraqi forces to the West Bank. As for the Federation, Meir said, Israel faced the problem that the West welcomed this 'creature' and would like to take it under its patronage. The diplomats agreed that Israel should be cautious and be careful not to appear as a factor that opposed this 'process' of unity. Israel should neither bless nor curse the unions and must realise its limited ability to change the situation because of the Cold War and the increasing domination of the Soviets in the region, and because the West favoured the Federation.[126]

Moshe Sasson emphasised that it was very important under the current circumstances that the Israeli Foreign Ministry should take a greater role and exclude the IDF from any diplomatic initiative. He recommended that Israel should be aware of the different interests of each country in the region and conduct its political efforts according to the various considerations of each country. However, the situation vis-à-vis Britain, he said, was very different because it was the only Western country not interested in peace between Israel and the Arabs. Britain, in his view, was the only power that still had colonial interests in the Middle East and was different therefore from France or the United States who were motivated mainly by economic interests.

> There is one colonial power, and her name is England [*sic*], and she is stationed in Aden, Kuwait, Bahrain etc. Iraq was also under her patronage and a member in the Baghdad pact. She [Britain] knows that the Arab world fight not only Zionism but Imperialism, and Imperialism means England. Britain therefore would not be interested to see an end to the dispute between us [Israel] and the Arabs because it would divert all the Arabs' attention on her.[127]

The Israeli Ambassador to London agreed with most of this analysis.

Although Israel adopted a cautious line, especially when expressing its view on the Arab Federation, it wanted the West to be aware of its anxiety about the present situation. Michael Comay, the Deputy Director of Foreign Affairs, told Rundall, on 4 February, that the slogan of Arab unity appealed to the Arabs and that consequently countries like Jordan were in danger. When Rundall asked him about the Israeli reaction to union between Jordan and Iraq, Comay reiterated that Israel and Iraq had no armistice agreement and that therefore the entrance of Iraqi troops into Jordan would cause alarm in Israel.[128]

Israel's cautious line was also expressed in Eban's discussions with the State Department. He told them that Israel had reservations towards the unions, but that his government felt that United Nations' members should recognise them. Eban said that in Israel's view the UAR would face difficulties because of its lack of cultural unity.[129] The Arab Federation, on the other hand, had more in common, for example resistance to communism. Eban said that Ben-Gurion wished to discuss with Dulles the implications for Israel. He said that Israel would have welcomed the act of unity if these states were peace-loving, but they were all anti-Israeli.[130] He emphasised once again that, although the Arab Federation was the lesser of two evils, Israel felt that it had the right to object to any move of Iraqi forces west of the River Jordan.[131] Eban said that Ben-Gurion wanted to reassure the Iraqis that they had no need to fear Israel, but they should be aware of Israel's security interests especially along the armistice lines.[132]

There are two interesting points that emerged from the Paris meeting and from the discussions between the Israeli diplomats and their British and American colleagues; first, the relatively moderate line in Israel's foreign policy, and, second, the greater role of the Israeli Foreign Ministry. We can assume that before Suez similar events in the Arab world would have met with a very different, more extreme Israeli reaction. The other interesting point is the important place of Britain in these discussions, and the great criticism of and suspicion shown towards it. The line represented by Sasson, and shared by the Israeli Ambassador in London, was still a common belief among Israeli decision-makers.

From Israel's point of view, British policy at the time did not suggest anything that would justify a reduction of Israel's suspicions and bitterness towards Her Majesty's Government. At the same time, it seems that the Israeli government placed hope and trust in the friendship of the Labour Party leaders towards their cause, as this had been evident in the dispute over Shell's withdrawal from Israel and on several other occasions during this period. The Israeli decision-makers saw Gaitskell and Bevan as loyal friends, although they were aware of their limited power and influence upon the Conservative government. During their Paris meeting, Meir told Elath to continue his connections with the Labour Party and stressed that every speech Gaitskell gave on Israel's behalf had some benefit.[133]

The Labour Party leaders at this time tried to press the government to adopt a more forthcoming attitude towards Israel and to supply it with arms. The official British policy following Suez was that under the UN resolution the British government was not permitted to supply certain countries in the region, including Israel, with arms. During 1957, Britain supplied Israel with some spare parts but unofficially adopted an arms embargo towards it. The official British view was that Israel was in a position to defend itself against Arab attack, especially with the arms it had captured in the Sinai.[134] At the end of July, Bevan told Lloyd that it was illogical that there was a ban on arms to Israel while at the same time the Syrians were obtaining arms from the Soviets and creating further tensions in the region.[135] Lloyd promised Bevan and Gaitskell that the British government would supply Israel with radar for the destroyers previously supplied to the Israeli Navy, and that arrangements for the overhaul of aircraft belonging to the Israeli Air Force were in hand. Lloyd said that he would like to proceed with the supply of Meteor fighters but it had to be remembered that the UN resolution was still in force. Macmillan added that it was important that Israel kept quiet about the arms it was getting from Britain.[136]

TENSIONS OVER MOUNT SCOPUS

In 1958, the Israeli government decided to have an official ceremony in Jerusalem to celebrate the tenth anniversary of the state, and planned to have a military parade. The parade was technically a breach of the Israeli–Jordanian armistice agreement, which required that no aggressive forces come within ten kilometres of the demarcation line.[137] This could only add more tension to the state of relations between Israel and Jordan, especially along the armistice lines.

There had, over the previous years, been many incidents along the border, particularly around Mount Scopus and in the area of Governor House. According to the armistice agreement Mount Scopus, which included the Hebrew university and HADASA hospital, remained under Israeli control. However, it was not easy for Israeli convoys, who had to go through an Arab neighbourhood to reach Mount Scopus, which was an isolated Israeli enclave within Jordanian territory. During July 1957, the Jordanians complained to the Security Council that Israel had started to plant trees in the Governor House area, south of Jerusalem,[138] and that Israel had started to work in no man's land between the armistice lines.[139] However, Israel was determined to continue and claimed that the planting of trees was simply in order to prevent soil erosion and that it had no military repercussions or significance.[140] The Jordanians, on their side, stopped a convoy to Mount Scopus on the grounds that it carried petrol.[141] According to the Israel–Jordan armistice line agreement, neither the armed forces of the two countries nor civilians could cross the demarcation line, but the planting area was to be in an area between the lines and not in the demilitarised zone. In a discussion between Dulles and Eban, the Ambassador said that Jordan was making a 'fuss of nothing'.[142] However, Dulles suggested that in view of the tension in the area, it was important that Israel should avoid any action which could appear provocative, particularly at a time when the US government was doing its utmost to convince the King that the real danger to Jordan and other Arab states was not from Israel but from communism and the Soviets.[143] At the end, however, Israel went on with the parade as was planned.

THE LEBANON ON THE BRINK OF CHAOS

While there were continuing problems along Israel's eastern frontier, the main concern for the Western powers and Israel from the spring of 1958 was the growing instability in the Lebanon.

The situation in the Lebanon started to deteriorate during the spring, thereby adding more tension and instability to the region. The crisis in the Lebanon was stimulated by pan-Arabism, and escalated when rumours started to spread that Kamil Chamoun, the Lebanese President, aimed to amend the constitution in order to ensure his re-election.[144] Lebanese politics were complicated by inter-family rivalries between the Maronites and the Sunni Moslems. Lebanon was ruled by the Christian Maronites, although in proportion to the Moslem Sunnis they formed a minority. For a long time, the Sunnis were reluctant to share the management of the affairs of their country. The Shi'ites, who formed the least advanced section of the population, could only play a minor role, and the Druzes, who were able and willing to co-operate, were a comparatively small group; thus Lebanese affairs were dominated by the Christians.[145] Even among the Christian Maronites there was growing opposition to Chamoun, but they were all terrified by the pan-Sunni role in Arab nationalism and by the prospect that the Sunnis, who were inspired by Nasser, would try to change the status quo. General Chehab, the Army Chief of Staff, was favoured by the Christians and Moslems but refused to be considered as a possible successor to Chamoun. In the first weeks of May, the split between the Moslems and Christians over a potential replacement for the President, and among pro-Western elements and the pan-Arabist sections, grew and by the middle of the month the situation had worsened, with Lebanon on the brink of chaos. On 8 May, the editor of an opposition newspaper, Nabib Matni, was assassinated. Violent actions were committed by both sides in certain parts of the Lebanon, which threatened to jeopardise the delicate co-existence between the different minorities. Chamoun rejected the opposition's demand, submitted on 10 May, that he, his Prime Minister and Foreign Minister should resign.[146] Chamoun was eager to ensure Western help in case of an emergency.

The US and British governments were agreed that it was important to assist Chamoun if the situation in the Lebanon deteriorated further. It appeared that for Macmillan and Eisenhower the Lebanon was a case where they could ill-afford to fail and they felt that the Lebanon was a test for Western readiness to help pro-Western countries in the region. However, although Eisenhower and Dulles promised to assist the Lebanon if the need arose, they had some reservations. Eisenhower stressed that American aid to the Lebanon had certain conditions; the United States would not send troops for the purpose of achieving an additional term for the President and the request should have the concrete support of some other Arab nations. American forces deployed to the Lebanon would be there to protect American lives and, at the same time, would assist the legal Lebanese government.[147] Dulles told Eban, on 30 June, that the problem with armed intervention was that it would intensify anti-Western sentiment and would weaken the position of Iraq and Jordan, and therefore the optimum solution would be a peaceful one.[148] The letter to the Lebanese government from Dulles, on 13 May, also emphasised American reservations. Dulles wrote that, although the United States was prepared to act upon an appropriate request from Chamoun and his government to send certain forces to Lebanon, there was a belief that such action was a grave step which could have the most serious and far-reaching implications, and therefore the request should only be made if the situation in the Lebanon was at a critical point. Dulles added that the US government also assumed that Chamoun would not push his candidacy if it divided Lebanese integrity or compromised the pro-Western orientation of the Lebanon.[149]

Chamoun also approached the British government to seek their assistance if this became necessary. He told the British Ambassador to Lebanon that there was increasing evidence of massive Egyptian aid to armed groups who were endeavouring to take control of the country. Chamoun asked the Ambassador whether the British government was willing to provide the Lebanon with military assistance within 24 hours of a formal request for the dispatch of forces.[150] Macmillan thought that it was very important to assist Chamoun if the situation in the Lebanon deteriorated. 'Thus once more', he wrote in his diary, 'we were faced with an aggressive action by Nasser threatening the stability of the whole Middle East.' He believed that Nasser's object was to force the Lebanon to join the UAR, and compared the situation in the Middle East with Austria and the Sudetenland position in 1938.[151] However, Macmillan realised that the loss of Britain's position at the Canal and the outcome of Suez had worsened its military position and limited its ability to undertake a military operation alone. He believed that this fact should not prevent Britain from helping the Lebanon and was anxious to ensure American support for military intervention. In his talks with Dulles and State Department officials, Sir Harold Caccia, the British Ambassador to the United States, referred to Sir Michael Wright's telegram, calling attention particularly to the opinion of King Faisal and Crown Prince Abdul-ilah of Iraq that, in the absence of an adequate alternative, it was better to support Chamoun's re-election even at the price of civil war, adding that Lloyd agreed with this point. It is clear that Macmillan wanted to prevent a repetition of Suez where the British had stood alone against the Arab world and against the wishes of the United States. He noted in his diary that the British view was supported by Eisenhower and Dulles: 'The world,' he wrote, 'learnt much in the last two years and we no longer stood alone.'[152] The British Cabinet agreed, on 13 May, that Britain should join the United States in any military intervention to preserve the independence of the Lebanon if the need arose,[153] and the British Ambassador to the Lebanon was authorised to inform Chamoun that Her Majesty's Government was prepared to give the Lebanon military assistance if requested.[154] On 22 May, the Lebanese government turned to the Security Council and asked the UN to take account of the massive activities by the UAR. On 11 June, the Security Council subsequently authorised the dispatch of an observation group to the Lebanon.[155] The British Ambassador in Washington was requested to tell Dulles that the British government believed it was very important to assist the Lebanon if requested, and that it was believed by Britain that any failure to help the Lebanon would be a greater defeat for the West than the withdrawal of British and French troops from Port Said, and might lead to the collapse of Jordan, Iraq, Libya and Sudan.[156]

DE GAULLE AND FRANCO-ISRAELI RELATIONS

At this stage it was not clear what France's reaction would be if the situation deteriorated, but it seemed that they would take a cautious line. France was going through a period of instability and upheaval; between September 1957 and April 1958 three governments had collapsed either directly or indirectly due to the situation in Algeria.[157] There were growing economic difficulties in France and a lack of public confidence in Parliament. Although the Suez crisis had not had such an immediate and grave political impact on France as on Britain, the war and its consequences escalated the general dissatisfaction with Parliament. On 16 April 1958, M. Gaillard's government resigned and it was only on 14 May that a new government was formed by Pierre Plimlin.[158] However, the day before he became premier there were growing demonstrations by the European settlers in Algeria, demanding a committee of public safety to be led by General de Gaulle.[159] On 24 May, French parachute troops from Algeria landed in Corsica making it clear that de Gaulle's accession could not be delayed.[160] De Gaulle seemed to be the remedy for many Frenchmen, and on 1 June, he received a vote of confidence from a large majority of the French assembly.[161]

The political changes in France brought considerable speculation and concern in Israel. As already emphasised, the friendship with France was seen by Israeli decision-makers as a unique asset to be valued and cherished. However, it was not clear whether de Gaulle would pursue the policy of his predecessors or would choose to take a more balanced attitude towards the Arab–Israeli dispute. Ben-Gurion wrote in his diary with optimism, but also with some caution, that he did not think de Gaulle was a fascist or a dictator, 'he believes he is France, he is a big and distinguished man, a bit egocentric, but means well'.[162] Pierre Gilbert, the French Ambassador to Israel, stressed publicly that the relations between Israel and France were excellent and would remain so; the French Prime Minister, he stressed, was one of Israel's great friends.[163] France continued to supply Israel with arms and during the summer the latter received 60 Fouga unarmed jet training aircraft.[164]

ISRAEL AND THE LEBANESE CRISIS

Meanwhile, the situation in the Lebanon worsened and a special US intelligence report estimated that the position of President Chamoun was in the balance and that the country was in a state of civil war. The report stated that it was likely that US intervention in the Lebanon would face hostility even from some of the Christians, but that on the other hand if Chamoun publicly asked for US aid and it was refused it could have serious consequences for the anti-Nasser elements in the Arab world, particularly Iraq and Jordan. The reaction in the Lebanon could be even worse, according to the report, if the British and especially French troops joined in.[165]

Events in the Lebanon caused anxiety and unrest in Israel. Lebanese–Israeli relations were relatively peaceful and the Israeli government favoured Christian rule in the Lebanon. Although Israel had no peace agreement with the Lebanon it saw the country as a 'different' Arab state, one which was naturally Western and basically not hostile to Israel. On these grounds, one could explain the growing uneasiness the Israeli government felt about recent developments in the Lebanon. The geographical position of the Lebanon was important because of its frontier with Syria, a member country of the UAR and one viewed by Israel as a 'Soviet satellite'. The Israeli decision-makers were in favour of military intervention if the situation in the Lebanon deteriorated and its own independence was put at risk. Eban told Dulles, on 13 May, that the United States should take the risk of intervention and added that the Arabs would respect any Western initiative, especially if it was successful.[166]

In a discussion between Rundall and Colonel Yehoshafat Harkabi, the Director of Military Intelligence, on 30 June, Harkabi said that the Lebanon was the key to major developments and changes in the Middle East. He stressed that in Israel's judgement, if the Lebanon fell to the UAR, there was no hope that the Federation of Jordan and Iraq could survive as an independent entity. If the Western world would not keep the Lebanon independent, its influence could totally collapse. Harkabi told Rundall that Israel's information was that the Lebanese army was being reorganised and many Moslem officers had resigned as they were regarded as unreliable.[167] Sir Francis Rundall was well aware that the situation in the Lebanon might awake the militarist tendency in Israel. 'There is', he wrote on 13 June, 'evidence that Israel is becoming seriously nervous over the Lebanese issue.' He went on to note that, 'Although there was no repetition of the policy of reprisals there was a new atmosphere of truculence and a tendency to flex more openly Israel's nationalist muscles.'[168] In his view, these changes resulted from a number of reasons such as the confidence Israel had gained in the Sinai war, a factor which was enhanced by the growing evidence of Arab weakness, and the loss of Western credibility due to their failure to bring about a satisfactory solution to the Lebanese issue. However, the Ambassador emphasised to the Foreign Office in London that the outcry in Israel could also be explained as typical Israeli behaviour in a crisis, as they were very concerned over the future of the Lebanon. 'Basically,' Rundall continued, 'Israel would prefer to see a peace settlement, but on the other hand there was also a different mood which combined military confidence, a faith in Israel's destiny and a feeling that the odds could move heavily against her almost overnight.' He added, '"This belief" led the man in the street and the government to the conclusion that conciliation was unprofitable and perhaps even dangerous.'[169]

Rundall's observation pointed to a significant dilemma in Israel's political behaviour. It appears that even today there are two ambivalent lines of Israeli foreign policy, and this was even more so in the period under study. The ambiguity between the desire for peace and, at the same time, the realisation that at least for a while peace was only a dream, gave birth to the belief that any sign of weakness, which an outside observer might describe as 'moderation', could from Israel's point of view lead only to disaster. With some caution one can say that a tendency towards militarism had strong roots in Israel, and it led to the feeling that only an 'iron fist' policy could preserve Israel's existence. This belief continued to exist during 1957–58, even though Israel's policy was more moderate and cautious than during the earlier period. The characteristic line of Israel's behaviour was dominated by a deep desire for a peaceful solution to the Arab–Israeli dispute, but at the same time great disbelief in this becoming a reality. Consequently, one can understand that any political event that might change the fragile status quo was almost certainly going to be perceived by the Israeli government as a real danger to its existence and thus strengthen her militaristic tendency.

At this stage, however, the Israeli government watched the events along its borders with great concern but refrained from taking any military action. The realisation that the Western powers were still reluctant to take action, and that Soviet penetration in the area had grown, forced Israel to consider its policy carefully. The Syrian crisis, which had caused much tension, had come to an end and there were no further indications that Syrian stability was in danger, although it was clear that the latter was moving towards closer relations with the Soviet Union. It seemed that Israel and the Western powers realised the region's delicate and flammable situation and the need for restraint.

Thus in the summer the situation in the Lebanon steadily deteriorated and Western intervention seemed increasingly inevitable. However, the events of 14 July in Iraq proved to be even more dramatic and horrific than anyone in London, Washington or Jerusalem could have foreseen.

NOTES

1. Benjamin Shwadran, 'The Kingdom of Jordan, To Be Or Not To Be', *Middle Eastern Affairs*, August–September 1957, Vol. 8, Nos 8–9, p. 276.
2. Harold Macmillan, *Riding the Storm 1956–1959* (London: Macmillan, 1971), p. 220.
3. Ibid.
4. Shwadran, *The Kingdom*, p. 278.
5. Ibid., p. 279.
6. PRO, FO371/127887/VJ10110/7, Johnston (Amman) to Lloyd, 9 October 1957.
7. PRO, FO371/127887/VJ10110/2, Mason (Amman) to Lloyd, 29 July 1957.
8. Ibid.
9. PRO, FO371/127878/VJ1015/29, Johnston to Lloyd, 14 April 1957.
10. Shwadran, *The Kingdom*, p. 282.
11. Ibid., p. 283.
12. *FRUS*, Vol. 13, 1955–57, telegram from the embassy in Jordan to the State Department, 3 August 1957, p. 122. Dwight D. Eisenhower, *The White House Years: Waging Peace, 1956–1961* (London: Heineman, 1966), pp. 194–5.
13. *FRUS*, Vol. 13, 1955–57, memorandum of conversation, 14 April 1957, pp. 92–3.
14. PRO, FO371/127878/VJ1015/12, Levant Department minute, 15 April 1957.
15. PRO, FO371/127878/VJ1015/27, Wright (Baghdad) to Lloyd, 15 April 1957.
16. *FRUS*, Vol. 13, 1955–57, memorandum of conversation, State Department, 24 April 1957, p. 104.
17. *FRUS*, Vol. 13, telegram from the State Department to the embassy in Jordan, 15 April 1957, p. 97, and see also note 3, p. 97.
18. *FRUS*, Vol. 13, telegram from the State Department to the embassy in Washington, 15 April 1957, note 3, p. 97.
19. ISA, HZ329/2, Golda Meir to Israeli embassies, 19 April 1957.
20. *FRUS*, Vol. 13, memorandum of conversation, State Department, 24 April 1957, p. 104.
21. Ibid., p. 105.
22. Eisenhower, *The White House*, p. 193.
23. David Ben-Gurion, *Kochavim Vaefer* [Like Stars Like Dust], essays from the government year book (Ramat-Gan: Masada, 1976), p. 296.
24. Ibid. See also, *FRUS*, Vol. 17, 1955–57, Richard to State Department, 4 May 1957, pp. 597–8.
25. *FRUS*, Vol. 17, 1955–57, Richard to State Department, 4 May 1957, p. 598.
26. Ibid., pp. 597–9.
27. *FRUS*, Vol. 13, 1955–57, special intelligence report on developments in Syria, p. 675.
28. J.S. Raleigh, 'The Middle East in 1957: A Political Survey', *Middle Eastern Affairs*, Vol. 9, No. 3, March 1958, p. 93.
29. Patrick Seale, *The Struggle for Syria: A Study in Post-War Arab Politics* (London: Tauris, 1968), p. 290.
30. Ibid., p. 289.
31. PRO, FO371/128236/VY1022/7, Scott (Beirut) to Rose (Foreign Office), 29 April 1957.
32. PRO, FO371/128107/VR1052/23, Lloyd to Rundall, 29 April 1957.
33. Ibid.
34. *FRUS*, Vol. 13, 1955–57, memorandum from the Assistant Secretary of State for Near Eastern Affairs (Rountree) to the Acting Secretary of State, 13 August 1957, p. 633.
35. Ibid.

36. Ibid.
37. *FRUS*, Vol. 13, 1955–57, telegram from the State Department to the embassy in Jordan, note 3, 14 August 1957, p. 637.
38. Nigel Ashton, 'A Great New Venture? Anglo-American Cooperation in the Middle East and the Response to the Iraqi Revolution July 1958', in *Diplomacy & Statecraft* Vol. 4 (London: Frank Cass, 1993), p. 61.
39. PRO, FO371/128241/VR10338/15, Hadow recommendation for the Cabinet, 1 September 1957.
40. Macmillan, *Riding the Storm*, p. 278.
41. Ibid.
42. PRO, FO371/128228/VY1015/22, Dixon (New York) to Lloyd, 17 September 1957.
43. Ashton, 'A Great New Venture?', p. 62.
44. Eisenhower, *The White House*, p. 198.
45. PRO, FO371/128227/VR1015/185, Lloyd to Caccia (Washington), 11 September 1957.
46. PRO, FO371/128224/VY1015/118, Macmillan to Dulles, 23 August 1957.
47. Macmillan, *Riding the Storm*, p. 280.
48. Eisenhower, *The White House*, p. 200. This significant point could not be found in the British documents, nor in the Israeli archives or in Macmillan's memoirs.
49. PRO, FO371/128224/VY1015/102, Beamout (Baghdad) to Lloyd, 21 July 1957.
50. PRO, FO371/128227/VY1015/186, minute, 11 September 1957.
51. Ibid.
52. PRO, FO371/128227/VY1015/186, Foreign Office minute, 11 September 1957.
53. Eisenhower, *The White House*, p. 199. See also, PRO, FO 371/128225/VY1015/138, Tesh (Foreign Office) minute, 28 August 1957.
54. PRO, FO371/128107/VR1052/23, Lloyd to Rundall, 11 September 1957.
55. PRO, FO371/128224/VY1015/118, Macmillan to Dulles, 23 August 1957.
56. *FRUS*, Vol. 13, 1955–57, telegram from the embassy in Israel to the State Department, 22 August 1957, p. 648.
57. Ibid.
58. *FRUS*, Vol. 13, telegram from the embassy in Israel to the State Department, 28 August 1957, p. 662.
59. *FRUS*, Vol. 13, telegram from the US embassy Tel-Aviv to State Department, pp. 662–3.
60. PRO, FO371/128225/VY1015/131, Rundall to Lloyd, 27 August 1957.
61. PRO, FO371/128225/VY1015/138, Rose, minute, 30 August 1957.
62. Ibid.
63. PRO, FO371/128225/VY1015/141, British embassy Istanbul to Levant Department, 30 August 1957.
64. Ibid.
65. *FRUS*, Vol. 17, 1955–57, memorandum of a conversation, State Department, 12 September 1957, p. 731.
66. PRO, FO371/128107/1052/23, Lloyd to Rundall, 11 September 1957.
67. PRO, FO371/128231/VY1015/306, Rundall to Rose, 26 September 1957.
68. Michael Bar-Zohar, *Ben-Gurion* (Tel-Aviv: Am-Oved, 1977), p. 1308.
69. *FRUS*, Vol. 17, message from Dulles to Ben-Gurion, 12 November 1957, p. 792.
70. Ibid., p. 793.
71. Bar-Zohar, *Ben-Gurion*, p. 1317.
72. Ashton, 'A Great New Venture?', p. 62.
73. Eisenhower, *The White House*, p. 201.
74. ISA, HZ2449/8, meeting of Israeli diplomats, Paris, 24–25 February 1958.

75. ISA, HZ330/14, Israeli Foreign Office to Avidar (Moscow), 1 October 1957.
76. Ibid.
77. Ibid.
78. PRO, FO371/128116/VR1072/90, Wright to Foreign Office, 2 November 1957.
79. PRO, FO371/129327/ZP24/14, Foreign Office minute for the Prime Minister's Commonwealth tour, 6 December 1957.
80. PRO, FO371/128114/VR1072/5, Foreign Office note, 19 February 1957.
81. *FRUS*, Vol. 17, draft prepared by the British embassy, 21 October 1957, p. 769.
82. *FRUS*, Vol. 17, memorandum of a conversation, State Department, 22 November 1957, note 2, p. 767.
83. Ibid., p. 768.
84. ISA, HZ/409/4, Maroz to Comay, 28 October 1957. This is confirmed in *FRUS*, Vol. 17, Rountree to Dulles, note 2, p. 767.
85. ISA, HZ409/4, Maroz to Comay, 28 October 1957.
86. *FRUS*, Vol. 17, memorandum of a conversation, State Department, 25 October 1957, p. 774.
87. *FRUS*, Vol. 17, memorandum of a conversation, State Department, 22 October 1957, pp. 767–8. (For a full analysis of Israeli immigration policy see Chapter 2.)
88. *FRUS*, Vol. 17, memorandum of a conversation, State Department, 5 December 1957, p. 843.
89. Ibid., p. 844.
90. *FRUS*, Vol. 17, memorandum of a conversation, State Department, 10 December 1957, p. 849.
91. *FRUS*, Vol. 17, memorandum of a conversation, State Department, 5 December 1957, p. 843.
92. Ibid.
93. ISA, HZ413/3 Israeli embassy London to Meir, 10 December 1957.
94. *Hansard*, Vol. 582, col. 1422, 20 February 1958.
95. *Hansard*, Vol. 582, col. 1425, 2 May 1958.
96. PRO, FO371/134292/VR1072/33, Rundall to Hadow, 28 February 1958.
97. Ibid.
98. ISA, FO 371/134284/VR1051/5, Lloyd to Rundall, 2 May 1958.
99. ISA, HZ413/3, Israeli embassy London to Meir, 10 December 1957.
100. PRO, CAB 134/2340, V1022/63, Rundall to Lloyd, 2 December 1957.
101. Ibid.
102. FO371/128118/VR1072/143, Hadow minute, 20 December 1957.
103. ISA, HZ412/30, Ben-Meir to all departments, 18 March 1958.
104. ISA, HZ412/30, IDF Intelligence Branch to Eban, 29 January 1958.
105. ISA, HZ412/30, a special survey by the Israeli Research Department, 7 February 1958.
106. ISA, HZ412/30, IDF Intelligence Branch to Eban, 29 January 1957.
107. ISA, HZ412/30, IDF Intelligence Branch to Eban, 17 April 1958.
108. PRO, FO371/137267/VR1081/6, conversation between Lloyd and the French Ambassador M. Chauvel, 3 February 1958.
109. PRO, FO371/133881/V1533/3, Fearhley (Foreign Office) brief for Gore Booth, 4 February 1958.
110. PRO, FO371/134292/V1072/30, Beely (Foreign Office) minute, 3 January 1958.
111. PRO, FO371/134387/VY52, Middleton (Beirut) to Lloyd, 6 February 1958.
112. PRO, FO371/134389/VY10316/104, Vallat (Legal Adviser, Foreign Office) minute, 24 February 1958.
113. PRO, FO371/134389/VY10316/115, record of special Baghdad Pact meeting, 29 January 1958.
114. *Middle Eastern Affairs*, attached agreement on the Iraq–Jordan agreement, Vol.

9, March 1958, pp. 111–12.
115. ISA, HZ412/30, MAHAV (United States Department, Israeli Foreign Office) to Israeli embassy Washington, 19 March 1958.
116. ISA, HZ412/30, Israeli Foreign Office internal survey, 26 March 1958.
117. ISA, HZ 412/30, MAHAV to Washington, 19 March 1958.
118. Ibid.
119. *Hansard*, Vol. 582, col. 1422, 20 February 1958.
120. ISA, HZ2449/8, Israeli diplomats conference in Paris, 24–25 February 1958.
121. Ibid.
122. Ibid.
123. ISA, HZ2449/6, MAHAV to the Director, 20 February 1958.
124. Ibid.
125. Ibid.
126. Ibid.
127. Ibid.
128. PRO, FO371/134388/VY10316/85, Rundall to Hadow, 4 February 1958.
129. ISA, HZ412/30, IDF Intelligence Branch to Eban, Washington, 17 April 1957. The report emphasised the economic difficulties the UAR might face.
130. *FRUS*, Vol. 13, 1958–60, memorandum of a conversation, State Department pp. 24–5, 27 February 1958.
131. Ibid., p. 26.
132. Ibid., p. 27.
133. ISA, HZ2449/8, Israeli diplomats meeting in Paris, 24–25 February 1958.
134. PRO, CAB133/237/PM(W), 21 October 1957.
135. PRO, FO371/128107/VR1052/20, Rose minute, 1 August 1957.
136. Ibid.
137. PRO, FO371/134300/VR1081/403, Foreign Office minute, 3 March 1958.
138. *FRUS*, Vol. 17, 1955–57, memorandum from the Director of the Office of Near Eastern Affairs (Rockwell) to Rountree, 21 August 1957, p. 709. See also: PRO, FO371/128149/VR1084/40, Hadow minute, 10 December 1957.
139. PRO, FO371/128149/VR1084/40, Hadow, minute, 10 December 1957.
140. *FRUS*, Vol. 17, 1955–57, memorandum from the Director of the Office of Near Eastern Affairs (Rockwell) to Rountree, 21 August 1957, p. 709.
141. PRO, FO371/128149/VR1084/32, Commonwealth Relations Office to High Commissions, 25 November 1957.
142. *FRUS*, Vol. 17, 1955–57, memorandum of a conversation, State Department, 31 October 1957, p. 779.
143. Ibid., p. 782.
144. According to the Lebanese constitution, the President was elected by the Parliament meeting as an electoral college. The President was elected for a term of six years and was not immediately re-eligible for office. If the President wanted to be re-elected a special amendment of the constitution was needed, *World Today*, p. 373.
145. Ibid., pp. 372–3.
146. PRO, FO371/134116/V1015/39, Middleton, (Beirut) to Lloyd, 12 May 1958.
147. Eisenhower, *The White House*, p 267. See also *FRUS*, Vol. 11, 1958–60, Dulles to US embassy Beirut, 13 May 1958.
148. *FRUS*, Vol. 11, 1958–60, State Department memorandum, 30 June 1958, p. 63.
149. Ibid., telegram from the State Department to the embassy in the Lebanon, 13 May 1958, p. 49.
150. Macmillan, *Riding the Storm*, p. 506.
151. Ibid.
152. Ibid.
153. Ibid.

154. Ibid.
155. PRO, FO371/134116/VL1015/147, Rose to Beirut, 15 May 1958.
156. Macmillan, *Riding the Storm*, p. 508.
157. Adam Watson, 'The Aftermath of Suez: Consequences for French Decolonization', in Wm Roger Louis and Roger Owen (eds), *Suez 1956: The Crisis and its Consequences* (Oxford: Clarendon Press, 1989), p. 342.
158. Dorothy Pickles, *The Fifth Republic* (London: Methuen, 1964), p. 16.
159. Macmillan, *Riding the Storm*, pp. 442–3.
160. Ibid., p. 443. See also Pickles, *Fifth Republic*, pp. 16–18.
161. Macmillan, *Riding the Storm*, p. 444.
162. Ibid. See also for further information: Adam Watson, 'The Aftermath of Suez', pp. 342–3, and Maurice Vaisse, 'Post-Suez France', in *Suez 1956*, pp. 342–3.
163. BGA, Ben-Gurion diary, 17 June 1958.
164. PRO, FO371/128093/VR10317/10, Rundall to Lloyd, 20 June 1958.
165. Ibid.
166. *FRUS*, Vol. 11, 1958–60, State Department to US embassy in Beirut, 13 May 1958, p. 49.
167. *FRUS*, Vol. 11, 1958–60, memorandum of a conversation, State Department, 30 June 1958, p. 61.
168. PRO, FO371/134123/VL1015/311, Rundall to Foreign Office, 13 June 1958.
169. PRO, FO371/134292/VR1072, Rundall to Lloyd, 24 June 1958.

—8—

The End of an Era: The Crisis of 1958 and Anglo-Israeli Relations

AT DAWN ON 14 JULY 1958, the Middle East was shaken: a coup d'état[1] had taken place in Iraq. The coup was led by a group of officers under the command of Colonel Abd Al-Karim Qassem. The battalions involved in the coup were originally to be sent to Jordan in order to reinforce King Hussein's vulnerable position, but instead they entered the Iraqi capital at 4.30 a.m., surrounded the royal palace and took possession of key installations in Baghdad. The same morning, the King, the Prince and other members of the royal family were executed.[2] The only survivor was Nuri el-Said, the Premier, but he was caught the following day when walking in the street dressed as a woman. Baghdad Radio announced the following day that Nuri had been captured and killed.[3] Nuri's body was brutally abused by the public in the streets of Baghdad.

The dramatic news shocked and surprised the West. It was immediately feared that this event might be followed by similar attempts in other pro-Western Middle Eastern states and might jeopardise the West's strategic, political and economic interests.

The British embassy in Baghdad was also attacked by an Iraqi mob. On the day of the coup, Iraqi soldiers entered the embassy in order to guard it but made no great effort to protect the embassy residents from the mob and the British Ambassador and other officials had to take shelter in the Registry. They were surrounded by an angry crowd who threatened to set fire to the room if the Ambassador and his companions did not leave it unarmed; they were eventually rescued and protected by the army.[4] The coup demonstrated the prevalence of nationalist, radical and anti-Western feeling among the Middle Eastern states and the growing resentment towards Nuri and the monarchy.

These events could only add to the sombre atmosphere in London. Britain's interests in Iraq and the belief that the latter was one of the main pillars of stability in the region meant that these developments were seen as a serious blow to Britain's position. It was described by Harold Macmillan as, 'destroying at a blow a whole system of security which successive British governments had built up'.[5] There were growing fears in Britain that the oil pipeline from Kirkuk to the Lebanon, which ran through Syria, could be cut and the flow of oil from Iraq stopped. The British government was quick to reinforce its forces in the Persian Gulf in order to secure and strengthen their position.

THE AMERICAN INTERVENTION IN THE LEBANON

The events in Iraq were of great importance, in themselves, but they were also significant because they threatened to create a precedent for other states in the region. In the coming months it would be the potential of revolution spreading to other Arab states, rather than the events in Iraq itself, that would dominate thinking in Britain, Israel and the United States. In particular, there was a concern that they would lead to the deterioration of the already fragile situation in the Lebanon. The radical elements in the Lebanon, opposed to Chamoun, might well be stimulated by the rise of pan-Arabism and seek to challenge the status quo there. They were already receiving, according to US sources, assistance and guidance from the UAR for their subversive activities.[6] On 6 June, Dr Charles Malik, the Lebanese Foreign Minister, presented a lengthy indictment of the UAR to the Security Council, which then decided to send military observers to the Lebanon.[7] The Americans decided to accede to the Lebanese request for American assistance and to send their troops immediately.

The Suez crisis had already contributed to a different American attitude towards the Middle East, as manifested in the Eisenhower doctrine. The American administration felt, therefore, that a failure to respond to an open Lebanese request for assistance would be seen in these circumstances as a move that would fatally undermine the doctrine. The US administration feared that any political compromise in the Lebanon might cause a further loss of US prestige and that the overthrown of Chamoun by anti-Western groups would weaken the ability of the United States to maintain its interests in the region. In addition, it might accelerate the UAR's efforts to undermine other pro-Western regimes in the Middle East.[8] However, the American government wanted to draw a distinction between Suez and their intervention in the Lebanon. The Americans were keen that it should not be seen in the same light.[9]

Eisenhower called for an emergency meeting of the United Nations Security Council on 15 July, having already discussed the matter with 22 Congress leaders on 14 July, resulting in an endorsement of the President's decision to intervene in the Lebanon.[10] Subsequently, on 15

July, American forces consisting of the 2nd marine regiment landed in Beirut.[11]

The British Cabinet had already decided in May that year that they would be willing to take part in any joint Anglo-American operation in the Lebanon if requested to do so.[12] However, Eisenhower believed that the American forces could cope with the situation without any additional assistance from the British, and also did not want it to appear as if the United States was collaborating with Britain.[13]

TENSIONS IN JORDAN: THE ANGLO-AMERICAN RESPONSE

At the same time as Chamoun's request to Washington, the British Cabinet received an informal request from King Hussein of Jordan for British and American assurances of immediate assistance if necessary. Macmillan believed that, in the light of the situation in Iraq and the Lebanon, Hussein should be urged to make a formal request at once in order to make the position clear, and sought US support for a possible intervention.[14] Macmillan and the British Cabinet were thus careful not to repeat the mistake of Eden's government in 1956. At the same time, however, they did not want to appear to have abandoned their commitments and interests in the region. 'Nothing', Macmillan wrote in his diary on 15 July, 'could be worse for our position in the Middle East than to find ourselves first exposed and then abandoned.'[15]

On 16 July, a formal request arrived from King Hussein and Shamir Rifai, the Jordanian Prime Minister. They sought the dispatch of British and American forces in order to enable Jordan's army and security forces to deal with a coup which they believed would be staged by the UAR in the West Bank, along the Syrian frontier and in Amman.[16] Hussein had been subjected for some time to hostile propaganda and incitements to rebellion from the UAR and was aware that a plot against him was taking place within his army and country.[17] Hussein's political and economic situation was desperate, the oil supply from Iraq had been cut off and, according to the British embassy in Amman, the country was left with less than one day's energy supplies for the electricity plant and the municipal pumping stations.[18]

When the British government received the formal request from King Hussein they were aware of the grave situation in Jordan and the Cabinet agreed that it was essential to assist Jordan as quickly as possible. It was assumed that a failure to respond would weaken the King's will to resist and might strengthen the UAR and Hussein's opponents. It was feared that if such a situation developed, the British position in the Gulf would be in jeopardy.[19]

Having learnt the bitter lessons of Suez, Macmillan was eager to secure US support before taking any action. Already, on 15 July, Macmillan had sent a message to President Eisenhower, expressing his government's support of US intervention in the Lebanon, and emphasising that a critical situation had developed not just in the Lebanon but throughout the Middle East as a whole. He asked the President for his support to restore the situation in Iraq and, if need be, in Jordan.[20] However, the US government did not want to commit itself to a combined Anglo-American operation in Jordan. In a telephone conversation between Macmillan and Dulles on 16 July, the latter expressed his reservations about the wisdom of military intervention in Jordan, and said it was better to wait until he could be sure that such an operation would be in Hussein's favour.[21] The American response caused disappointment within the British Cabinet, but Macmillan was determined to seek some US approval. When Hussein's formal request was finally presented to the British and American governments, Macmillan informed Dulles that the British Cabinet had decided to accede to the King's request without delay. Dulles' attitude now became more forthcoming and he promised Macmillan that the American government would stand behind the British decision and would support it both publicly and in the UN. He also said that the United States would assist Britain with logistical support as the situation developed, and agreed that the demonstration flights which US aircraft were to make over Israel and Jordan the following day (17 July) should coincide with the British operation.[22]

The British government was disappointed to learn that the Americans would not commit themselves to a joint operation, but they were partly comforted by America's political and moral support. The British government could therefore inform Hussein that they had decided to accede to Jordan's request and would dispatch troops from Cyprus immediately.[23] In order not to risk a day's delay, Macmillan ordered the flights to Jordan to start on the night of 16 July.[24] On that day, Macmillan informed Parliament that the British government had received a formal request from Hussein and the Jordanian Prime Minister to assist Jordan by sending British troops to Amman immediately, and that the British government had decided to accede to Hussein's request. He explained that the purpose of the operation was to help the King to stabilise the situation in Jordan, and to help the Jordanian government to maintain the integrity and independence of the country. He assured Parliament that the British operation enjoyed full US support.[25] Macmillan argued that it was essential to help Jordan in order to prevent a chain reaction in which other Arab states, especially the Gulf states, would fall victim to the UAR and their supporters.[26] Macmillan also said that the British government must assist Jordan, whose independence was under threat because of conspiracy and subversion.[27]

The RAF had to fly to Jordan by the shortest and quickest route possible, but the flight paths available were limited. As a result of the Suez crisis an air barrier had been established in the region. The British found that it was impossible to use the quickest route through Saudi Arabia because the Saudis would not allow the RAF to use their airspace and thus they had to find an alternative route. The Saudi objection can be explained on the grounds that they did not want to be seen as associating with one side or another. It was quite clear that Nasser opposed Hussein and one can assume that the Saudis, who were unsure about the outcome in Jordan, did not want to alienate Egypt more than necessary.

The only quick route available was over Israel. This created a most strange situation in which Hussein's existence was threatened by his Arab neighbours while his survival depended on its enemy, Israel. Hussein and Shamir Rifai were aware that, following the Saudi refusal to permit flights through Saudi airspace, it might be necessary for British troops to be flown over Israel and that they would have to be reinforced and maintained by the same route.[28] However, they were reconciled to this as they knew they stood alone without Arab support.[29]

ISRAEL AND THE JORDANIAN CRISIS

The British government had already approached the Israeli government on 15 July for permission to fly through Israeli airspace. Barbara Salt, the British Chargé d'Affaires in Tel-Aviv, asked Ben-Gurion whether Israel would permit British troops to overfly Israel if the need arose. Ben-Gurion replied that although Israel was interested to see the present status quo in Jordan continue, he could not give an answer without consulting the Cabinet first.[30]

The Israeli government was very worried by the coup in Iraq and Ben-Gurion feared that similar events could follow in Saudi Arabia, Sudan and Jordan.[31] According to Professor Harkabi, at that time Head of IDF Intelligence, the coup came as a total surprise to Israel and there was growing speculation about the political orientation of the conspirators.[32] Ben-Gurion wrote to Eisenhower during the crisis that the new regime in Iraq should be treated with deep scepticism because it was closer to communism than Nasser himself.[33] At the same time, the Israelis also feared that Nasser might be behind the coup because Abd al-Salam Aref (Qassem's deputy) was seen as a pro-Nasserist.[34] However, before Israel even had time to consider the British request seriously in the light of these events it was faced with a *fait accompli*, as the British Cabinet, assuming that the Israelis would not raise any objections, began their flights.[35]

The first RAF planes flew over Israel on 16 July without prior clearance, and advanced troops of the 16th Parachute Regiment arrived at Amman airport at about noon. However, the rest of the troops were turned back to Cyprus when Israeli jets scrambled and fired on the British planes.[36] The Israeli government told the British government that their request was under 'active consideration', but that the earliest they could expect a reply was not before midday on 17 July. The British Chargé d'Affaires was puzzled by Israel's apprehension and assumed that Ben-Gurion did not want to be blamed for supporting a military action in which Israel would have no voice.[37] Salt anticipated that Israel opposed the operation because it might prevent Jordan's collapse, and that Israel would prefer to see the fall of Jordan in order to annex the West Bank.[38] She also believed that Ben-Gurion was a 'master of his Cabinet and did not need two days to decide on his price'.[39] However, in her own mind she felt that it was in Israel's interest to keep Nasser and the UAR away from Jordan and that therefore they should favour British action.[40]

However, Ben-Gurion had concerns about the further implications of British action, and although he was a powerful and influential figure, his power over this decision was limited. As opposed to his firm control over defence issues, where Ben-Gurion consulted very few people, here the Israeli Prime Minister had to convince the members of his coalition government to support his decision. Ben-Gurion also wanted to avoid any overt involvement in the upheaval in the Arab world and preferred, in this case, to remain in the background. Unlike in the Suez crisis, Ben-Gurion was now aware of two influential actors whose support he was keen to secure: world public opinion and the United States. Michael Bar-Zohar, Ben-Gurion's biographer, notes that the British request did not seem to Ben-Gurion so urgent as to justify immediate government consultation and Ben-Gurion also wanted to be sure that the United States supported Britain's request and action.[41] The Suez war had, after all, demonstrated the decline of Britain's power in the region and the great importance of the United States, and Ben-Gurion was anxious this time to play his cards carefully. He also did not want to alienate the Soviet Union and to expose Israel to any danger from the Soviets.[42] Above all, Ben-Gurion had strong doubts about whether the stationing of British forces in Jordan was in Israeli interests, because he suspected Britain's real motives.[43] This deep suspicion of the British led him to protest to Macmillan on 17 July that Israel was faced with a *fait accompli* and to express his hope that such incidents would not happen again. 'We cannot', he concluded, 'acquiesce in the sovereignty of our country being violated.'[44] Thus, he insisted that, prior to any agreement by his government, he should be assured that the United States supported Britain's action in Jordan.[45] Subsequently, in a late-night telephone conversation on 17 July, Dulles assured Ben-Gurion that British intervention in Jordan enjoyed full American support.[46]

Meanwhile, Macmillan addressed the question of overflying Israel in a formal parliamentary debate on 17 July, and justified the decision on the grounds that it was most urgent to send British planes to Amman.[47] However, in private he was aware that the Israelis might complain about British action and in his diary entry of 17 July admitted that the overflying of Israeli territory on 16 July without prior permission from the Israeli government was a 'major mistake'.[48] Macmillan, aware of the risk to the future operation, apologised to Ben-Gurion and assured him on 18 July, that as soon as he was aware that the overflight had not been granted prior permission by Israel, he had given orders to postpone the operation.[49] He also promised Ben-Gurion that British troops were in Jordan to save King Hussein and would not intervene in any incidents along the Jordanian–Israeli border.[50]

The episode proved that the British government had not previously taken into consideration a situation where Israel's assistance would be necessary to save an Arab leader, nor the fact that it could be a beneficial player in a time of crisis in the Middle East. Furthermore, Israel's willingness to co-operate with the British was taken for granted on the assumption that Israel preferred to maintain the status quo. It proved that there was no British military planning for such an action and that decisions were being taken on the spot. Thus, Macmillan found himself eventually in a situation where he and his government had to plead for Israeli help and sympathy.

DISCUSSIONS AT THE UN

Britain and the United States also took the issue of intervention to the United Nations in order to ensure an international solution to the problem. On 18 July, nine Security Council members supported a Japanese resolution calling for additional measures to be taken in order to uphold the integrity and political independence of Lebanon, which it was hoped might make US withdrawal possible. The resolution was vetoed by the Soviet Union, who condemned the action and stated that the whole affair had an 'acute smell of oil'.[51] On the same day, Nikita Khrushchev, Chairman of the Council of Ministers of the USSR, presented a letter to Eisenhower in which he warned that the American and British intervention in the Lebanon and Jordan posed a threat to the peace and stability of the region and therefore called for a summit of the USSR, Britain, United States, France and India, with the possible attendance of the UN Secretary-General, in order to discuss the situation in the Middle East.[52]

Both the Americans and the British objected to the proposal, and Dulles felt strongly that they must avoid anything that could provide an opportunity to present the problem as American aggression against the Lebanon.[53] The British shared the American view and Lloyd observed that it was most important to complete the Lebanese and Jordanian operations before any discussions with the Soviets.[54] The Israelis, too, objected to such a summit, with Ben-Gurion stating his belief in regard to the proposal that 'no good can come to Israel but only evil'.[55]

FRENCH REACTION

The only party in favour of the Soviet proposal was France. This was part of de Gaulle's policy, after he became Premier of France on 1 June, of breaking away from close co-operation with the Anglo-Saxon countries in search of a more independent policy.[56] The Israelis viewed the development of this new French attitude with anxiety, but they were aware that France was less hostile towards the Soviets than other Western countries. However, they believed that this difference was not an obstacle to their close relations, as the Israelis still regarded France as their main ally and supporter. However, they were uncertain what line and direction de Gaulle would adopt. The Israeli government was informed by Guy Mollet, the French Prime Minister, on 24 July, that de Gaulle had great sympathy towards Israel, but had some reservations on the subject of open co-operation which arose from his basic political outlook and not from a lack of sympathy towards Israel. De Gaulle preferred, Mollet added, to leave the impression that Israel and France might sign a treaty, because it could strengthen France's position in the region.[57] De Gaulle's personal attitude, as revealed in his memoirs, both towards Zionism and the state of Israel, was sympathetic. 'I could', he wrote, 'not fail to be attracted by the grandeur of an enterprise which consists in re-establishing an autonomous Jewish nation.'[58] He went on to say that, from a human point of view, it was some compensation for all the suffering Jews had endured through generations. However, although the existence of Israel was more than justified, one could not and should not ignore the problems it created in the Arab world. Israel should therefore be aware of these difficulties and treat its Arab neighbours, whose pride was wounded, with great caution.[59] Moreover, de Gaulle wanted to restore France's former position in the Middle East, in both Cairo and Damascus.[60] De Gaulle appreciated the heavy burden of the involvement in Algeria, its impact on France's relations vis-à-vis the Arab world and the political price paid for it. His outlook on the matter was bound to affect his relations with Israel, and when he succeeded to power he wanted to change the nature of the Franco-Israeli relationship. De Gaulle, however, did not favour this form of close relations because he viewed the situation in the Middle East differently to his predecessors and thought that foreign relations should be conducted by the Quai d'Orsay and not by the Defence Ministry. In his letter to Ben-Gurion, dated 30 July, de Gaulle emphasised his sympathy and concern for Israel's security, but also stressed his belief in non-interference in the internal affairs of regional states, as well as the necessity to adopt a reasonable attitude towards the extreme groups in the Middle East.[61]

This belief that there were larger interests relating to the Algerian situation, and the fact that control of foreign affairs was given back to the Quai d'Orsay, had an impact on Franco-Israeli relations and on France's policy in the region. After all, the significance of Franco-Israeli relations arose from the fact that they were conducted between defence ministries which had very similar views on the Middle East, Nasser and the Algerian problem. The Quai d'Orsay held a different view and was concerned to re-establish good relations with the Arab world.

The first signs of change came in July 1958 when an initial agreement was signed between the UAR and the Suez Canal company, and in August, when France and Egypt signed an agreement in Zurich, which paved the way for a renewal of relations between the two countries.[62] The Israeli Ambassador to Paris, Yacov Zur, had already warned in 1956 that, although the French Defence Ministry was powerful, one should bear in mind that the civil service dominated the formation of French foreign policy. 'Governments come and go,' he concluded, 'but the civil service forever stays.'[63] His view proved to be more than accurate. Although at this stage there were no clear signs of a shift in policy, nonetheless in private conversations between French and British officials there were some references to the different nature of relations the new government was going to pursue.

The French Foreign Minister, Couve de Murville, had already told Selwyn Lloyd at the end of June that in future Franco-Israeli relations would be conducted in a less provocative fashion.[64] De Gaulle also assured Macmillan that the nature of the relations would be slightly modified.[65] Still, Israeli decision-makers wanted to believe that these changes were cosmetic rather than fundamental. At this stage they could still hang on to this notion because de Gaulle did not raise any obstacles to good Franco-Israeli relations or indicate the arrival of any major changes. Yet, Israeli concerns were to be confirmed all too soon. The Algerian question, the very issue that paved the way to a close Franco-Israeli relationship, proved subsequently to be the core issue which divided them. This French change of heart, as a result of De Gaulle's accession to power, did not indicate an imediate, fundamental change in Franco-Israeli relations, but it was a sign that future relations might not be as close as they had been. Israel had always sought a closer relationship with the United States and Britain, and the crisis seemed like a good opportunity for Israel to expand its ties with other Western states.

THE UNITED STATES, BRITAIN, ISRAEL AND THE OVERFLIGHTS

Meanwhile, on 17 July, the American government also requested permission to overfly Israel as a demonstration of US intentions and their support for the pro-Western powers in the region.[66] This was an easier decision for the Israelis to make than that concerning British overflights because, first, it was a request by America, a country for which Israel had special sympathy and with which it had close economic relations, and, second, in Israel's view, the situation in the Lebanon seemed in essence very different to the one in Jordan. Since 1949, after the first Arab–Israeli war, the Israeli–Lebanese border had been a quiet frontier and Israel perceived the Lebanon as a different and more moderate country. During the May crisis, Israel had even indicated to the Lebanese that it would not exploit the situation if Lebanese forces stationed on the northern border were withdrawn in order to reinforce troops in Beirut.[67] Ben-Gurion told Sir Francis Rundall on 19 July, that, if Chamoun fell from power, there would be other forces which could pursue a pro-Western line in Lebanon, unlike Jordan where its pro-Western policy depended only on the King.[68]

However, around this time, Ben-Gurion also began to change his policy towards Jordan. Although he still had grave doubts about Hussein's ability to survive, he and the Israeli Cabinet decided to support the British and American decision to aid the King. In part, this was because the aid was an indication of Western determination to assist

Middle Eastern states in their resistance against Nasser and his powerful influence.

The Israelis began to see that they might be able to use the opportunity of the coup in Iraq to try to persuade the West once again that Israel was the only loyal stronghold in the region. Ben-Gurion, in particular, was determined to use the moment to the full. When he met Rundall on 19 July, he repeated his frustration at the British overflights occurring without prior agreement, but then followed this by proposing a partnership between Britain and Israel. Rundall, who was quite surprised by this sudden approach, told Ben-Gurion that collaboration between the two countries already existed. Ben-Gurion, however, disagreed and said that partnership meant in his view a British arms supplies to Israel[69] and concluded that at present, 'Anglo-Israeli relations did not exist'.[70]

At first, this initiative failed to elicit a response from the British. Faced with continuing concern about the situation in Jordan and the lack of a positive response concerning overflights from the Israeli government, the British government finally lost its patience. Rundall told Ben-Gurion, on 20 July, that if Israel did not accede to British overflights a fatal imbalance of power between East and West might be established, and Britain therefore believed that the Israeli government must allow the airlift to Jordan to continue.[71] This kind of language and tone could only stiffen Israel's position. After all, it was Israel and not any Arab country that was being traversed by the overflights; it was Israel whose territory made possible assistance to a country with whom its relationship could hardly be described as friendly.

However, it did not take long for the British to be forthcoming. Macmillan, realising that only positive action could ensure Israel's goodwill, wrote Ben-Gurion a letter on 21 July explaining that Britain had no intention to mislead Israel about the scope of the operation or the number of troops involved.[72] Macmillan assured Ben-Gurion that Britain was making efforts to open an alternative route, which would reduce the number of flights over Israel. The highlight of the letter was, however, Macmillan's response to Ben-Gurion's partnership proposal, in which he expressed his willingness to discuss the latter's ideas and concluded optimistically that, 'In spite of the seriousness of the present situation I hope it may be the beginning of a new fruitful stage in our relations.'[73]

In part, this move appears to have arisen from mere expediency. The problem of policy towards Israel was important because the situation in Jordan remained unstable and the British feared that unless Hussein's position was reinforced there was a real danger of a coup taking place right under their noses.[74] It was therefore necessary to placate Israel in order to save Jordan. This is not, however, the whole story, for there do appear to have been other, wider factors at play. One of these was the realisation that Israel's acceptance of the overflights was not an easy decision for Ben-Gurion to take, for it opened up the possibility of new security threats to Israel. If this was the case, it was only right that Britain should reciprocate by responding positively to Ben-Gurion's overture. It is important to note here that Sir Francis Rundall played an important role in pushing the British decision-makers into taking some positive action towards Israel. Although he later viewed Ben-Gurion's proposals as 'mere blackmail' and accused the Israelis of demonstrating 'emotional overtones in their political manoeuvring as in their personal relations',[75] he realised at the time that Ben-Gurion had taken considerable risks and might find it hard to continue co-operation without a more forthcoming attitude from the British. He therefore stressed, in a telegram to the Foreign Office on 19 July, that it was important that Britain should indicate its willingness to enter into some commitment to Israel on a basis of equality.[76] He feared that without such a move the British could face further difficulties in regard to their overflights.[77]

Also, there is the possibility that Macmillan was motivated by an awareness that, at least in this area, Britain had to act independently, as it could not entirely rely on the Americans. Certainly, it seems that the American attitude regarding the situation in Jordan was quite different to that of the British. Although Dulles was aware that the situation in Jordan was still dangerous, he thought that the King's position had stabilised. At a meeting of the National Security Council in Washington on 24 July, Dulles said that Hussein had indicated to him that there was no real need for US forces in Lebanon, although the King still believed that in Jordan they would be useful as a symbol of American intentions rather than as a real safeguard.[78]

It is quite clear that the British government viewed the situation very differently and were not informed by the American government of their view of Hussein's situation. We can only assume that Dulles had his own reasons not to pass on this information, which could be explained by his desire to keep away from any direct association with Britain, in his view a colonial power, and that he also had some reservations about the value of any intervention in Jordan.[79]

The fact that Britain needed an alternative policy to that of reliance on the United States was shown in the days following Macmillan's letter to Ben-Gurion. In particular, this was evident when the British proposed that the Americans should commit ground troops to Jordan. In such a case, they thought, their overflight difficulties could be eased because the Americans were in a better position to deal with 'Israeli blackmail'.[80] Therefore, on 22 July, Macmillan asked the Americans for assistance.[81] However, the American president was unwilling to commit ground forces, which he justified by noting that it could cause difficulties both in Congress and with public opinion. He did, however, state that he was willing to allow use of American Globemaster aircraft to help with the air logistics to Jordan.[82]

The difficulties caused by the American attitude over the Jordan issue can also be seen when the Israelis made their own overtures in Washington. At a State Department meeting on 21 July, Eban argued that Israel's territorial position had made the airlift operation possible, but that the Americans and the British would eventually leave the region, while Israel would remain there and might find that as a result of the operation it was threatened. Therefore, he claimed, it was only sensible that Israel's military capacity should be strengthened.[83] The Americans were, however, reluctant to accept this argument and Dulles stressed that the administration believed that the Eisenhower doctrine gave sufficient guarantees to Israel.[84]

Although in the short term Britain needed Israel and was almost totally dependent on Ben-Gurion's goodwill, it would be wrong to suggest that only its short-term needs contributed towards a different attitude. With the fall of Nuri, one of the main pillars of British policy in the region had collapsed, and the Foreign Office had to admit, as it later noted to the Washington embassy in October, that, 'We can look back over years and see that our previous attitude towards Israel in fact got us little credit with the Arabs, who are never likely to be satisfied on this score, nor did it in the end help to bolster our friendship in the Arab world.'[85]

However, despite the soothing words used by Macmillan on 21 July, Ben-Gurion remained sceptical. He wrote in his diary, 'I do not have great hopes that British foreign policy will change, but we shall wait and see.'[86] Elath, the Israeli Ambassador in London, was also surprised and excited when Lloyd told him, on 23 July, that Britain was interested to hear Israel's views regarding Jordan. Elath told the Foreign Secretary that such an approach would do more than anything to reduce Israeli suspicions towards British policy in the region. This approach, he said, had made his eight years in London worthwhile.[87] However, when Ben-Gurion asked Elath's opinion on the current nature of Anglo-Israeli relations, Elath privately noted that he doubted whether any real change in British policy towards Israel had taken place, and stated his belief that, although Macmillan showed some genuine goodwill, the old officials in the Foreign Office still clung to their traditional hostile attitude, and that Selwyn Lloyd was a nonentity.[88]

Despite his doubts, Ben-Gurion could still see, however, that a policy of co-operation could be advantageous and therefore, on 22 July, Ben-Gurion decided simply to ignore the flights and told Rundall that for the moment he did not have daily contact with the Israeli air force and that only in two or three days could he be sure whether foreign aircraft were flying over Israel.[89] Taking into account Ben-Gurion's links to the defence circles this was quite unbelievable, especially since all who stood on their balconies in Tel-Aviv could spot the large British aircraft.[90] Ben-Gurion decided that he would ignore the flights until he received replies from Britain and the United States to his requests. He was hoping that the changing situation in the Middle East would convince the two countries to reshape their policies. The Israelis believed that they had 'crossed the Rubicon', and that their co-operation during the crisis was stronger proof than the Suez affair of Israel's affiliation with the Western camp.[91] It was therefore the moral duty of the West to ensure that Israel would not suffer as a result.[92]

THE ISRAELI THREAT TO OCCUPY THE WEST BANK

The Israeli government was also worried about Jordan's future. They feared that Hussein's regime might collapse and therefore believed that some settlement for its future should be arranged, even with the new Iraqi regime. On 27 July, Eban told Dulles that Israel thought that the West Bank belonged to the Palestinians, and therefore it might be possible to unite the eastern portion of Jordan with Iraq, while the western part, although still a politically autonomous unit, could be brought into a union with Israel.[93] To anyone familiar with Israeli fears of Iraq, this sounds almost unbelievable. Ever since the 1948–49 war, Israel had genuine fears that Iraqi troops might enter Jordan and alter the status quo and the balance of power. Iraq was a major concern of Israel's decision-makers, since the Iraqis had never signed an armistice agreement with Israel. Already, in autumn 1956, Israel had rejected the idea of Iraqi forces entering Jordan, and one might even speculate that the Qalqilya operation was initiated partly for this reason. During the crisis of summer 1958, however, Israel appears to have been more tolerant towards Iraq, which is particularly surprising taking into account that there was now a new more radical regime, of which the Israelis were very suspicious. The immediate question, therefore, is what was Israel's policy vis-à-vis Iraq, especially towards Iraqi co-operation with Jordan. There is no definite answer to this question, because many of the documents in the Israeli archives are not accessible to researchers.[94]

Israel's change of attitude might be understood if we take into consideration the different circumstances of the Iraqi coup. The troops that initiated the coup originally had orders to proceed to Jordan to assist in maintaining public order. Since this was a decision taken by the Arab Union, and the British were not involved, Israel viewed it differently to 1956. At this stage (July 1958), Israel also had to consider what the favourable outcome would be, or at least the less damaging one if Jordan collapsed; would Iraq or the UAR have the dominant influence in Jordan? If we analyse Israel's behaviour during spring–autumn 1958, we might conclude that Iraq was seen at the time as the lesser of the two evils. The other answer is that it was an opportunity for Israel to expand its territory.[95] Still, it is hard to explain the contradiction between Ben-Gurion's letter to Eisenhower on 24 July, in which he expressed his deep suspicion towards Qassem and emphasised his belief that Iraq was now under the domination of Nasser and very close to communism,[96] and the impression one could get that the Israelis were willing to see the Iraqis closer to their border than ever before. What the Israeli leaders had in mind at the time remains a mystery.

SOVIET PRESSURE ON ISRAEL

Israel's situation became even more delicate as a result of the Soviet note sent to Prime Minister Ben-Gurion on 1 August. The Soviets protested against the British overflights, which in their view were in support of an invasion of Jordan, and warned Israel that by supporting the British flights they had become associated with aggressive actions that might endanger Israel's national interests. Consequently, Ben-Gurion believed that Israel's position had become vulnerable and he ordered the British and American governments to stop their flights immediately.[97] The United States tried to convince Ben-Gurion that their mission was near to completion and that it was important that they be permitted to continue flying over Israel until 6 August. However, Ben-Gurion believed that the United States had no right to ask Israel to take a risk for Hussein's sake and he was determined to stop the flights.[98] Although Ben-Gurion's decision might appear tactical, he felt genuinely threatened by the Soviet Union's hostile attitude.[99] In the period following Suez, the Soviets had increased their involvement in the Middle East and, to large extent, become Israel's neighbours, and Ben-Gurion believed that without any special security guarantees he could not take any risks.

The British and American governments were furious with the Israeli response, which they viewed as a 'surrender' to the Soviets. The situation in Jordan remained critical and the British government was anxious to extend its operations. 'It is a most difficult and dangerous situation in Amman', Macmillan wrote, 'bad enough without this extra problem in Tel-Aviv.'[100]

Rundall's argument to Ben-Gurion on 4 August, that Israel was guaranteed by the Eisenhower doctrine and that Israel should not allow the Soviets to gain a major political success, fell on deaf ears. Ben-Gurion argued in response that the British overflights had no practical importance and told Rundall that this assumption had been confirmed by Dulles in a conversation with Eban. Therefore he asked that the flights should not be resumed for at least another week. He told Rundall that he had already informed his Cabinet that the airlift was over and that he would not reverse his decision.[101] Ben-Gurion summarised the discussion in his diary: 'Rundall badgered me for half an hour.'[102]

The Foreign Office, in its desperation, was even willing to consider special guarantees to Israel to protect it against any adverse consequences, but they wanted American approval for such a move.[103] However, the American government was not prepared to consider any special commitment towards Israel and went on to criticise Israeli determination to stop the airlift. On 3 August, Dulles told Eban that it was shocking to learn that Israel had taken such a decision without first consulting the United States. If Israel no longer stood with Britain and the United States, Dulles said, he would like to know about it. Such a decision, he warned, could have further political implications for the Soviet Union's position in the region, and he wanted to know for future reference whether Israel felt so threatened that it would do whatever the Soviets requested.[104]

The United States was informed by its embassy in Moscow that there was little chance that the Soviets would take military action in the region, though perhaps they might intervene by sending so-called 'volunteers' if action were taken against Iraq, while American intelligence reported that the Soviets would create maximum political alarm but would be cautious about making any military commitment.[105] It is hard to know whether this information was passed to the Israelis. Although there were intelligence ties between the two countries, according to Isser Harel, former head of 'Mossad', it was Israel that normally provided the Americans with information and not the other way around.[106]

Ben-Gurion was disappointed to learn of the American reaction and suspected that their harsh response was prompted by the British.[107] Ben-Gurion's suspicions were not based on anything substantial, as it was quite clear that the British government was now proving more forthcoming than the Americans regarding Israel's request for arms supplies and closer co-operation, but his assumption demonstrated once again his deep mistrust of the British Foreign Office. Ben-Gurion, who appreciated and valued America's support of Israel, wanted to avoid a breach between the two countries, and in his reply to Dulles on 5 August, he extravagantly praised Jewish heroism through the generations and stated that Israel would never be subservient to the Soviet threat. He noted that Israel had been promised that an alternative route would be found, but that three weeks after the start of the operation this had not been done. Ben-Gurion believed he was entitled to an answer about this issue without any challenge to his basic sympathy towards the West. Israel, he said, had the impression that the United States did not regard the new airlift as vital, but if the administration believed it was important they should reach an agreement satisfactory to both governments.[108] Eventually, Ben-Gurion agreed to the continuation of the overflights.

In his reply to the Soviets, Ben-Gurion argued that Israel had permitted the flights for a limited period only, as a matter of urgency, until an alternative route could be found. Furthermore, there had been no complaint from the Jordanian government that the action had been taken against its will.[109]

Ben-Gurion's decision to allow some overflights to continue was influenced by his belief that in order to secure future US–Israeli relations, and get the former's support even on a limited scale, Israel ought to show some goodwill. He had a hard task convincing some of the member parties within his Cabinet, who, he believed, did not understand the special nature and value of US friendship, and he blamed some of them for being infected with an anti-American virus. Ben-Gurion permitted the Americans to proceed with their logistical assistance to Jordan and Lebanon and allowed occasional flying until 10 August.[110]

THE CRISIS IN JORDAN AND THE RISK OF ISRAELI INVASION

The situation in the Lebanon began to stabilise after General Fuad Chehab, the Chief of Staff, an acceptable candidate to many Lebanese, was elected President on 31 July, but unrest still continued and it was estimated that at least 60 per cent of the country was out of control.[111] However, this instability was seen as being mainly criminal in nature and lacking political dimension.[112] Chehab appointed Rashid Karami, leader of the former opposition party, as Prime Minister, and he formed a government that was a balance between pro-Nasserist, pro-Western and neutralist opinion.[113]

Unlike in the Lebanon, the situation in Jordan remained unstable and it became clear that it would be necessary to find an international framework in order to safeguard Jordan's independence before the British could afford to withdraw their forces.

On 11 August, Lloyd told the Americans that, in Britain's view, it was desirable to leave a small force behind and to co-ordinate their withdrawal with them.[114] This was reinforced when the British Ambassador in Amman, Sir Charles Duke, warned the Foreign Office that an early British withdrawal could carry the risk of a coup, and he urged London to subsidise the Arab Legion with additional Bedouin units, loyal to the King.[115]

A further concern of the British and American governments in planning their withdrawal was the possibility that Jordan might still collapse and that in such a situation Israel might occupy the West Bank. Since the beginning of the crisis, there had been growing speculation about such a possibility. The British believed that Israel could not stand aside and see the whole of Jordan taken by Nasser. British suspicions were strengthened by the Americans, who estimated that Israel would occupy the West Bank and Aqaba, if only on a temporary basis, in order to deny their use to Nasser.[116] Rundall was reluctant to agree with the American assumption because he believed it could ruin Israel's claim to occupy the West Bank.[117] However, he also believed that Israel could not stand aside if Jordan collapsed and the UAR took advantage of the situation. 'All the indications are,' he wrote to the Foreign Office on 5 August, 'that it would be an extremely swift operation.'[118] Israel, he warned, could mobilise almost overnight, as it had before the Sinai campaign.[119] All the parties involved still feared that King Hussein would not be able to hold on to his position. In particular, American intelligence estimated that if Hussein continued his present policy after Britain's withdrawal, it would only be a few months before he would be overthrown, and although Israel would hold back its forces for a while, it would not tolerate a move by the UAR to annex Jordan.[120]

On 11 August, Dulles told Viscount Hood that if Israel occupied the West Bank it would create total chaos, because the UAR would suffer an international defeat, the USSR consequently would feel obliged to join in, and the West would have to assist Israel. 'The area', Dulles concluded, 'would be off to what at least could be something like the Spanish civil war.'[121] However, the British and American governments believed that there was a positive side to the threat because it would act as a deterrent to Nasser's ambitions. Dulles anticipated that the Israeli threat served as a restraint upon the UAR's ambitions and might also help to secure the establishment of UN forces in Jordan.[122]

The Jordanian royal family also knew that Israeli action was, in a way, their best safeguard against the UAR. In fact, Queen Zein of Jordan told the British Ambassador in Amman, on 11 August, that she and the King were distressed by an Israeli broadcast which had stated that if there was a coup in Jordan, Israel would not occupy the West Bank.[123] On 10 August, Golda Meir told Selwyn Lloyd that Israel was concerned at the prospect of taking over a territory in which 850,000 Palestinians lived, but, at the same time, it could not stand aside if the UAR took over Jordan. Meir emphasised, therefore, that Israel would be happy for Britain to remain in Jordan.[124] Indeed, Meir also told Sir Francis Rundall, on 29 August, that Israel did not want to take over the West Bank, but that if Jordan collapsed Israel would have to take Mount Scopus, the old city of Jerusalem and strategic grounds on their side of Jordan.[125]

Meir's announcement that Israel welcomed British presence in Jordan, at least until the crisis was over, can be seen as a change in Ben-Gurion's attitude, for in July he had still been worried about the British forces stationed in Jordan. It seems that the more positive relations and the greater understanding between the two countries had reduced his suspicions. Meir also said that the present frontier between Israel and Jordan could be tolerated if there was some kind of international force in Jordan. This is quite surprising, especially taking into account that Israel had no great confidence in the ability of any international force to protect its existence. It is interesting to note that later that year, Selwyn Lloyd received a very different response from the Israeli Ambassador in London. In a conversation in December, Lloyd asked Elath what Israel's reaction would be if an international force was stationed partly in Jordan and partly in Israel, and Elath replied to the Secretary of State by stating categorically that it was unacceptable and that Israel's attitude would be similar to the British reaction if an international force were stationed along both sides of the Irish border to protect the citizens of Northern Ireland.[126]

Rundall assumed correctly that Israel had already planned for an occupation of the West Bank if necessary.[127] As revealed in Ben-Gurion's diary, Israel had plans to occupy the Hebron mountain area and the northern mountain ridge from Jerusalem to Nablus. The possibility of such an action was discussed with the Israeli Chief of Staff as early as 14 July, but Ben-Gurion had suggested at the time giving priority to diplomatic and political methods.[128]

The question is, did Israel really intend to occupy the West Bank during the summer and autumn of 1958? In answering this we should take into consideration the different atmosphere of 1958 to that of autumn 1956. This time, events remained regional and did not develop into a full international crisis. Israel's foreign policy had not changed fundamentally since the winter of 1956, but Israeli military victory in the Suez campaign contributed to a more relaxed, secure climate. At the same time, Israeli leaders realised that the Middle East had become a part of the Cold War rivalry; hence, every Israeli action might have further, global implications and could bring the Soviets into the picture. Israel also now had to acknowledge its great dependence on the United States, and unlike in 1956, France, Israel's main ally, did not take a major role. It was quite clear that de Gaulle would not support an Israeli action, let alone co-operate in one. In addition, Moshe Dayan, who had previously presented a very militant line, completed his term of office as Chief of Staff, a fact that might have contributed to a more moderate attitude. It is quite clear that the personnel change had an impact. This was true when Ben-Gurion succeeded Sharett and when Macmillan succeeded Eden, but we should also take into consideration the fact that events are sometimes a stronger factor than personnel change.

Already, during the Sinai war, Ben-Gurion had appreciated the complicated issue of the Palestinian refugees. He was aware that if Israel occupied the West Bank it would have to incorporate a massive Palestinian population, which could cause Israel great difficulties. At that stage in his career he understood that Israel's problem was a lack of Jews and not a lack of space.[129] An occupation of the West Bank could therefore cause internal problems, might damage Israel's efforts to secure arms and security guarantees, and ruin its relations worldwide. Thus, Israel was prepared to take action if the situation in Jordan became hopeless and the West stood aside, but it did not seek to engineer such an opportunity. The statements of Ben-Gurion and other Israeli officials were intended to serve as a deterrent to Israel's Arab neighbours rather than as a declaration of intent. It was a fundamental characteristic of Israel's foreign policy that it aimed to deter the Arab countries from taking aggressive action against Israel.

THE CRISIS DRAWS TO AN END

Fortunately, during August, the situation in Jordan stabilised and the King gained control over the rebel forces. The threat of Israeli annexation of the West Bank receded, and Britain could start planning its withdrawal from Jordan. In addition, there was progress on the international front to ensure that Britain could withdraw safely without fear of further Iraqi or UAR intervention. An opportunity for international agreement offered itself after the UN General Assembly opened its session on 12 August. The United States and Britain were concerned to ensure that the Soviet Union would not exploit this occasion for its own advantage, and therefore supported a resolution put forward by the Arab states on 21 August, to solve the problem themselves. The resolution pledged non-interference among the Arab states in each other's affairs and instructed the UN Secretary-General to arrange an agreement for the withdrawal of British and American forces.[130] It placed obligations on the Arab states themselves, and offered Britain and the United States the opportunity to end their military action.

When the British finally started to plan their withdrawal in October, they were faced with the question of which route to choose. It was agreed that they would use UAR airspace through Syria, but they wanted to make sure that this move would not lead to hostile interference by the UAR. Dag Hammarskjold, the UN Secretary-General, assured them, on 5 October, that he had UAR agreement for Britain to use their airspace without interference.[131] The Chiefs of Staff and the Air Ministry believed, however, that the most efficient route for withdrawal was through Israel because its air traffic control was much more efficient than that of Syria, and, although the plan was to withdraw through Syria, the British wanted to keep the Israeli option as an alternative. Francis Rundall was also worried that the Israelis might get the impression that they were being 'dropped out' of the operation. The Israeli government, however, did not think this. Michael Comay, the Assistant Director-General of the Israeli Foreign Ministry, assured the Ambassador on 7 October that Israel would not feel 'dropped' in the slightest, because it had always believed that the withdrawal of British forces was not its concern and was part of the UN resolution. He stated that Israel was willing to grant permission for more overflying, although he emphasised that a different route would be preferred.[132] On 25 October, American forces left the Lebanon, and the British evacuated their forces from Jordan by air on 2 November. The route chosen for the withdrawal was through Amman–Bannias–Sidon to Nicosia.[133]

With the end of the crisis, it is important to analyse its nature and to understand why it remained local and did not develop into an international one. First, it is essential to examine the different roles of the powers involved, and to see, as with Israel, that the lessons learnt from Suez contributed to very different behaviour. In addition, the positive role of the United States, in contrast to its behaviour in 1956, placed events in a very different perspective. This time the Americans did not undermine Britain's plans, standing by it and co-ordinating their efforts. Moreover, the Western powers responded to a clear request from Jordan and the Lebanon with the active participation of the UN.

It was an open move without secret and mysterious figures and exotic hiding places, and it was therefore hard for the Soviet Union or the UAR to score points on the grounds that it was an imperialist conspiracy.

THE CRISIS AND ITS IMPLICATIONS ON ISRAELI FOREIGN POLICY

As the crisis came to an end, the Israeli leaders were keen to harvest the fruits of their co-operation with the West. One of the main targets was the United States. Although finally the United States was willing to sign a formal defence agreement with Turkey, Iran and Pakistan, it was reluctant to sign a similar agreement with Israel or to supply Israel with arms. Yet, there was some change in its policy later that year. Israel needed financial assistance in order to pay Britain for 55 Centurion tanks at an estimated cost of $8–10 million, which Israel did not have.[134] On 17 October, Eban emphasised the urgent need to obtain this aid, because there were growing signs of an improvement in Anglo-Israeli relations, to which Israel attached great importance, and it would not like to fail to benefit because of a lack of economic strength.[135] The Americans were willing to help and provided a programme of assistance which enabled Israel to purchase approximately 58 Centurion tanks.[136] The Americans were also willing to supply Israel with S-58 Sikorsky helicopters with multiple-barrelled machine-guns. However, they proved unwilling to release 200 Patton tanks from France and Italy.[137] The United States, Dulles told Meir, had made an important exception in its policy of not being a major supplier of arms to Israel, but their basic policy had not changed and it would be better if Israel did not raise great expectations.[138] It would take another nine years for the real turning point in US–Israeli relations to come.

ISRAEL AND THE PERIPHERY TREATY

Although Ben-Gurion believed that the America of Eisenhower and Dulles was in a period of temporary decline, he still felt that friendly relations with the United States were of great importance for Israel.[139] Ben-Gurion also realised that the United States could help with a different issue which had enormous importance for Israel: the 'Periphery Treaty'. In the midst of the crisis Ben-Gurion was quick to realise the benefits of US support for Israel's plan to expand its relations with regional states outside the circle of the Arab–Israeli dispute. He wrote to Eisenhower that Israel wanted to create a group of countries, not necessarily under a formal umbrella, which by mutual political and economic assistance could create a buffer against Nasser's expansion and influence. He tried to get the American president to help Israel by indicating to the countries concerned that the initiative enjoyed the support of the United States.[140] On this matter the Americans were forthcoming and Dulles told Eban, on 21 July, that he had told the Shah that the administration viewed Israel's initiative with sympathy.[141]

As emphasised previously, Israel had tried after Suez to reach a closer relationship with these African and Asian countries, and these efforts were now enhanced by the events of July. This was especially true in the case of Turkey, a country which had, up to then, hesitated over the question of a closer relations with Israel. The coup in Iraq caused concern among the Turkish leaders, who sought to explore the opportunity of a closer relationship with Israel and indicated that they would like to see full political co-ordination between the two countries.[142] Consequently, it was decided that a high-level meeting should take place in Turkey, and Ben-Gurion flew to Ankara on 28 August to discuss the matter with his Turkish colleagues. Like many events and actions in Israel's history and foreign affairs, the entire affair was shrouded in secrecy and only a few people knew about Ben-Gurion's destination. The meeting with the Turks proved to be very productive and the Turkish government decided to raise the level of diplomatic representation in Israel and to broaden economic and political co-operation.[143]

TOWARDS A NEW ERA: THE SHIFT IN THE ANGLO-ISRAELI RELATIONSHIP

Israeli co-operation during the crisis of July 1958 and its willingness to assist the British flights to Jordan, combined with Nuri's fall, finally brought a much closer co-operation between Israel and Britain, and Ben-Gurion was determined to use the opportunity to cash in on Britain's goodwill. It is now that a real shift in the Anglo-Israeli relationship can be seen, beginning with the visit to London of Golda Meir, Israel's Foreign Minister, in early August. The main issues on the agenda were: first, British policy towards the Middle East, second, arms supply, and third, the eternal issue of the Guildhall plan.

The Israelis were obsessed with the 'Guildhall' question and they had not forgotten or forgiven the British government for its part in ALPHA. Although the US government was also behind ALPHA, the Israeli government always blamed the British for taking the initiative for the plan. For Israel, therefore, the British attitude towards 'Guildhall' was a test of the mood in Whitehall. Golda Meir told Selwyn Lloyd, on 12 August, that there was an uneasy atmosphere between the two countries because of the Guildhall speech and Israel believed that in order to create a firm base of understanding with Britain it was essential to clarify the issue.[144] Lloyd tried to emphasise that Britain had forgotten all about the Guildhall speech and that it belonged to the past.[145] Foreign Office officials also tried to convince the Israelis that a 'Guildhall plan' had never existed and there was no intention to translate the speech into a programme. The speech, they argued, would have been forgotten if Israel had not raised it again and again. Eventually, they admitted that at the time they thought that the speech could be used as a basis for an Arab–Israeli settlement, but this hope had faded away after the Sinai campaign.[146] This assurance brought great relief to the Israelis and Ben-Gurion commented in his diary: 'The Guildhall affair ceased to exist – a new chapter is open and there are chances for a better relationship and understanding between Israel and Britain.'[147]

The second issue was arms supply to Israel. The British government had to find a middle way which avoided jeopardising their future relations with friendly Arab governments and with the new Iraqi regime, but at the same time showed some positive approach towards the Israeli request for arms. They also realised that it would be against the spirit of their present relations with Israel to quibble over minor items and that there should be a certain relaxation of their former strict embargo.[148] The Israelis had a long shopping list which included Centurion tanks, submarines and guided missiles. The British government was willing to supply Israel with submarines, although they hesitated to supply the tanks, fearing a negative reaction from Jordan. Lloyd told Golda Meir, when they met in New York at the United Nations on 26 September, that it would therefore be better if the United States could supply the tanks, but Meir said that Jordan should not be worried because it was not under any threat from Israel as long as King Hussein could maintain his position and his country's independence.[149] The British government decided, therefore, to take the risk of hostile Arab propaganda and to supply Israel with the tanks and also with submarines, which were to be refitted and shipped from Malta.[150]

The Israeli government also suggested co-operation in the commercial, military and intelligence fields. In regard to commercial relations, the Israelis sought Britain's assistance in simplifying the bureaucratic procedures for obtaining cover for its exporters and, at the same time, encouraging Israel's imports of United Kingdom machinery and other manufactured goods. France, Belgium and the United States gave credit cover up to certain limits for various types of machinery, which enabled the Israeli authorities to plan imports ahead from those countries and simplified the import licence and convertibility guarantee documentation. The Israelis, therefore, wanted Britain to approve a global limit of credit cover for certain types of machinery.[151] The Israelis also wanted to test Britain's sincerity in opening a new chapter in relations between the two countries by putting forward the idea that Britain should help Israel in its economic relations with Europe. They suggested that Britain should help Israel to strengthen its relations with European organisations. It is not clear from the documents whether the Israelis meant the EEC or whether they wanted Britain to help them in the Council of Europe, where the Chancellor of the Exchequer was the chairman of the Council of Ministers.[152] This issue in any case highlighted Israel's desire to expand its trade with Britain in the belief that Britain was still an economic power that held influence over certain European institutions. It also demonstrates that Israel was eager to extend its trade with Europe, and was aware of the growing importance of these markets. One should bear in mind that most of the Israeli decision-makers at the time, and Israel's founders, were European-orientated and they shared the belief that Israel could ensure its superiority in the region only if it adopted Western methods and values. Ben-Gurion believed these relations were of prime importance to Israel because they would have a positive effect on its position vis-à-vis Europe. In this he was influenced by Shimon Peres, the General Director of the Ministry of Defence and a very influential figure at the time, who opposed the view that Israel should try to integrate itself in the region. Peres argued instead that Israel was linked to the Middle East only geographically, but on all other matters should seek closer co-operation with Europe, which was culturally and politically Israel's natural ally.[153] The British government, however, did not find that it was in their interests to help Israel, largely because it would have led to similar requests from other countries outside the EEC.[154]

The Israelis wanted the British government to encourage oil companies to invest in Israel and to contribute towards the development of their new pipeline from Eilat to the Mediterranean.[155] In addition, Israel was interested in closer military ties with the British army. The Israeli armed forces were founded on the British model and many of their officers had served during the Second World War in the British forces. Haim Laskov, Israeli Chief of Staff at the time, was, for example, a product of the British army. He, in addition to other officers, saw the British forces as a role model and therefore favoured closer ties between the two. In this sphere the British were more forthcoming as they believed it was a way of gaining influence over the IDF, which was a key establishment and had a great influence over Israeli decision-makers. In particular, the British were keen to co-operate with the Israelis in the intelligence sphere, because they appreciated Israel's expertise in assessing Arab thinking and tactics.[156]

The British were forced to conclude during the crisis that the best method of reducing Israel's anxiety would be to supply arms. As Rundall argued, on 12 September, it would boost Israel's feeling of security and convince it that it would not stand alone if faced with aggressive action, thus preventing a return to the state of affairs that existed in Israel before the Sinai campaign.[157] The Foreign Office therefore decided that Israel should be treated just like any another country with which Britain enjoyed normal relations and should be supplied with arms.[158]

Accordingly, in December 1958, the British government decided to supply Israel with the Centurion tanks, although they were eager to keep this secret for as long as possible.[159] The British hoped that the United States would adopt a similar policy. After all, one of the characteristic lines of British foreign policy at that time was Britain's effort to conduct its policy in the Middle East in harmony with the United States. However, the British found that in regard to Israel, their starting point was different and that therefore they had to introduce a more forthcoming approach than the Americans. Although the British government believed that there were no great differences between themselves and the American government, and agreed with Dulles' basic assumption that Western involvement with Israel was, in general, an obstacle to the pursuit of Western interests,[160] they had to admit that their previous policy, compared with that of the United States, could be described as frigid and even hostile.[161]

Thus, to overcome memories of the past, the British government realised that it had to be more positive than the United States. Rundall also realised that Israel might take desperate action, if unable to obtain arms,[162] and also noted that if Israel felt insecure, it might adopt a harsh attitude because it would prefer 'to be morally indefensible now than to being militarily indefensible later'.[163]

The Foreign Office also realised that British arms supplies to Israel would increase Britain's popularity in Israel to a degree that had never existed before, a popularity which might also enable the British to gain more influence over Israel's decision-makers. The British hoped that, although they could not provide Israel with financial aid (as the Americans could), their recent benevolent policy and more forthcoming attitude would lead Israel to a better understanding of British interests in the region.[164] Rundall believed that this potential influence was very important and could be maintained not solely by arms supply, but also by small benign gestures. He emphasised that it was important not to lose the opportunity, because 'The present honeymoon, will not last forever.'[165] Viscount Hood in Washington also argued that because of Soviet penetration in the Middle East and the rise of Arab nationalism, Israel in the short and long term was a force that could combat Nasser and Soviet penetration.[166] It is interesting to point out that on the subject of Nasserism the Israelis and the British shared the same view, likewise on the far-reaching implications of Soviet penetration in the area. Both parties were reluctant to admit that Nasser was admired by many in the Arab world, enjoyed great popularity and represented much more than the command of power by a small group of authoritarian officers based on the traditional Ottoman model.

The American government, for its part, watched quietly the British arms supply to Israel, and in that respect there was a continuation of their previous policy of preferring other countries to supply arms to Israel, thus relieving the pressure on themselves. Rountree, the American Assistant Secretary of State for Middle Eastern and African Affairs, told Francis Rundall on 20 August that it was dangerous to supply Israel with submarines because it would station them in the Gulf of Aqaba which would lead to confrontation in the Gulf.[167] The American view did not change later on, and on 19 October, Dulles told Lloyd that the supply of the submarines to Israel caused quite a storm, but agreed that it had reduced Israel's tension and anxiety.[168] Lloyd argued that it was the right policy to supply Israel with arms because it relaxed Israel's tension and at the same time deterred Nasser. Israel, Lloyd added, was the only factor in the area that Nasser was afraid of, and concluded, 'At some time in the future we might be quite glad to have one friend in the Middle East.'[169] This discussion proved a change in British perceptions of Israel and shows that at that point the British government was more sympathetic towards Israel than the United States. Furthermore, as the dust settled over the crisis, the British government sent a message to Golda Meir on 5 November expressing its gratitude for Israeli assistance and offering assurance that the British would do everything in their power to see that the Israel–Jordan border would remain in its current position.[170] The same day, Harold Macmillan attended a party for the Israeli Ambassador on his departure from London. It was the first time that a British Prime Minister paid such attention to an Israeli Ambassador. In his speech at the party, Macmillan addressed the common interests between Israel and Britain, and emphasised his optimistic belief that relations between the two countries would be formulated in the future on a basis of mutual sympathy and understanding.[171] It impressed Ben-Gurion so much that he commented in his political testament that, for the first time ever, Britain, who had always before presented itself as a true and loyal friend of the Arabs, declared its sympathy towards Israel.[172]

THE CRISIS AND ITS IMPLICATIONS ON BRITISH FOREIGN POLICY

Against the background of the new developments in the region, the British government had to address the following issues: first, their future relationship with Iraq and the Baghdad Pact; second, the future strategic requirements and the military possibilities open for Britain; and third, the lessons to be learned from the events of 1958.

The British government came very quickly to the belief that it was in its interests to recognise the new Iraqi regime under Qassem, because the new administration was clearly in power and, although nationalist, its members were free from Nasser's control. Moreover, Iraq depended heavily on Western trade and it was therefore in Iraq's interests to keep all channels open. Above all, the British wanted to prevent a situation where Iraq might feel isolated by the West and consequently driven into Nasser's camp.[173] The Iraqis also emphasised their willingness to maintain friendly relations with Britain. As early as 15 July, Qassem himself had apologised to Sir Michael Wright, the British Ambassador in Baghdad, for the unfortunate events at the British embassy the day before, stressing his hope that they would not damage future relations between Iraq and Britain.[174] Then, on 17 July, Muhammad Hadid, the Iraqi Finance Minister, assured the British that his government had no intention of nationalising the oil industry and would respect the principles of the UN Charter. Iraq, he added, would maintain friendly relations with the UAR but would not join it.[175] Britain's attitude towards the regime was also influenced by the fact that the member states of the Baghdad Pact, at a meeting on 28 July, had already expressed their willingness to recognise it.[176] The only exception was King Hussein of Jordan, who objected to such a move and told the British that he was aware of its interests in Iraq, but he hoped that the British would delay their recognition. Such a move, he warned, might encourage military conspirators everywhere in the region to follow the Iraqi example.[177] Nonetheless, the British proceeded with recognition, which was formally announced on 1 August.[178]

The future of the Baghdad Pact and Iraqi participation in it was a fundamental question for the British. It was assumed that one of

Qassem's first steps would be to terminate Iraq's membership of the Pact because it had always been criticised by Arab nationalists, and any continuation of its membership could be seen as a sign of Qassem's political weakness and used by his opponents against him.[179] The British thought they should wait for an Iraqi decision on whether to terminate their membership of the Pact. The Foreign Office assumed that if Iraq was going to have any future link with the Pact it would only be in the economic sphere.[180]

The new situation in the Middle East also brought some changes in British military and strategic thinking, leading to the reorganisation of the new Middle Eastern command and the creation of two separate commands based at Cyprus and Aden respectively, as well as the adoption of the concept of strategic mobility, which had been implemented successfully during the intervention in Jordan. The Baghdad Pact was still regarded as having political advantage with minimum financial support. The Iraqi position was also important for future British military requirements in the region. Britain's position had already been weakened as a result of the Suez war, and an air barrier had been created, making Britain's manoeuvres in the region difficult. The 1958 crisis proved the great importance the British attached to the Middle East at a time when their options were more limited. However, they believed it was essential, with the increase in Soviet involvement, to enhance the West's foothold.[181] The best way to secure Britain's position in the Middle East was by closer co-operation with the United States. This belief had already existed in Britain but was accentuated by the crisis.[182] The American government, however, did not favour close co-operation with the British and preferred to conduct their policy without consulting them.

The British government believed it was essential to keep their bases in Cyprus and the Persian Gulf, in order to support both NATO (in a global war) and the Baghdad Pact. It was also of great importance to secure air and sea communication routes in the Middle East. The strategic importance of the Persian Gulf grew as a result of the stormy events of 1958. Britain's share of Gulf oil was still more than 30 per cent and most other remaining oil imports came from that region or from neighbouring states.[183] As nearly all the oil sold by the Middle East to Europe, except Saudi oil, was traded in sterling, it had great importance for Britain's economy. The loss of this oil would mean that Britain would have to use dollars to buy oil and lose its oil revenues. Thus it was decided to strengthen the forces in the Gulf and to reinforce Aden and Kenya.[184] The importance of Iran as a major base also grew as a result of the crisis.[185]

In assessing the short-term consequences of their operation, the British government could be satisfied. The situation in Jordan and in the Lebanon had been stabilised, as well as that of Iraq. However, the situation in Iraq deteriorated during 1959 and Qassem's regime faced further upheavals.

TOWARDS A NEW BEGINNING

The future of the Anglo-Israeli relationship at this point seemed to be more promising, and there is room to suggest a shift in relations between the two countries. Golda Meir's visit to London during the summer of 1958, the British arms supply and the disappearance of the Guildhall plan as an issue, all contributed to a much better atmosphere between the two countries. Anglo-Israeli co-operation during the 1958 crisis was very different to that in 1956. Then, the directors of British policy tried to hide any involvement with Israel, even from their own people, whereas in 1958, co-operation was openly discussed and led to Britain's realisation that Israel's existence in the region had a positive side and not merely a negative one. However, it would be wrong to regard the development in their relations as being on the same basis as those with France during the 1950s, or US–Israeli relations following the Six-Day war. Close relations did not emerge; nonetheless, the progress from almost hostile and frigid relations to a much warmer and sympathetic climate cannot be denied. Israel's position strengthened and it was seen as a true friend of the Western world; however, it still felt isolated and did not succeed in getting any special guarantee or in concluding any specific alliance with the United States. Not until 1967 would a special relationship be established between the two.

As the dust settled on the Middle Eastern crisis, the region entered a relatively quiet period, but this was only a hiatus: in another nine years the storm would begin to blow again.

NOTES

1. The coup is sometimes referred to as revolution, but in this book only the word 'coup' will be used.
2. Hana Batatu, *The Old Social Regime and the Revolutionary Movement in Iraq* (Princeton, NJ: Princeton University Press, 1978), p. 801.
3. PRO, FO371/134199/VQ/72(9), Wright (Baghdad) to Lloyd, 15 July 1958.
4. Ibid.
5. Harold Macmillan, *Riding the Storm, 1956–1959* (London: Macmillan, 1971), p. 511.
6. *FRUS*, Vol. 11, 1958–60, special national intelligence estimate, 5 June 1958, p. 94.
7. Dwight D. Eisenhower, *The White House Years: Waging Peace 1956–1961* (London: Heineman, 1966), p. 269.

8. *FRUS*, Vol. 11, 1958–60, special national intelligence estimate, 5 June 1958, p. 95.
9. Eisenhower, *The White House*, p. 271.
10. Ibid., p. 272.
11. US declassified documents, US85/1366, 21 July 1958.
12. Macmillan, *Riding the Storm*, p. 506.
13. Eisenhower, *The White House*, p. 273.
14. PRO, CAB128/32, C.C.(58)55, 14 July 1958.
15. Macmillan, *Riding the Storm*, p. 514.
16. PRO, FO371/134038/VJ1091/1G, Mason (Amman) to Lloyd, 16 July 1958.
17. Uriel Dann, *King Hussein and the Challenge of Arab Radicalism, Jordan 1955–1967* (Oxford: Oxford University Press, 1989), p. 86.
18. *FRUS*, Vol. 11, 1958–60, US embassy to State Department, 15 July 1958, p. 302.
19. Ibid.
20. PRO, CAB128/32, C.C.(58)57, 15 July 1958.
21. PRO, CAB128/32, C.C.(58)58, 16 July 1958.
22. Ibid.
23. Ibid.
24. Ibid., see also *Hansard*, Vol 591, col. 1438, 16 July 1958.
25. *Hansard*, Vol. 591, col. 1439, 16 July 1958. For the full parliamentary debate on the situation in the Middle East and in Jordan, see *Hansard*, Vol. 591, col. 1240–371, 16 July 1958, and pp. 1438–46, 17 July 1958.
26. Ibid., col. 1509–10, 17 July 1958.
27. PRO, CAB128/32, C.C.(58)58, 16 July 1958.
28. PRO, FO371/134038/VJ1091/1G, Mason to Lloyd, 16 July 1958.
29. United States declassified documents, US85/1375, intelligence report, 23 July 1958.
30. BGA, Ben-Gurion diary, 15 July 1958.
31. BGA, Ben-Gurion diary, 14 July 1958.
32. Yehoshafat Harkabi letter to Orna Almog, 12 November 1993.
33. United States declassified documents, US89/518, Ben-Gurion to Eisenhower, 24 July 1958.
34. Harkabi letter to Almog, 12 November 1993.
35. PRO, CAB128/32, C.C.(58)58, 16 July 1958.
36. *FRUS*, Vol. 11, 1958–60, editorial note, pp. 316–17. This information could not be found anywhere but in the American sources. It seems that it was passed from the US embassy in Tel-Aviv to Washington. It is mentioned, however, in British Cabinet documents that the leading British aircraft carrying the commander of the British troops had disregarded Israel's orders to turn back. (Cab 128/32, 17 July 1958) We can therefore assume that the Israeli fire was a response and warning to the British troops not to proceed with their flights without the authorisation of the Israeli government.
37. PRO, FO371/134345/VR1222/6, Salt (Tel-Aviv) to Foreign Office, 16 July 1958.
38. Ibid.
39. Ibid.
40. Ibid. See also Orna Almog, 'An End of an Era: The Crisis of 1958 and the Anglo-Israeli Relationship', *Contemporary Record*, Vol. 8, No. 1, Summer 1994.
41. BGA, Ben-Gurion diary, 16 July 1958.
42. Ibid.
43. PRO, FO371/134345/VR1222/6, Ben-Gurion to Macmillan, 17 July 1958.
44. Ibid.
45. *FRUS*, Vol. 11, 1958–60, White House memorandum, 17 July 1958, p. 321. See also Eisenhower, *The White House*, p. 270.
46. *Hansard*, Vol. 591, col. 1556, 17 July 1958.

47. Macmillan, *Riding the Storm*, p. 519.
48. PRO, FO371/134345/VR1222/7, Macmillan to Ben-Gurion, 18 July 1958.
49. Ibid.
50. Moshe Perlman, 'Mid-Summer Madness', *Middle Eastern Affairs*, Vol. 9, Nos 8–9, August–September 1958, p. 252.
51. *FRUS*, Vol. 11, 1958–60, editorial note, 22 July 1958, p. 339.
52. *FRUS*, Vol. 11, 1958–60, White House memorandum, 20 July 1958, p. 349.
53. *FRUS*, Vol. 11, 1958–60, memorandum of a conversation, 20 July 1958, p. 345.
54. BGA, Ben-Gurion diary, 25 July 1958.
55. Adam Watson, 'The Aftermath of Suez: Consequences for French Decolonisation', in Wm Roger Louis and Roger Owen (eds), *Suez 1956: The Crisis and its Consequences* (Oxford: Clarendon Press, 1989), p. 344.
56. BGA, Ben-Gurion diary, 24 July 1958.
57. Jean Lacouture, *Charles de Gaulle: The Ruler 1945–1970* (London: Harvill, 1991), p. 436.
58. Ibid.
59. Charles de Gaulle, *Memories of Hope* (London: Weidenfeld & Nicolson, 1971), p. 264.
60. Charles de Gaulle, Letters, *Notes et Carnets, June 1958–December 1960* (Paris: Plon, 1985), p. 57.
61. Michael Bar-Zohar, *Gesher Al Hayam Hatichon* [Bridge Over the Mediterranean] (Tel-Aviv: Am-Hassefer, 1964), p. 203.
62. ISA, HZ192/15, Zur (Paris) to Bartur (Economic Department Israeli Foreign Ministry), 26 December 1958.
63. PRO, PREM11/2326/20431, record of visit of Macmillan and Lloyd with de Gaulle, 29–30 June 1958.
64. Ibid.
65. Michael Bar-Zohar, *Ben-Gurion* (Tel-Aviv: Am-Oved, 1977), pp. 1334–5, and BGA, Ben-Gurion diary, 17 July 1958.
66. BGA, Ben-Gurion diary, 26 June 1958.
67. Ibid., 19 July 1958.
68. BGA, Ben-Gurion diary, 19 July 1958.
69. PRO, FO371/134284/VR1051/12, Rundall (Tel-Aviv) to Lloyd, 19 July 1958.
70. PRO, FO371/134345/VR1222/15, Rundall to Lloyd, 20 July 1958.
71. PRO, FO371/134346/VR1222/30, Macmillan to Ben-Gurion, 21 July 1958.
72. Ibid.
73. PRO, FO371/134039/VJ1091/35, Lloyd to Makins, 22 July 1958.
74. PRO, FO371/134298/V10710/4, Rundall to Stevens, 26 November 1958.
75. PRO, FO371/134284/VR1051/12, Rundall to Lloyd, 19 July 1958.
76. PRO, FO371/134345/VR1222/13, Rundall to Lloyd, 19 July 1958.
77. Ibid., National Security Council meeting, 24 July 1958, p. 383.
78. Ibid., conference with Eisenhower, 20 July 1958, p. 348.
79. PRO, FO371/134039/VJ1091/35, Lloyd to Caccia, 22 July 1958.
80. PRO, PREM11/2380/T342/58, Macmillan to Eisenhower, Nos 5030 and 5031, 22 July 1958.
81. *FRUS*, Vol. 11, 1958–60, Eisenhower to Macmillan, 23 July 1958, p. 378.
82. *FRUS*, Vol. 13, 1958–60, State Department memorandum, 21 July 1958, p. 69.
83. *FRUS*, Vol. 13, 1958–60, State Department memorandum, 3 August 1958, p. 82.
84. PRO, FO371/134298/V10710/1, Stevens (Deputy Under-Secretary of State) to Hood (Washington), 7 October 1958.
85. BGA, Ben-Gurion diary, 22 July 1958.
86. PRO, FO371/134284/VR1051/13, Lloyd to Rundall, 23 July 1958.
87. BGA, Ben-Gurion Diary, 18 September 1958.
88. Ibid., 22 July 1958.

89. Bar-Zohar, *Ben-Gurion*, p. 1338.
90. PRO, FO371/134284/VR1051/13, Lloyd to Rundall, 23 July 1958.
91. Ibid.
92. *FRUS*, Vol. 13, 1958–60, memorandum, 27 July 1958, pp. 74–5.
93. The Israel Defense Forces Archive is closed to most researchers, though some researchers are privileged enough to have special access to its documents. The ISA documents are available for most researchers, unless they contain any defence or security issues. The Ben-Gurion Archive in Sde-Boker is open to researchers, but again some of the material is closed to most researchers.
94. Harkabi letter to Orna Almog, 12 November 1993.
95. US declassified documents, US98/518, 24 July 1958.
96. *FRUS*, Vol. 13, 1958–60, Israeli embassy Washington to State Department, 2 August 1958, pp. 80–1.
97. BGA, Ben-Gurion diary, 24 July 1958.
98. During the Suez war Marshal Bulganin wrote a letter to Ben-Gurion warning him that the Soviet Union would not tolerate Israel's action. Ben-Gurion was furious and commented that such a letter could have been written by Hitler. He also believed that the Soviet action in Hungary proved what these 'Nazis Communists' could do. See Bar-Zohar, *Ben-Gurion*, p. 1280, in Ben-Gurion diary, 8 November 1956. Ben-Gurion also quoted Sharett who said that the Soviet propaganda against Israel and the arms deal with Egypt escalated Israel's worries, see David Ben-Gurion, *The Rebirth and Destiny of Israel* (London: Thomas Yosellof, 1959), p. 490.
99. Macmillan, *Riding the Storm*, p. 525.
100. PRO, FO371/134347/VR1222/60G, Rundall to Lloyd, 4 August 1958.
101. BGA, Ben-Gurion diary, 4 August 1958.
102. PRO, FO371/134347/VR1222/55G, Foreign Office to Washington, 3 August 1958.
103. *FRUS*, Vol. 13, 1958–60, Dulles to Eban, 3 August 1958, pp. 82–3.
104. US declassified documents, US85/1375, 23 July 1958.
105. Isser Harel, *Bithaon ve Demokratiya* [Security and Democracy] (Tel-Aviv: Edanim, 1989), p. 338.
106. BGA, Ben-Gurion diary, 4 August 1958.
107. *FRUS*, Vol. 13, 1958–60, Ben-Gurion to Dulles, 5 August 1958, pp. 86–7.
108. PRO, FO371/134347/V10338/60G, Rundall to Lloyd, 4 August 1958. See also FO371/134278/VR10338/8, Rundall to Foreign Office, 13 August 1958.
109. BGA, Ben-Gurion diary, 10 August 1958.
110. Bar-Zohar, *Ben-Gurion*, p. 1341.
111. *FRUS*, Vol. 11, 1958–60, US embassy Lebanon to State Department, 29 August 1958, p. 539.
112. Perlman, p. 254, 'Mid-Summer Madness'.
113. Yaacov Shimoni, *Medinot Arav* [The Arab States] (Tel-Aviv: Am-Oved, 1990), p. 484.
114. *FRUS*, Vol. 11, 1958–60, telegram from the embassy in the United Kingdom to the State Department, 11 August 1958, p. 452.
115. *FRUS*, Vol. 11, 1958–60, US embassy London to State Department, 24 August 1958, p. 578.
116. PRO, FO371/134313/VR1093/11G, Rundall to Johnston (Amman), 6 September 1958.
117. Ibid.
118. PRO, FO371/134313/VR/1093, Rundall to Hoyer Millar (Permanent Under-Secretary of State), 5 August 1958.
119. Ibid.
120. *FRUS*, Vol. 11, 1958–60, special national intelligence estimate, 28 October

1958, p. 620.
121. *FRUS*, Vol. 11, 1958–60, Dulles to Lloyd, 12 August 1958, p. 458.
122. PRO, FO371/134313/VR1093/5G, Hood to Lloyd, 11 August 1958.
123. PRO, FO371/134313/VJ1093/6, Johnston to Foreign Office, 11 August 1958.
124. *FRUS*, Vol. 11, 1958–60, London to State Department, 12 August 1958, p. 458.
125. PRO, FO371/134313/VR1093/5G, Rundall to Foreign Office, 29 August 1958.
126. ISA, HZ328/28, Elath to Israeli Foreign Ministry, 29 December 1958.
127. PRO, FO371/134313/VR1093/5, Rundall to Hoyer Millar, 5 August 1958.
128. BGA, Ben-Gurion diary, 14 July 1958.
129. Ibid., 19 August 1958, and Bar-Zohar, *Ben-Gurion*, p. 1342.
130. Eisenhower, *The White House*, pp. 287–8.
131. PRO, FO371/134043/VJ1091/146, Hadow to Rundall, 5 October 1958.
132. PRO, FO371/134043/VJ1091/146, Rundall to Lloyd, 7 October 1958.
133. PRO, FO371/134044/VJ1091/177, Foreign Office to Dixon, 15 October 1958.
134. *FRUS*, Vol. 13, 1958–60, Golda Meir to Dulles, 2 October 1958, p. 96.
135. Ibid., State Department memorandum, 17 October 1958, p. 102.
136. *FRUS*, Vol. 13, 1958–60, Golda Meir to Dulles, 2 October 1958, p. 96, and Rountree memorandum to Dulles, 9 October 1958, p. 98.
137. Ibid.
138. Ibid., p. 96.
139. Bar-Zohar, *Ben-Gurion*, p. 1361.
140. US declassified documents, US98/518, Ben-Gurion to Eisenhower, 24 July 1958.
141. *FRUS*, Vol. 13, 1958–60, memo of a conversation, 21 July 1958.
142. Bar-Zohar, *Ben-Gurion*, p. 1327.
143. Ibid., pp. 1329–30.
144. PRO, FO371/134283/VR1051/29, Lloyd to Rundall, 12 August 1958.
145. Ibid.
146. ISA, HZ334/6, Israeli embassy London to MABAR, 20 August 1958.
147. BGA, Ben-Gurion diary, 12 August 1958.
148. PRO, FO371/133858//V1194/232, Hadow (Levant department) minute, 10 September 1958.
149. PRO, FO371/134286/VR1057/49, Dixon (UN New York) to Foreign Office, 26 September 1958.
150. PRO, FO371/134344/VR1212/3, Hadow minute, 19 August 1958.
151. PRO, FO371/134286/VR1051/53, Rundall to Lloyd, 18 October 1958.
152. ISA, HZ321/8, Israeli Foreign Office economic department to Golda Meir, 24 August 1958.
153. Bar-Zohar, *Gesher*, pp. 192–3.
154. PRO, FO371/134337/VR1151/37, Foreign Office minute, 30 October 1958.
155. PRO, FO371/13460/VR1531/31, Rundall to Wright (Assistant Under-Secretary of State), 21 August 1958.
156. PRO, FO371/134286/VR1051/53, Rundall to Lloyd, 18 October 1958.
157. PRO, FO371/134313/VR1093/8G, Rundall to Hadow, 12 September 1958.
158. PRO, FO371/134295/VR1076/6, Foreign Office to certain of Her Majesty's representatives, 17 October 1958.
159. PRO, FO371/133859/V1194/326, Foreign Office to Paris, 5 December 1958.
160. PRO, FO371/134347/VR1222/55G, Foreign Office to Tel-Aviv, 3 August 1958.
161. PRO, FO371/134298/VR1071/1, Stevens to Hood, 7 October 1958.
162. PRO, FO371/134313/VR1093/8G, Rundall to Hadow, 12 August 1958.
163. PRO, DEFE7/1288/81/045/49, Rundall to Lloyd, 24 August 1958.
164. PRO, FO371/134298/VR10710/1, Stevens to Hood, 7 November 1958.
165. PRO, FO371/134298/VR10710/4G, Rundall to Stevens, 26 November 1958.
166. PRO, FO371/134279/VR10345/12, Viscount Hood (Washington) to Sir William

Hayter, 9 September 1958.

167. PRO, DEFE7/1288/81/045/49, Dixon (New York) to Lloyd, 20 August 1958.
168. Ibid.
169. PRO, FO371/133823/V1078/28, Lloyd to Dulles, 19 October 1958.
170. PRO, FO371/134288/VR1051/60, Hadow to Rundall, 5 November 1958.
171. PRO, FO371/134286/VR1051/59, Macmillan speech, 5 November 1958.
172. David Ben-Gurion, *Yehud Veichud* [Singularity and Mission] (Tel-Aviv: Ma'arachot, 1972:1982), p. 317.
173. PRO, FO371/134216/V1041/23, Foreign Office to Johnston, 29 July 1958.
174. PRO, FO371/134199/VQ1015/98, Wright to Lloyd, 15 July 1958.
175. PRO, FO371/134199/VQ1015/109, Wright to Lloyd, 16 July 1958.
176. PRO, FO371/134216/VQ1041/24, Foreign Office to Basra, 30 July 1958.
177. PRO, FO371/134212/VQ1041/23, Johnston (Amman) to Foreign Office, 27 July 1958.
178. PRO, FO371/134216/VQ1041/36, Foreign Office to British embassy Helsinki, 31 July 1958.
179. PRO, FO371/132921/EB10345/41(b), Whitwell (Foreign Office) minute, 5 December 1958.
180. Ibid.
181. PRO, DEFE5/84/COS(58)193, 11 August 1958.
182. PRO, DEFE6/52/JP(58)135, 17 August 1958.
183. Philip Darby, *British Defence Policy East of Suez* (London: Oxford University Press, 1973), pp. 134–5.
184. *Hansard*, Vol. 591, col. 961, 28 July 1958.
185. PRO, DEFE6/52/JP(58)145, 27 October 1958.

Epilogue

WITH THE OVERTHROW OF Nuri el-Said, the traditional system of co-operation between Britain and the Middle East came to an end. The Anglo-American intervention gained its objectives and the position of pro-Western forces in the Lebanon and Jordan was restored. Yet, some problems continued to overshadow the Middle East. The greatest enigma was Iraq's future. Iraq suffered from internal instability due to rivalry between different factions such as the Ba'athists and the communists. These forces had been suppressed under Nuri, but arose again under Qassem and struggled to gain dominance over Iraq. The rivalry between them brought a long period of internal instability and upheaval.

The Ba'athists and the Istiqlalists were in favour of an immediate merger with the UAR, and enjoyed the support of Abd'as' Salam Arif, the Minister of the Interior and the Prime Minister's deputy. The communists, on the other hand, opposed such a move due to the fear that Nasser might suppress them. Qassem himself, in contradiction to all the early assumptions, did not favour such a move and wished to be, 'A part of the Arab world but not a part of a part of it.'[1] Qassem did not hesitate, therefore, to take action against Arif, the main supporter of union with the UAR, dismissing him from his posts and appointing him Ambassador to the German Federal Republic. Arif was finally arrested in Baghdad on 4 November, after he returned to Iraq without permission.

The tensions in Iraq escalated during March 1959 as a result of riots in Mosul which were suppressed by communist and loyalist forces. Iraq's accusation that pro-Nasserist elements were behind these disturbances added an extra dimension to the hostility between Cairo and Baghdad. In his speech on 12 March, Nasser praised Arif as the true hero of the revolution and accused Qassem of having deployed a terrorist system worse than that of Nuri el-Said. He also attacked the communists for being a counter-force to Arab nationalism: a minority group that attempted to impose their views by dictatorship.[2] The Iraqi government retaliated by closing the Egyptian Middle East news agency office in Baghdad on 9 March, and by expelling, on the following day, nine members of the UAR embassy in Baghdad for alleged encouragement of the revolt.

It was obvious that the initial excitement and sympathy in Egypt for the Iraqi coup had now turned into a bitter rivalry between Cairo and Baghdad, and Nasser's hopes that Iraq would join the UAR were in vain. For some time after the revolution, it seemed that the pro-communist forces would take over and Qassem would embark on a pro-communist policy, as his relations with the Soviet Union had blossomed during the first year of his premiership. After the crisis of summer 1958, the Soviets realised that they lacked a strategic foothold and bases in the Mediterranean that would give them the flexibility to intervene in the region and add an extra dimension to their deterrence.[3] Iraq therefore seemed a natural ally which the Soviet Union could support and identify with. However, the honeymoon between Iraq and the Soviets was short due to a change in Qassem's policy from mid-1959 and his shift towards centre and right-wing forces.[4]

The Kirkuk riots drove Qassem to take action against the communists who, for some time, had enjoyed great freedom. In July 1959, during the celebrations of the first anniversary of the Iraqi revolution, a clash between Kurds and Turks took place in Kirkuk and this time the communists stirred up the incident. Qassem reacted by removing the most dangerous communist elements from the army, and at the same time restoring the authority of the security service and government officials.[5] However, he was challenged again when, on 7 October, while travelling by car through Rhasid Ali, he was fired upon and slightly wounded in the shoulder. This attempted assassination was carried out by the Ba'athists.

In spite of the instability of Qassem's regime and his 'zig-zag' policy, the British government believed it should support him because he seemed to be trying to stabilise his country and to take a neutral, non-hostile policy towards the West. Moreover, if the West rebuffed Qassem it might only strengthen the anti-Western forces and push Qassem closer to the Soviets. Although Qassem did not wish to continue close relations with Britain on the model of Nuri, neither did he wish to turn his back on Britain. Instead, he conveyed to the British Ambassador his country's wish to keep Britain as the main source of arms supply for the Iraqi forces.[6] The British government was hoping that Qassem would succeed in pursuing a neutral policy in spite of the internal difficulties he faced, and the opposition to his authority inside and outside the army.

One of the significant steps Qassem took was to terminate the Baghdad Pact on 24 March 1959. The Pact, which had been signed for five years in 1955, and raised so many hopes in the West, especially in Britain, was now dead and buried. On 31 March, the last RAF personnel left the Iraqi base at Habbaniya, and, on 22 June, Iraq left the sterling area and terminated its military agreements with the United States. The Baghdad Pact was recontracted without Iraq in August 1959, under a new title – the Central Treaty Organisation (CENTO) – between the United States, Iran, Pakistan and Turkey.

At the same time, Britain tried to re-establish its position in the region and to restore its relations with the UAR. An Anglo-Egyptian agreement was signed on 28 February 1959, under which the UAR agreed to release British properties that were under dispute, and to pay a lump sum of £27.5 million to compensate for British private property that had been nationalised or compulsorily acquired and to cover claims for the damage to the property.[7] This paved the way for the resumption of diplomatic relations between the UK and the UAR at the level of Chargé d'Affaires announced on 1 December 1959.[8]

In conclusion, although Britain suffered greatly as a result of Suez, it gradually managed to recover and restore its relations with the Arab world. The regional states, however, were more than ever caught up in a bitter struggle over their claims to hegemony. The Iraqi coup and its resulting upheavals gave the impression that Iraq was soon to fall prey to communist dominance. These fears, however, eventually seemed to be unfounded when it became clear that, although he had departed from Nuri's affiliation with the West, Qassem still favoured good relations with Britain and was struggling to embark on a neutral policy. The union between Syria and Egypt was short-lived and ceased to exist when, in September 1961, as a result of a coup in Damascus, Syria withdrew from the UAR. After that Nasser lost his momentum and it would take another six years for him to be able to unite the Arab world against one target – Israel.

Israel viewed the upheavals in Iraq with great interest and adopted (probably for the first time) a similar outlook to Britain's. Eliahu Elath told Lloyd, on 10 February 1959, that it was important that Qassem should be given every chance and that he be supported by the West or else he might join forces with Nasser or the communists.[9] Elath's remark was a small but significant sign of the transformation of the Anglo-Israeli relationship and of Israel's growing political maturity.

Following the 1958 crisis, Israel's position in the world changed dramatically. In her speech in the Knesset on 30 March 1959, Golda Meir praised extravagantly Israel's achievements in pursuing better relations with foreign states, in particular its relations with France and the countries of Black Africa.[10] Israel had tremendous success in its relations with the newly independent countries, especially the African states, and trade with the latter increased, particularly during the 1960s. Although Israeli financial aid to these countries was relatively small, compared to that of the Soviet Union, France, Britain and the United States, for Israel's mood and position it had great importance. Israel concentrated on small and self-contained projects which aimed to bring immediate benefit to the receiving country. Israel also succeeded in signing technical agreements with countries in Africa between 1960 and 1966, and also provided professional training for thousands of Africans in Israel between 1958 and 1966.[11] These improved relations proved themselves able to withstand Nasser's propaganda and the Arab League attempts to destroy them. Ben-Gurion's political vision in this respect proved to be very prudent and far-reaching.

Franco-Israeli relations continued to blossom, although they lacked the passion of earlier times. De Gaulle aspired to design a more balanced Middle Eastern policy, and aimed to restore France's prestige in the region, which had suffered a great setback due to French policies during the Suez and Algerian crises. In a broadcast on 16 September 1958, de Gaulle mentioned for the first time the importance of Algerian self-determination. In addition, Pierre Gilbert, the French Ambassador to Israel, was withdrawn from Tel-Aviv, which was seen as a bad sign.[12] This caused great concern in Israel and was seen as a sign of France's attempt to embark on a new policy. One of the bases for co-operation between France and Israel was the similarity in their views on Middle Eastern events and, especially, French interests in Algeria. If this fundamental element was eliminated, France's interests in Israel would diminish. In May 1961, talks between the French government and the FLN were held in Evian. These eventually paved the way for the Evian accord of 19 March 1962, whereby the two parties agreed to a ceasefire and France agreed to recognise Algerian independence. This was approved in both France and Algeria, and on 3 July Algerian independence was officially proclaimed.[13] Even so, on 30 October a Franco-Israeli cultural agreement was signed, and in June the previous year, Ben-Gurion and de Gaulle had met for the first time.

American-Israeli relations warmed as a result of the events of 1958. It was probably the first time that the State Department reassured Israel of its value, but although relations recovered from the setback they suffered during Suez, they did not undergo a real transformation. Only when Kennedy succeeded Eisenhower at the White House did US policy begin to shift towards a more pro-Israeli direction. During his presidency, the United States supplied Israel with new and modern arms for the first time. In September 1962, the Kennedy administration announced its willingness to sell Israel the short-range defensive Hawk missiles.[14] The shift in US policy can be understood in relation to the increasing Soviet military supply to Egypt, Iraq and Syria, and the growing concern in the United States that this might lead to an Arab attack on Israel, or to a preventive war by Israel on its Arab neighbours.

Ever since the Iraqi coup in the summer of 1958, the Soviet Union had attempted to secure its foothold in the region. Despite Nasser's attack on the Communist Party in Iraq and Syria, the Soviets were not deterred from seeking close relations with Nasser. The Soviet Union was willing to help Nasser with the construction of the Aswan Dam, and, on 27 December, an agreement on economic and technical aid was signed between the two countries. The Soviets granted Egypt a loan of 400 million rubles as well as equipment and machinery for work on the Dam.[15] The Soviets' ambition to expand in the region grew during the 1960s and they became the main arsenal of many regional states. Soviet–Iraqi relations flourished in the first year after the revolution, but started to cool from mid-1960 onwards. The Soviets continued to supply Iraq with economic and military assistance and, on 18 August 1960, a new agreement between the two countries for military, technical and economic aid was signed. At the same time as the Soviets moved closer to the Arab states, their relations with Israel continued to deteriorate, although Israel succeeded in maintaining better relations with some of the eastern European states.

Although this period was marked by calmer Arab–Israeli relations, partly because the Arabs were engaged in their own internal rivalry, it did not see any lessening of their hostility towards Israel or any real attempt at a peace settlement. On the contrary, this was the only issue that could unite countries such as Iraq and Egypt. Accordingly, on 29 February 1960, the Arab League Council adopted a resolution on the Palestinian question, condemning the Zionists for attempting to liquidate the question of Palestine and the Arab states and calling for an international framework in which the Palestinian refugee problem would be solved. There again the Arab states did not show any real sign of attempting to resolve the problem themselves. On the contrary, the Council rejected the idea of forming a Palestinian army and decided to postpone discussion of this issue until a later date.

The Palestinian refugee problem, although relatively minor at the time, was a time bomb and would eventually become an additional obstacle to any possible Middle Eastern settlement. In 1959, a group of young Palestinians, led by Yasser Arafat, founded the FATAH movement for the liberation of Palestine, and at the first Arab summit in Cairo, Egypt initiated the foundation of the PLO. This demonstrated the fallacy of Israeli hopes for an end to the issue and the belief that 'the Palestinian problem' was only of secondary importance. The problem remained alive and proved to be one of the main obstacles to any Arab–Israeli agreement, and one of the most acute challenges to Israel's existence.

Israel's leaders realised that the Middle East had become an arena of superpower rivalry and that their actions might provide the Soviets with a pretext and opportunity to act against Israel. However, when Israel felt it was necessary to strike, it did not hesitate to use armed force. During the 1960s, Israel took limited action against some trouble spots in Syria and Jordan, for example when the Syrians used their strategic advantage of positions on the Golan Heights to shell Israeli settlers in Lake Hachulha and the Sea of Galilee area. In response, the IDF took actions against Tawfik, south of the Sea of Galilee, in 1960, and in 1962, at Nukeib, east of the Sea of Galilee. The Jordanian–Israeli border was relatively quiet after 1958, but there was still some terrorist penetration of Israel's territory. This led Israel to take action, in 1966, against the village of Samoa, located south of the Hebron mountain.[16]

Overall, however, Israel was more careful about the use of military retaliation and instead attempted to use the UN, not because Ben-Gurion or his successor had any greater belief in this institution, but because this avoided actions that might endanger Israel.

All in all, the post-Suez period saw the end of an era in the Middle East. Gradually the dust of Suez settled down, but its impact had far-reaching consequences. It was evident that the region stood at the beginning of a new epoch; old alliances ceased to exist and new ones had been formed. A chapter in the region's history had come to an end and a new one was about to begin.

Indeed, a new storm struck again in June 1967. A total war between Israel and its neighbours started, resulting in Israel's swift victory. The war changed the balance of power in the region and brought the superpowers' intervention to its height. The new situation had a far-reaching impact on the Middle East and on the international arena as a whole.

NOTES

1. PRO, FO371/142304/VR1052/11, notes for a lecture to the Anglo-Jewish Association, 26 September 1959.
2. Royal Institute of International Affairs (RIIA), *Survey of International Affairs*, ed. Geoffrey Barraclough (London: RIIA, 1959), pp. 293–59.
3. Arieh Yodfat, *Brit Hamoazot Vehamizrach Hatikhon* [The Soviet Union and the Middle East] (Tel-Aviv: Israel Defence Ministry Press, 1973), p. 37.
4. Ibid., pp. 38–9.

5. PRO, FO371/1439839/EQ 1011/1, Trevelyan (Cairo) to Lloyd, 1 January 1960.
6. PRO, FO371/142304/VR1052/111, notes for a lecture for the Anglo-Jewish Association, 29 September 1959.
7. Ibid.
8. RIIA, *International Affairs*, p. 34.
9. PRO, FO371/142304/VR1052/6, Lloyd to Rundall (Tel-Aviv), 10 February 1959.
10. PRO, FO371/142726/VR1022/4, Rundall to Lloyd, 3 April 1959.
11. Shimon Peres, *David's Sling: The Arming of Israel* (London: Weidenfeld & Nicolson, 1970), pp. 158–9. See also Michael Bar-Zohar, *Ben- Gurion* (Tel-Aviv: Am-Oved, 1977), p. 1359.
12. Michael Bar-Zohar, *Gesher Al-Hayyam Hatichon* [Bridge Over the Mediterranean] (Tel-Aviv: Am-Hassefer, 1964).
13. Ibid., p. 240.
14. Shimon Peres, 'American Arms for Israel', in Itamar Rabinovich and Jehuda Reinharz (eds), *Israel and the Middle East: Documents and Reading on Society, Politics and Foreign Relations, 1947–present* (Oxford: Oxford University Press, 1984), p. 173.
15. RIIA, *International Affairs*, p. 336.
16. Martin Gilbert, *The Arab–Israeli Conflict: Its History in Maps* (London: Weidenfeld & Nicolson, 1974), p. 61.

Conclusion

IN JUNE 1959, in one of his last dispatches, Sir Francis Rundall wrote:

> I shall leave Israel next week rather like someone who has been called out of an exciting play or film before the end: with real regret but also with the realisation that what I have been watching for a little over two years has had increased impact largely because it has been played upon so small a stage.[1]

This flattering remark was not characteristic of Anglo-Israeli relations for the period covered by this book; on the contrary, these years were loaded with bitterness, bad feelings and suspicion. Rundall's comments show, therefore, the significant change in Anglo-Israeli relations during the later part of this period, mainly from summer 1958 onwards.

It was an era of radical change in the Middle East, in terms both of Britain's position in the area, and of Anglo-Israeli relations. The early stage, 1955–56, was marked by Israel's militancy, with its retaliation policy intended to deter its Arab neighbours. It was a difficult time for Israel, a young country struggling with mass immigration, heavy financial burdens and security problems on its borders. These problems, coupled with its futile attempts to gain Western security guarantees, increased its feelings of isolation in hostile surroundings. During this period, Israel succeeded in gaining one close ally, France. It was a significant achievement, which gave Israel a sense of confidence and had a major impact on its foreign policy.

Israel's relations with the Arab states deteriorated during this period, due, in large part, to its fears about the growing influence of the Arab National Movement led by Gamal Abdul Nasser. The situation was further aggravated by the Fedayeen infiltration into Israel's territory and the brutal murders of Israeli citizens, but Israel's retaliation policy only added fuel to the fire, leading to an escalating cycle of reprisals and counter-reprisals.

Britain's position at this stage was still guided by its traditional interests, which were essentially to keep the oil supply routes open and to secure its strategic position in the area. These interests, and its special affiliation with Iraq and Jordan, led to a policy that leaned towards the Arabs, and meant that Britain tended to see Israel as an obstacle to the achievement of its goals. Although Britain's imperial status was slipping, its decision-makers were still wrapped up in sweet memories of Britain's glorious days in the Middle East and tried to preserve this stake in the region to the bitter end. Their refusal to relinquish the heyday of empire, and the delusion that Britain was still able to dominate affairs in the region, led in the end to catastrophe. The Suez war highlighted the descent from power of France and Britain, the old colonial powers who tried to use military methods in order to impose their will. It demonstrated their lack of understanding of the transformation that the Middle East had gone through, as well as their failure to realise that their own positions were declining and that the power of the United States and the USSR was growing.

Anglo-Israeli relations were always overshadowed by Britain's traditional position in the region, and from November 1955, Anthony Eden's speech at the Guildhall came to symbolise for the Israelis the unsympathetic attitude of the British government. As long as the Israeli leaders believed that the 'Guildhall spirit' still existed in Whitehall there was little hope of a real understanding between Britain and Israel. Israel's perception was that the British were willing to compromise Israel's security to maintain their power in the region and to sustain their relations with the Arab states. It is quite evident that British policy at the time was not favourable towards Israel, and the fact that Britain publicly admitted that Israel's borders could not be seen as final was a major concern for Israel.

However, Israel's militant policy at the time also made closer relations more difficult. The retaliation policy adopted by Ben-Gurion and Moshe Dayan became a major obstacle to Anglo-Israeli relations. It gave the Foreign Office an excuse to suspend arms sales to Israel and place Israel under heavy criticism and condemnation. This criticism, however, only led to stronger feelings of isolation among the Israeli public and the decision-makers.

The Suez operation did not contribute in any notable way to a greater understanding between Britain and Israel, and the cautious co-operation that occurred during the Suez war was not followed by a blossoming of relations immediately afterwards. It is therefore important to emphasise that, although Suez had a major impact on Britain's worldwide position and on the Conservative party, it did not bring about a fundamental change in Anglo-Israeli relations.

Notwithstanding the fact that the hostility between Israel and Britain did lessen to a degree, there is little hard evidence that British policy became fundamentally different, although there was greater appreciation in Whitehall of Israel's military ability. However, there was little to suggest that major political revision was undertaken in Whitehall or the Foreign Office in regard to the general outlook on Israel. It would be right to point out that in the period immediately after Suez, the British were busy licking their wounds and restoring their relationship with the United States.

It was only the consequences of Suez and the upheavals during the summer of 1958 that eventually opened the way for closer relations and better understanding between the two countries. Thus, it was the internal changes in the Middle East that largely contributed to a real shift in the Anglo-Israeli relationship. Israel's policy following Suez, and the greater restraint it demonstrated during July–August 1958, presented it in a different and more positive light, enabling this new state to be seen for the first time as a reasonable partner for the West. Ben-Gurion proved willing to learn the lessons of the past and was clever enough to adopt a more mature, understanding policy in order to break out of Israel's virtual diplomatic isolation.

As for Anglo-Israeli relations – after the summer of 1958, they should be analysed from the different premisses the United Kingdom operated on after the coup. The shift in Anglo-Israeli relations can also be seen in the different policy Israel adopted during summer 1958. Whereas previously Israeli decision-makers had been quick to press the trigger, they eventually reached the stage where they could afford to adopt more mature and restrained behaviour. Ben-Gurion, a master in his own country, proved to be a master in foreign relations during the crisis of 1958 and managed to manoeuvre the situation to Israel's benefit in a most extraordinary fashion.

The dramatic events of summer 1958 brought about a fundamental change in the Middle East. For Britain the future looked grim; Nuri's downfall destroyed the traditional system under which Britain had operated for a long time. The Iraq of Nuri no longer existed and the Baghdad Pact was buried with him. Qassem's decision to withdraw from the Pact led to the collapse of one of Britain's fundamental pillars in the region. These events, however, eventually turned to Britain's benefit, as it was able to restore some of its relations with the Arab states, for instance with the UAR. Nuri's fall and Hussein's delicate position demonstrated the great vulnerability of the pro-Western states in the region. Israel, on the other hand, proved for the first time it could be valued as a loyal ally. The Suez episode, in this respect, should be seen only as one of a series of changes in the Middle East rather than the direct cause of the later wars. Some historians note that at first sight it seems that Israel did not obviously gain any great benefits from its participation in the Suez war. This is a valid argument, and adds weight to the view that it was the experience of summer 1958 which eventually brought about the breakthrough in Israel's worldwide position, especially in its relations with Britain.

Anglo-Israeli relations never reached the same degree of co-operation as Israel had enjoyed with the French or later enjoyed with the United States, but the bitter emotions, the anger and the suspicion faded away. For Israel, a country that attached great importance to its foreign relations, this was an important achievement. Ever since the establishment of Israel, its leaders had placed special emphasis on their relations with Britain. The greater understanding that was eventually accomplished therefore brought great satisfaction and relief to Israel. Britain was finally seen among Israeli leaders as a friendly, trustworthy power. The positive course relations took after summer 1958 was highlighted in Meir's speech of March 1959 in the Knesset. She stressed that the relations between Israel and Britain were closer than ever before and paid special tribute to Macmillan's contribution to the greater understanding between the two countries. Meir referred specifically to the excellent state of economic relations between the two countries and expressed the hope that these would continue to develop, especially with regard to air communications and British investment in Israel. Macmillan's election victory in October 1959 was welcomed in Israel because he was considered a sincere friend.[2] Meir's speech reflected again the overwhelming positive feelings among Israeli leaders towards Harold Macmillan, and the overall belief that Macmillan's appointment as Prime Minister had enabled the Anglo-Israeli relationship to move forward and contributed to a better understanding between Britain and Israel.

Most important of all was the transformation in Israel's feelings and mood. As Meir said: 'We no longer regard ourselves as a country standing alone in the world.'[3] This shift in Israel's policy also enabled British officials to conduct their Middle Eastern policy in an easier atmosphere.

In his valedictory dispatch, Francis Rundall stressed that, although the Israelis always looked to the United States as the chief source of financial aid, they had always had great admiration for Britain and its way of life, coupled with the feeling that the British were more experienced and predictable in conducting international affairs than the United States. Rundall emphasised that Israel realised the Anglo-Israeli relationship could not be built on the Franco-Israeli model of 'undying love and fidelity', and that the nature of Anglo-Israeli relations would be different and had to be built on modest achievements. He concluded optimistically:

> The time may come when we may want closer relations with Israel at short notice ... but until then we should be able to maintain our position if we steer a course between neglect, the most unforgivable insult to this sensitive people, and the uneasy emotionalism of Franco-Israeli relations ... A relationship embodying mutual respect for each other's interests and a spirit of consultation and understanding is perhaps the best contribution we can at present make to Israel's future ... We have succeeded during the past year in laying I hope permanently the ghost of the Guildhall plan and establishing an understanding of our position as genuinely in its own interests.[4]

The end of an era for the British position in the Middle East paved the way for a new, more co-operative relationship between Israel and Britain. The way from Guildhall to the eventual breakthrough in 1958–59, was long and painful, yet it seemed that the two were ultimately able to embark on a new calm dawn in the perpetually stormy Middle East.

NOTES

1. PRO, FO371/142273/VR1015/9, Rundall valedictory dispatch, 4 June 1959.
2. PRO, FO371/142276/VR1022/4, Rundall to Lloyd, 3 April 1959.
3. Ibid.
4. PRO, FO371/142273/VR1015/9, Rundall valedictory dispatch, 4 June 1959.

Bibliography

UNPUBLISHED SOURCES

UNITED KINGDOM

DOCUMENTS
Public Record Office (PRO), Kew, Surrey.

Cabinet Papers
CAB128 & CAB129: minutes and memoranda.
CAB130: Cabinet Committee files.
CAB134: Cabinet Committee (standing) files.

Defence Papers
DEFE4: Chiefs of Staff Committee, minutes of meetings.
DEFE5: Chiefs of Staff Committee, memoranda.
DEFE7: general series.
DEFE11: Chiefs of Staff Committee, register files for official correspondence and memoranda.
DEFE13: Private office papers.
AIR20: Operation Musketeer, foreign and allied air forces.
ADM1: Secretariat papers.

Foreign Office Papers
FO371: Foreign Office: general correspondence: political
FO800: Private collections
FO115: General correspondence.

Prime Minister's Office Papers
PREM11: Prime Minister's office, correspondence and papers.

Treasury Papers
T225: Defence policy and material division, register files.
T234: Home and overseas planning staff division.
T236: Overseas finance division.

War Office
WO32: Register files general series.

Private Papers
B. Earl of Avon Papers, University of Birmingham.

ISRAEL

Ben-Gurion Archive (BGA), Sde Boker.
Beit-Ariela, Newspapers Library Collection, Tel-Aviv.
Israeli State Archive (ISA), Jerusalem.

INTERVIEWS
Eliahu Elath, Jerusalem summer 1988.
Mordechai Bar-On, Jerusalem summer 1989.
Professor Yehoshafat Harkabi, Jerusalem winter 1993.
Michael Bar-Zohar, Jerusalem April 1990.
Gershon Avner, Jerusalem April 1990.

PUBLISHED DOCUMENTS AND RECORDS

FOREIGN RELATIONS OF THE UNITED STATES

Vol. 4, The Arab–Israeli dispute.
Vol. 13, 1955–57, The Near East, Jordan, Yemen.
Vol. 14, 1955–57, The Arab–Israeli dispute, 1955.
Vol. 15, 1955–57, The Arab–Israeli dispute, 1 January–26 July 1956.
Vol. 16, 1955–57, The Suez Crisis, 26–31 December 1956.
Vol. 17, 1955–57, The Arab–Israeli dispute (1957).
Vol. 11, 1958–60, Lebanon, Jordan.
Vol. 12, 1958–60, The Near East, Iraq, Iran, Arabian Peninsula.
Vol. 13, 1958–60, The Arab–Israeli Dispute.
Hansard, House of Commons Debates, 1955–58.
US Declassified Documents Reference System.

SECONDARY SOURCES (HEBREW)

MEMOIRES AND DIARIES

Dayan, Moshe, *Avnei Derech* [Story of my Life] (Tel-Aviv: Edanim/Jerusalem: Dvir, 1976).
Elath, Eliahu, *Mibhad Learafel Haymim* [Through the Mist of Time, Reminiscences] (Jerusalem: Yad Ithak Ben-Zvi, 1989).
Harel, Isser, *Bithaon ve Demokratiya* [Security and Democracy] (Tel-Aviv: Edanim, 1989).
Meir, Golda, *Hayay* [My Life] (Tel-Aviv: Sifriat Ma'ariv, 1978).
Rafael, Gideon, *Besod Leumim* [Destination Peace] (Jerusalem: Edanim, 1981).
Sharett, Moshe, *Yoman Ishi* [Personal Diary], Vol. 5–6 (Tel-Aviv: Ma'ariv, 1978).

BOOKS

Bar-On, Mordechai, *Etgar Vetigra* [Challenge and Quarrel: The Road to Sinai, (Beer-Sheeva: Ben-Gurion University, 1991).
Bar-On, Mordechai, *Sharei A'za, Medinut H'chuz Vehabithon shel Medinaht Israel 1955–1957* [The Gates of Gaza: Israel's Defence and Foreign Policy 1955–1957] (Tel-Aviv: Am-Oved, 1992).
Bar-Zohar, Michael, *Gesher Al Hayam Hatichon* [Bridge Over the Mediterranean]

(Tel-Aviv: Am-Hassefer, 1964).

Bar-Zohar, Michael, *Ben-Gurion* (Tel-Aviv: Am-Oved, 1977).

Ben-Gurion, David, *Hazon Vaderech* [Vision and Destination], Vol. 3, (Tel-Aviv: Am-Oved, 1957).

Ben-Gurion, David, *Medinhat Israel Hamechudeshet* [The Revival of the State of Israel] (Tel-Aviv: Am-Oved, 1969).

Ben-Gurion, David, *Kochavim Vaefer* [Like Stars Like Dust], essays from the government year book (Ramat-Gan: Masada, 1976).

Ben-Gurion, David, *Yehud Veichud* [Singularity and Mission] (Tel-Aviv: Ma'arachot, 1971:1982).

Brecher, Michael, *Diplomatia Betzel Imut* [Diplomacy and Confrontation], selected issues in Israel's foreign relations 1947–78, ed. Benjamin Neuberger (Tel-Aviv: Everyman's University, 1981).

Cohen, Eliezer and Lavi, Zvi, *Hashamim Eynam Ha-gvul* [The Sky is Not the Limit] (Tel-Aviv: Ma'ariv, 1990).

Evron, Yosef, *Be'Yom Sagrir: Su'ets Me'ahorei Ha-klayim* [In Stormy Days: Suez Behind the Scenes] (Tel-Aviv: Otpaz, 1968).

Shimoni, Yaacov, *Medinot Arav* [The Arab States] (Tel-Aviv: Am-Oved, 1990).

Yizhar, Michael, *Harzot Habrit Vehamizrach Hatichon* [The United States and the Middle East] (Tel-Aviv: Am-Hassefer, 1973).

Yodfat, Arieh, *Brit Hamoazot Vehamizrach Hatikhon* [The Soviet Union and the Middle East] (Tel-Aviv: Israeli Defence Ministry Press, 1973).

ARTICLES (Hebrew)

Bialer, Uri, 'David Ben-Gurion Ve-Moshe Sharett, Hitgabshut Shtei Oraintaziot Mediniot Bithoniot Bchevra Haisralit' [David Ben-Gurion and Moshe Sharett, The Formulation of two Political–Strategic Orientations in the Israeli Society) *Medina Vemimshal*, Vol. 2, Ch. 1 (Haifa: Shikmona Publishers, 1972).

Bar-On, Mordechai, 'Haiska Ha-Checit-Mizrit, Shela shel-Tiaruch' [The Czech-Egyptian Arms Deal – A Question of Date], *Ma'arachot*, Israeli Defence Ministry, December 1986–January 1987.

Dayan, Moshe, 'Military Activities in Peace Time', *Bamachane* (Israel Defense Forces weekly magazine), Vol. 51, October 1954.

Horowitz, Dan, 'Doctrinat Habitchon shel Israel, Hatfisa Ha-israelit shel Bytachon Leumi (1948–1972)', in Benjamin Neurberger (ed.), *Diplomatia Betzel Eymut* ['Israeli Security Doctrine', in *Diplomacy and Confrontation*, Selected Issues in Israel's Foreign Relations, 1948–1978] (Tel-Aviv: Everyman's University, 1984).

Kedouri, Eli, 'Hamavar Min Haeidan Habriti Leidan Hamerikai Ba-Mizrach Hatichon' [The Transformation from the British to the American Era in the Middle East] in Eitan Rabinovich and Chaim Shaker (eds), *Harzot Habrit Ve-hamizrach Hatichon* [The United States and the Middle East] (Tel-Aviv: Am-Oved, 1986).

Neheman, Yuval, 'Kesher Eim Ha-tzorfatim ve-Habritim Bmarechet Sinai' [Connections with the British and the French during the Suez Operation], *Ma'arachot*, December 1986–January 1987.

Shefer, Gabi, 'Sharett, Ben-Gurion Vemilchemet Habriera be-1956' [Sharett, Ben-Gurion, and the Option to Engage in War] *Medina, Mimshal ve-Yachasim Benleuim*, No. 27, Winter 1956.

Staff of the Israel Defense Forces, 'Shuk Haneft Haolami' [The World Oil Market] *Skeira Hodshit*, Israeli military monthly review, November 1957.

MEMOIRES AND DIARIES (English)

Ben-Gurion, David, *Israel: A Personal History* (New York: Funk and Wagnalls/Tel-Aviv: Sabra Books, 1971).
Burns, E.L.M., *Between Arab and Israeli* (London: Harrap and Co., 1962).
Gaitskell, Hugh, *The Diaries of Hugh Gaitskell*, P.M. Williams (ed.) (London: Jonathan Cape, 1983).
Dayan, Moshe, *Diary of the Sinai Campaign* (New York: Harper and Row, 1966).
Eban, Abba, *An Autobiography* (New York: Weidenfeld & Nicolson, 1977).
Eden, Anthony, *Full Circle* (London: Cassell, 1960).
Eisenhower, Dwight D., *The White House Years, Waging Peace 1956–1961* (London: Heineman, 1966).
Gaulle, Charles de, *Memories of Hope* (London: Weidenfeld & Nicolson, 1971).
Gaulle, Charles de, *Letters, Notes et Carnets, June 1958–December 1960* (French) (Paris: Plon, 1985).
Glubb, General Sir John Bagot, *A Soldier with the Arabs* (London: Hodder & Stoughton, 1957).
Glubb, General Sir John Bagot, *Britain and the Arabs* (London: Hodder & Stoughton, 1989).
Heikal, Mohammed, *Cutting the Lion's Tail: Suez Through Egyptian Eyes* (New York: Arba House, 1987).
Lloyd, Selwyn, *Suez 1956 – A Personal Account* (London: Book Club Associates, 1978).
Macmillan, Harold, *Riding the Storm, 1956–1959* (London: Macmillan, 1971).
Nasser, Gamal Abdul, *Egypt's Liberation: The Philosophy of the Revolution* (Washington, DC: Public Affairs Press, 1955).
Nutting, Anthony, *No End of a Lesson* (London: Constable, 1971).
Peres, Shimon, *David's Sling: The Arming of Israel* (London: Weidenfeld & Nicolson, 1970).
Shuckburgh, Evelyn, *Descent to Suez, Diaries, 1951–1956* (London: Weidenfeld & Nicolson, 1986).

BOOKS

Abadi, Jacob, *British Withdrawal from the Middle East: The Economic and Strategic Imperatives* (Princeton, NJ: Kingston Press, 1982).
Ashton, Nigel, *Eisenhower, Macmillan and the Problem of Nasser: Anglo-American Relations and the Problem of Nationalism 1955–1959* (Basingstoke: Macmillan, 1996).
Bartlett, C.J., *The Long Retreat: A Short History of British Defence Policy 1945–1970* (London: Macmillan, 1972).
Bar-Zohar, Michael, *Suez, Ultra Secret* (Paris: Fayard, 1964).
Batatu, Hana, *The Old Social Regime and the Revolutionary Movement in Iraq* (Princeton, NJ: Princeton University Press, 1978).
Ben-Gurion, David, *Rebirth and Destiny of Israel* (London: Thomas Yosselof, 1959).
Bialer, Uri, *Between East and West: Israel's Foreign Policy Orientation 1948–1956* (Cambridge: Cambridge University Press, 1990).
Brecher, Michael, *Decisions in Israel's Foreign Policy* (New Haven: Yale University Press, 1974).
Campbell, John, *Defence in the Middle East* (New York: Harper, 1985).
Carlton, David, *Britain and the Suez Crisis* (Oxford: Basil Blackwell, 1988).
Cohen, Michael, *Fighting World War III From the Middle East: Allied Contingency Plans 1945–1954* (London: Frank Cass, 1997).
Cohen, Michael J. and Kolinsky, M. (eds), *Demise of the British Empire in the Middle East, British Responses to Nationalist Movements, 1943–55* (London: Frank Cass,

1998).
Dann, Uriel, *King Hussein and the Challenge of Arab Radicalism, Jordan 1955–1967* (Oxford: Oxford University Press, 1989).
Dann, Uriel, *Iraq Under Qassem, A Political History 1958–1963* (New York: Praeger, 1969).
Darby, Philip, *British Defence Policy East of Suez* (London: Oxford University Press, 1973).
Devereux, David, *The Formation of British Defence Policy Towards the Middle East 1948–1956* (Basingstoke: Macmillan, 1990).
Eisenstadt, Yacov, *The Transformation of the Israeli Society: An Essay in Interpretation* (London: Weidenfeld & Nicolson, 1985)
Fawzi, Mohamad, *Suez 1956: An Egyptian Perspective* (London: Shorouk International, 1987)
Gilbert, Martin, *The Arab–Israeli Conflict: Its History in Maps* (London: Weidenfeld and Nicolson, 1974).
Gorst, Anthony, Johnman, Lewis, and Lucas, Scott W. (eds), *Post-War Britain, 1945–1964, Themes and Perspectives* (London: Pinter, 1989).
Horne, Alistair, *Macmillan*, Vols I and II (London: Macmillan, 1988 and 1989).
Karsh, Efraim (ed.), *Between Peace and War* (London: Frank Cass, 1996).
Kcrosbie, Sylvia, *A Tacit Alliance: France and Israel from Suez to the Six Day War* (Princeton, NJ: Princeton University Press, 1974).
Kyle, Keith, *Suez* (London: Weidenfeld & Nicolson, 1992).
Lacouture, Jean, *Charles de Gaulle: The Ruler 1945–1970* (London: Harvill, 1991).
Lamb, Richard, *The Failure of the Eden Government* (London: Sidgwick & Jackson, 1987).
Louis, Roger and Owen, Roger (eds), *Suez 1956: The Crisis and its Consequences* (Oxford: Clarendon Press, 1989).
Lucas, Scott W., *Divided We Stand: Britain, the US and the Suez Crisis* (London: Hodder & Stoughton, 1988).
Morris, Benny, *Israel's Border Wars, Arab Infiltration, Israel's Retaliation and the Countdown to the Suez War 1949–1956* (Oxford: Clarendon Press, 1993).
Ovendale, Ritchie, *The Origins of the Arab–Israeli Wars* (New York: Longman, 1984).
Ovendale, Ritchie, *Britain, the United States and the Transfer of Power in the Middle East* (London: Leicester University Press, 1996).
Pappé, Ilan, *Britain and the Arab–Israeli Conflict, 1948–1951* (Basingstoke: Macmillan, 1988).
Peri, Yoram, *Between Ballot and Bullets: Israeli Military in Politics* (Cambridge: Cambridge University Press, 1983).
Perlmutter, Amos, *Military and Politics in Contemporary Israel* (London: Frank Cass, 1969).
Pickles, Dorothy, *The Fifth Republic* (London: Methuen and Company, 1964).
Rabinovich, Itamar, and Reinharz, Jehuda (eds), *Israel and the Middle East:, Documents and Reading on Society, Politics and Foreign Relations 1947–present* (Oxford: Oxford University Press, 1984).
Rhodes, James Robert, *Anthony Eden* (London: Weidenfeld & Nicolson, 1986).
Roi, Ya'acov, *Soviet Decision Making in Practice, The USSR and Israel 1947–1954* (Somerset, NJ: Transaction Books, 1980).
Royal Institute of International Affairs, *British Interests in the Mediterranean and the Middle East: A Report by Chatham House Study Group* (Oxford: Oxford University Press, 1958).
Safran, Nadav, *From War to War, the Arab–Israeli Confrontation 1948–1967: A Study of the Conflict from the Perspective of Coercion in the Context of Inter Arab and Big Powers Relations* (New York: Pegasus, 1969).
Safran, Nadav, *Israel's the Embattled Ally* (Cambridge, MA: Bellknap Press, 1978).

Schiff, Ze'ev, *A History of the Israeli Army* (New York: St. Martin's, 1985).
Seale, Patrick, *The Struggle for Syria: A Study in Post-War Arab Politics* (London: Tauris, 1968).
Shwadran, Benjamin, *The Middle East, Oil and the Great Powers* (Jerusalem: Israel Universities Press, 1973).
Thomas, Hugh, *The Suez Affair* (London: Weidenfeld & Nicolson, 1967).
Troen, Selwyn Ilan and Shemesh, Moshe (eds), *The Suez–Sinai Crisis 1956: Retrospective and Reappraisal* (London: Frank Cass, 1989).
Venn, Fiona, *Oil Diplomacy in the Twentieth Century* (London: Macmillan, 1986).
Watt, Donald Cameron, *Documents on the Suez Crisis* (London: Royal Institute of International Affairs, 1957).
Wilson, Harold, *The Chariot of Israel* (London: Weidenfeld & Nicolson, 1981).
Yergin, Daniel, *The Prize, The Epic Quest for Oil, Money and Power* (London: Simon & Schuster, 1991).
Ziegler, Philip, *Mountbatten: The Official Biography* (London: Collins, 1985).

ARTICLES

Almog, Orna, 'An End of an Era – The Crisis of 1958 and the Anglo-Israeli Relationship', *Contemporary Record*, Vol. 8, No. 1, Summer 1994.
Ashton, Nigel, 'The Hijacking of a Pact: The Formation of the Baghdad Pact and the Anglo-American Tensions in the Middle East 1955–1958', *Review of International Studies*, 1993.
Ashton, Nigel, 'A Great New Venture? Anglo-American Cooperation in the Middle East and the Response to the Iraqi Revolution July 1958', *Diplomacy & Statecraft*, Vol. 4 (London: Frank Cass, 1993).
Bialer, Uri, 'Our Place in the World: Mapai and Israel's Foreign Policy Orientation 1947–1952', *Jerusalem Papers on Peace Problems*, No. 33 (The Hebrew University, 1981).
Cohen, Stuart, 'A Still Stranger Aspect of Suez: British Operational Plans to Attack Israel, 1955–1956', *International History Review*, No. 10, 1988.
Dayan, Moshe, 'Israel's Border and Security Problems', *Foreign Affairs*, Vol. 33, No. 2, January 1955.
Doodley, Howard, 'Great Britain's "Last Battle" in the Middle East: Notes on Cabinet Planning during the Suez Crisis of 1956', *The International History Review*, No. 11, 3 August 1989.
Golani, Motti, 'The Historical Place of the Czech–Egyptian Arms Deal, Fall 1955', *Middle Eastern Studies*, Vol. 31, No. 4, October 1995.
Hertzberg, Arthur, 'Israel and the Diaspora: A Relationship Re-examined', *Israel Affairs*, Vol. 2, Nos 3–4, Spring–Autumn 1996.
Hurewitz, J.C. 'The Historical Context', in Wm Roger Louis and Roger Owen (eds), *Suez 1956, The Crisis and its Consequences* (Oxford: Clarendon Press, 1989).
Jasse, Richard L., 'The Baghdad Pact: Cold War or Colonialism?' *Middle Eastern Studies*, Vol. 27, No. 1, January 1992.
Johnman, Lewis, 'Defending the Pound: The Economics of the Suez Crisis, 1956', in A. Gorst, L. Johnman and W. Scott Lucas (eds), *Post-War Britain 1945–64, Themes and Perspectives* (London: Pinter, 1989).
Kent, John, 'The Egyptian Base and the Defence of the Middle East, 1945–1954', in Robert Holland (ed.), *Emergencies and Disorder in the European Empires* (London: Frank Cass, 1994).
Kunz, B. Diane, 'The Importance of Having Money: The Economic Diplomacy of the Suez Crisis', in Wm Roger Louis and Roger Owen (eds), *Suez 1956, The Crisis and its Consequences* (Oxford: Clarendon Press, 1989).
Levey, Zach, 'Anglo-Israeli Strategic Relations, 1952–1956', *Middle Eastern Studies*, Vol. 31, No. 4, October 1995.

Little, Douglas, 'The Making of the Special Relationship: The United States and Israel, 1957–68', *Middle East Studies*, Vol. 25, 1993.

Little, Douglas, 'His Finest Hour? Eisenhower, Lebanon and the Middle East Crisis', *Diplomatic History*, Vol. 20, No. 1, 1996.

Menken, Jules, 'Problems of Middle Eastern Strategy', in H.G. Thursield (ed.), *Brassey's Annual, The Armed Forces Year Book 1956*, Ch. 8.

Oren, Michael, 'Canada, the Great Powers and the Middle Eastern Arms Race, 1950–1956', *International History Review*, Vol. 12, No. 2, May 1990.

Ovendale, Ritchie, 'Great Britain and the Anglo-American Invasion of Jordan and Lebanon in 1958', *The International History Review*, Vol. 6, No. 2, May 1994.

Peres, Shimon, 'American Arms for Israel', in Itamar Rabinovich and Jehuda Reinharz (eds), *Israel and the Middle East:, Documents and Reading on Society, Politics and Foreign Relations 1947–present* (Oxford: Oxford University Press, 1984).

Perlman, Moshe, 'Mid-Summer Madness', *Middle Eastern Affairs*, Vol. 9, Nos 8–9, August–September 1958.

Peterson, J.A., 'The Politics of the Middle East Oil', *Middle East Institute*, 1983.

Raad, Zeid, 'Nightmare Avoided: Jordan and Suez 1956', *Israel Affairs*, Vol. 1, No. 2, Winter 1994.

Raleigh, J.S., ' The Middle East in 1957: A Political Survey', *Middle Eastern Affairs*, Vol. 9, No. 3, March 1958.

Shamir, Shimon, 'The Collapse of Project Alpha', in Wm Roger Louis and Roger Owen (eds), *Suez 1956: The Crisis and its Consequences* (Oxford: Clarendon Press, 1989).

Shefer, Gabriel, 'Has Israel Really Been a Garrison Democracy? Sources of Change in Israel's Democracy', *Israel Affairs*, Vol. 3, No. 1, 1996.

Sheffy, Yigal, 'Unconcern at Dawn, Surprise at Sunset: Egyptian Intelligence Appreciations before the Sinai Campaign', *Intelligence and National Security*, July 1990.

Shlaim, Avi, 'Conflicting Approaches to Israel's Relations with the Arabs: Ben-Gurion and Sharett, 1953–1956', *Middle East Journal*, Vol. 37, 1983.

Shwadran, Benjamin, 'The Kingdom of Jordan, To Be or Not To Be?', *Middle Eastern Affairs*, Vol. 8, Nos 8–9, 1957.

Shwadran, Benjamin, 'Formulation of the United Arab Republic and on the Iraqi–Jordanian Federation Agreement', *Middle Eastern Affairs*, Vol. 9, No. 3, August–September 1958.

Tal, David, 'The American–Israeli Security Treaty: Sequel or Means to the Relief of Israeli–Arab Tensions, 1954–55', *Middle Eastern Studies*, Vol. 31, No. 4, October 1995.

Vaisse, Maurice, 'Post-Suez France', in Wm Roger Louis and Roger Owen (eds), *Suez 1956: The Crisis and its Consequences* (Oxford: Clarendon Press, Oxford, 1989).

Watt, Donald Cameron, 'The High Dam at Aswan', in *Dams in Africa* (London: Frank Cass, 1968).

Watson, Adam, 'The Aftermath of Suez: Consequences for French Decolonization', in Wm Roger Louis and Roger Owen (eds), *Suez 1956: The Crisis and its Consequences* (Oxford: Clarendon Press, 1989).

Zak, Moshe, 'Israel and Jordan: Strategically Bound', *Israel Affairs*, Vol. 3, No. 1, Autumn 1996.

'G.L.', 'Suez and its Consequences: The Israeli View', *The World Today*, Vol. 13, No. 4, April 1957.

THESES

Tenembaum Yoav, 'British Policy Towards Israel and the Arab–Israeli Dispute 1951–1954' (PhD thesis, St Antony's College, Oxford, 1991).

Index